Madness and Death in Philosophy

SUNY SERIES IN CONTEMPORARY CONTINENTAL PHILOSOPHY

Dennis J. Schmidt, editor

MADNESS AND DEATH IN PHILOSOPHY

FERIT GÜVEN

STATE UNIVERSITY OF NEW YORK PRESS

Published by
STATE UNIVERSITY OF NEW YORK PRESS
ALBANY

For information, address
State University of New York Press
90 State Street, Suite 700, Albany, NY 12207

Production, Laurie Searl
Marketing, Anne M. Valentine

Library of Congress Cataloging-in-Publication Data

Güven, Ferit, 1966–
    Madness and death in philosophy / Ferit Güven.
      p. cm. — (SUNY series in contemporary continental philosophy)
    Includes bibliographical references and index.
    ISBN 0-7914-6393-1 (hardcover : alk. paper) — ISBN 0-7914-6394-X (pbk. : alk. paper)
    1. Death—History. 2. Insanity—History. 3. Philosophy—History. I. Title. II.
Series.
BD444.G88 2005
128'.5—dc22

                                                              2004007829

10   9   8   7   6   5   4   3   2   1

This book is dedicated to

Leyla Mélis Miller Güven

and Sofi Nur Miller Güven

Contents

Acknowledgments

Even though the themes of madness and death suggest a radical solitude, this book was certainly not written in solitude. I want to acknowledge Elaine P. Miller and Daniel Price for their contributions throughout this work. They not only read earlier versions and gave me criticism and suggestions, but they have been rare "philosophical friends" over the years.

I want to thank the entire community of the DePaul University Philosophy Department, especially Michael Naas, who was very supportive from the start of this project. Angelica Nuzzo and William McNeill were kind enough to read an earlier version of the manuscript.

I also want to acknowledge the contributions of members of the Earlham College community. I would especially like to thank JoAnn Martin, who read an earlier version of the manuscript and was extremely encouraging even when I was in doubt. Tanja Stähler was probably the first person to insist on seeing the manuscript in print. Elizabeth Kesling was very skillful in editing the manuscript. I also want to thank Earlham College for supplying a Professional Development Fund during the writing of this work.

Jane Bunker and Laurie Searl of SUNY Press were extremely helpful at several stages of the publication. I also want to thank the two anonymous readers of the manuscript for their helpful comments.

My family has always been supportive in many different ways that cannot be described. I want to thank my mother Nurten Güven, my brothers Engin Güven and Murat Güven, my nephew Derin Güven, my niece Yasemin Güven and my aunt Yüksel Inankur.

Finally, I want to again thank Elaine Miller publicly (especially because I do not do it enough privately), without whom I would not have been able to write a meaningful sentence, let alone a book. She has always been present throughout this project, critical yet always supportive, as the best possible partner.

Abbreviations

CHM   Jacques Derrida, *"Cogito et Histoire de la folie,"* in *L'écriture et la différence* (Paris: Editions du Seuil, 1967). "Cogito and the History of Madness," in *Writing and Difference*, Jacques Derrida, trans. A. Bass (Chicago: University of Chicago Press, 1978).

Enz.   G. W. F. Hegel, *Enzyklopädie der philosophischen Wissenschaften im Grundrisse* (1830) Dritter Teil, *Die Philosophie des Geistes, mit den mündlichen Zusätzen, Werke* 10 (Frankfurt a.M.: Suhrkamp, 1970). *Hegel's Philosophy of Mind:* Part Three of the Encyclopaedia of the Philosophical Sciences, G. W. F. Hegel, trans. W. Wallace, together with the Zusätze in Boumann's Text (1845), trans. A.V. Miller (Oxford: Clarendon Press, 1971).

GdP   Martin Heidegger, *Grundfragen der Philosophie: Ausgewählte "Probleme" der "Logik" GA.* 45 (Frankfurt a.M.: V. Klostermann, 1984). *Basic Questions of Philosophy: Selected "Problems" of "Logic,"* Martin Heidegger, trans. R. Rojcewicz and A. Schuwer (Bloomington: Indiana University Press, 1994).

H   Martin Heidegger, *Hegel GA.* 68, Martin Heidegger (Frankfurt a.M.: V. Klostermann, 1993).

HBE   Martin Heidegger, *"Hegels Begriff der Erfahrung,"* in *Holzwege* (Frankfurt a.M.: V. Klostermann, 1950). *Hegel's Concept of Experience*, Martin Heidegger (New York: Harper and Row, 1970).

HF   Michel Foucault, *Histoire de la folie à l'âge classique* (Paris: Gallimard, 1972). *Madness and Civilization: A History of Insanity in the Age of Reason*, Michel Foucault, trans. R. Howard (New York: Vintage Books, 1965).

HPP   Jean Hyppolite, "Hegel's Phenomenology and Psychoanalysis," in *New Studies in Hegel's Philosophy*, Jean Hyppolite, ed. W. E. Steinkraus (New York: Holt, Rinehart and Winston, 1971).

HPS   Martin Heidegger, *Hegels Phänomenologie des Geistes* GA. 32 (Frankfurt a.M.: V. Klostermann, 1980). *Hegel's Phenomenology of Spirit*, Martin Heidegger, trans. P. Emad and K. Maly (Bloomington: Indiana University Press, 1988).

OT   Michel Foucault, *The Order of Things: An Archaeology of the Human Sciences*, Michel Foucault (New York: Vintage Books, 1970).

Phen.   G. W. F. Hegel, *Phänomenologie des Geistes*, *Werke* 3, (Frankfurt A.M.: Suhrkamp, 1970). *Phenomenology of Spirit*, G. W. F. Hegel, trans. A. V. Miller (Oxford: Clarendon Press, 1977).

S   Martin Heidegger, *"Die Sprache im Gedicht: Eine Erörterung von Georg Trakls Gedicht,"* in *Unterwegs zur Sprache* (Pfullingen: Günther Neske, 1959).

SpA   Martin Heidegger, *"Der Spruch des Anaximander,"* in *Holzwege* (Frankfurt a.M.: V. Klostermann, 1950). "The Anaximander Fragment," in *Early Greek Thinking*, Martin Heidegger, ed. D. F. Krell (New York: Harper and Row, 1984).

SZ   Martin Heidegger, *Sein und Zeit*, 17th ed. (Tübingen: Max Niemeyer, 1993). *Being and Time*, Martin Heidegger, trans. J. Macquarrie and E. Robinson (New York: Harper and Row, 1962). *Being and Time: A Translation of* Sein und Zeit, trans. J. Stambaugh (Albany: State University of New York Press, 1996).

TO   Maurice Blanchot, Michel Foucault, *Foucault/Blanchot:* "Maurice Blanchot: The Thought from Outside," Michel Foucault, trans. B. Massumi; "Michel Foucault as I Imagine Him," Maurice Blanchot," trans. Jeffrey Mehlman (New York: Zone Books, 1990).

Z   Martin Heidegger, *Zollikoner Seminare: Protokolle-Zwiegespräche-Briefe* (Frankfurt a.M.: V. Klostermann, 1987). *Zollikon Seminars: Protocols-Conversations-Letters*, trans. F. Mayr and R. Aksay (Evanston: Northwestern University Press, 2001).

Madness and Death

I would like to make a Book that will derange men, that will be like an open door leading there where they would never have consented to go, in short a door that opens onto reality.

—Artaud

We forget that we are all dead men conversing with dead men. My course of study was philosophy.

—Borges

TOO LATE

THIS WORK ARRIVES too late, because it arrives after the event of madness. By the event of madness I refer to an inflation in discourses on madness in the last three decades.[1] The scholarly curiosity about madness has long passed, even though interest in the question of death seems to be more persistent. Madness appears to be once again silenced, this time not by exclusion, but by exhaustion. This silencing exemplifies an insidious dimension of scholarship. The radicality of any discourse can be mitigated and the discourse stripped of radicality by becoming an "object" of study, a "theme" of what is "mainstream" in academic scholarship. Even if madness once "represented" everything that was contrary to this rational movement of producing works, now it is yet another topic among others. Therefore, madness has once again been excluded, not by silencing the mad, but through the verbosity of reason on madness. Today one has to start a book on madness with a different analogy to leprosy: at the end of the twentieth century, madness disappeared from the Western world.[2] This disappearance of madness is not yet another stage in a continuous exclusion of madness, but a symptom of a much more general tendency of research, namely, a tendency to control, to pacify

1

the radicality of any topic by *studying* it. Yet perhaps there is always something more to say, which indicates not only the driving force of rationality, but also its closure.

The present work tries to explain madness as well. The question of whether this work is yet another rational discourse on madness is one of its central problems. I contend that it is unfair to treat madness as a contemporary focus of interest, one which should ultimately give way to more fashionable topics. Madness, I will try to show throughout this work, is one of the notions that philosophy has always relied upon in constituting its identity. The role of madness, in this respect, has always been parallel to the theme of death. Thus, I treat these two notions together throughout the history of philosophy. Evidently, madness and death are two distinct issues. They have their separate fields and experts. Yet they both concern the human body. They are both inscribed within the relationship between the body and language. Madness and death are the opposites of two characteristics that define the human being as a *rational living being*. Madness and death, therefore, always stand for negativity, that which is other than what the human being strives to be.

Therefore, I will interpret madness and death as instances of negativity; I will argue that they are the driving forces behind the history of philosophy, but I will not simply criticize the way in which philosophy relies on these notions. The pressing question is not whether we are for or against the history of philosophy, for or against reason, for or against any position or author represented in this work, but whether there is any possibility of continuing to think philosophically given this fundamental tendency within philosophy. In the examples of madness and death one can observe how philosophical thinking relates itself to its other. This complex relationship takes the form of a simultaneous exclusion and incorporation. If one is to approach the history of philosophy critically, it is not possible to do so by simply opposing it. In other words, if one were to object to the main strategy of philosophy, namely, its simultaneous appropriation and exclusion of negativity, one could not do so by reversing the role of madness and death from negativity to positivity. Such a move would be naïve and end up affirming the fundamental operation of the metaphysical tradition. I argue that unless one thinks the relationship of philosophy to its other differently, one cannot continue to think, at least not in a meaningful way. The compulsion for thinking comes from outside, from the other. Unless one allows this alterity to invade philosophical thinking, one cannot continue to think. The main conceptual problem of this work, which is really a paradox, is that the continuity of thinking secured by dialectical movement, which reduces difference to opposition, undermines the very possibility of thinking. Therefore, throughout this work I will concentrate on a possible interruption of a certain way of thinking. Hence, my argument is that as long as we continue to think the way we do, we cannot continue to think. The concepts of madness and death will demonstrate how philosophical thinking brings on its own closure through the way in which it thinks negativity.

THE BEGINNING

This work grew out of a conviction that the relationship between rationality and madness is one of the most elusive philosophical oppositions, and that this opposition constitutes the most problematic paradigm of the relationship of the same and its other. Perhaps only the opposition of life and death is as elusive. Indeed, madness and death are related to each other because they are both instances of negativity within philosophical discourse. Philosophy has always been a discipline that strives for rationality. No doubt rationality can be regarded as a broad term that tries to gather together the ancient conception of *logos* with the modern conception of reason. In its search for rationality, philosophy has almost always appealed to a type of madness in characterizing itself. It relied on madness, not in terms of listening to the mad, but rather by regarding madness as a specific configuration of negativity. We are not going to come to a definitive conclusion through this study as to whether this operation of reason constitutes a contradiction, or whether or not it is legitimate. The question is going to be both more modest and more troublesome: *how* does philosophy constitute itself in relation to madness and death? It is true that these terms are not always used consistently in the history of philosophy, designating different notions in different instances. This fact leads one to question whether that to which they refer can ever be the subject of philosophical scrutiny. There is, however, quite a consistency within the philosophical conceptions of madness[3] as well as of death. The philosophical tradition has been consistently ambiguous towards madness and death, and my aim here is not to resolve this ambiguity in order to explain madness and death. Instead, I will try to trace the consistency of this ambiguity in order to understand, perhaps not these notions themselves, but at least certain features of traditional philosophical discourse. Indeed, even my aim is a typically philosophical one. This can be best expressed in terms of the question of madness, but it is also applicable to death. One consistent claim surrounding philosophical discussions of madness is that these discussions do not *really* concern madness, but rather that the term *madness* stands as an index for something else. We will see that madness is that which cannot be spoken or written about in its own terms. One cannot correct this situation by trying to give a voice to madness, because madness would thereby become something other, something rational. Hence, one has to distinguish two seemingly different questions concerning the relationship between madness and rationality. One can say that madness itself does not have a truth, that the madman is quite simply wrong concerning the external world. Yet there is also a truth to madness, one that is accessible only to reason. Unfortunately, the difficulty is that these questions cannot be easily separated. What we designate as truth seems already to be defined by what we designate as rational. This is not as strong a claim as Hegel's statement that what is rational is the real. It only suggests that the terms of rationality seem to be parallel to the terms of truth. It is rational to believe what is true, and it is not rational not to believe in what is true—unless of course one's judgment concerning what is true is mistaken. Hence, even if the mad establishes the truth of madness this truth does not belong to madness; one cannot explain the truth of madness if one is mad. We will return to the relationship between madness and truth at several junctures in this work. The central point emerging from these observations is that madness always gives way to something other than itself within philosophical discussions. Madness and death have remained philosophical concepts in a somewhat strange fashion, namely, by not quite reaching the status of a concept. As we will see, they have sustained philosophy; they are defined and explained by philosophy, yet they are never quite regarded as *proper* philosophical concepts.

To be sure, the reason why madness has remained a concept that concerns philosophy is related to the earliest task philosophy set for itself. Rendering a rational account *(logos)* of the world requires a delimitation of *logos* itself. This need for delimitation is explicitly recognized by Kant, whose "critical" project literally signifies a separation or division *(krinein)* of the limits of reason. However, this requirement is already at work in Plato, especially in the dialogue *Phaedo*, where Socrates is faced with the question of the soul investigating itself. This relationship of *logos* (reason or thinking) to itself proves to be *the* philosophical problem in Western metaphysical thinking. In Plato, the soul gives itself the task of understanding itself. Similarly, in Kant, and in the subsequent tradition of German Idealism, reason has to understand itself. In each case philosophical discourse is faced with reflexivity. This reflexivity takes on different forms. Thinking initially relates to itself in the form of an other. Socrates' dictum "know thyself" becomes a seminal, yet always elusive philosophical problem. *Logos* (or reason) requires a division within itself, a division which is necessary for *logos* to know itself. Hegel recognizes this necessity and embraces this alterity. Yet the other in Hegel affirms the unity of reason, as radical alterity transforms itself into self-identity. For Hegel this is possible only on the basis of alterity as radical opposition. The fact that alterity transforms itself into opposition is the most important aspect of dialectic, and constitutes the power of the dialectic. Yet how can *logos* relate to itself as other? Is this relation not at least a formal determination of madness, namely the other of *logos*? Plato transforms this opposition, first by setting up the opposition between madness and *logos*, and then by unifying madness and *logos*. Madness thereby gets to be "set up": first as everything that is non-logical, and then as the excessively logical, namely, as philosophical madness. Hence, Plato both embraces (because the element of alterity is necessary for the soul to investigate itself) and condemns madness (because ultimately the unity of *logos* has to be recuperated). Hegel distinguishes madness as a relationship of the soul to itself from other types of self-relationality. He designates the first relationship as madness, but the others are not even to be understood as madness anymore: it is rational to be divided as a thinking subject, to be the other, to come back from the site of alterity. Yet I contend that Hegel cannot contain madness once he defines it in terms of reason's relationship to itself as its other. Beyond the limits of reason is "by definition" madness, and we have to be beyond these limits in order to delimit what is "within" these limits. Therefore, in Hegel's philosophy, the question of madness should not only be regarded as a distinctive relationship of the soul to itself. For Hegel himself, madness exclusively concerns the soul. Hegel restricts madness to this specific relationship because he trusts that reason is going to ascertain its power by overcoming the possibility of madness. However, I argue that the question of madness has to be taken to another domain within Hegel's thinking. The question of madness has to be raised with respect to phenomenology, as well as the system as a whole. In the domain of thinking and spirit, madness proves to be a much more serious problem. Plato and Hegel stand at the beginning and the end of the philosophical tradition. Therefore, I focus on them as the "limits" of this tradition. Their treatment of madness exemplifies the traditional philosophical gesture, which seems to have been relatively consistent over two thousand years. Yet I do not mean to suggest that Plato and Hegel address the question of madness in the same way.

Admittedly, madness becomes a distinctive problem in modernity. Madness is related to the rise of subjectivity as the predominant philosophical mode of thinking in modernity. Hence, the question of madness will enable us to raise the question of subjectivity on a different level. In modern philosophy, the problem of subjectivity proves to be more than simply interpreting human beings as subjects, and thereby giving the status of a ground. Subjectivity as a relation of the self to itself is constituted at the level of discourse. Hegel, for example, is quite clear that his logic does not require, indeed displaces, the necessity of a thinking subject. Yet this does not mean that Hegel is entirely beyond the question of subjectivity. One has to concentrate on the way in which thinking as a logical "process" assumes the form of subjectivity. Hence, subjectivity indicates one possible relationship of thinking to itself at the level of logic. I will try to show that Hegel is committed to a certain relationship of thinking to itself in order to articulate the dialectical movement. The question of subjectivity concerns the nature of this relationship and of this movement. Therefore, madness, in relation to the problem of subjectivity, has to be read as a problem of the *logos* itself, rather than of the human being (the human subject). Hence, this study will concentrate not only on what philosophers say about madness, but also on how their discourses are articulated in such a way that the question of madness becomes relevant and subversive.

Another consistent dimension of the philosophical conception of madness, for my purposes, is its relationship to death. This relation assumes different forms and takes place at different levels. In the most straightforward sense, madness is the death of the soul. For Plato, however, both madness and death concern the articulation of philosophy as an engagement. Both of these themes attempt to dissociate philosophy from an exclusively intellectual activity. As a merely intellectual activity, philosophy would have been inseparable from sophism. Plato's strategy against sophistry is first to articulate the distinction between philosophy and sophism in terms of an engagement. However, Plato subsequently transforms this engagement into a "content" in an effort to preserve philosophical discourse from the danger of ultimately losing its constant presence to forms. The famous distinction Plato draws between the world of being and the world of becoming ultimately excludes madness from the domain of "proper" philosophy. The distinction between being and becoming proves to be the inception of philosophy as well as the inception of its disintegration.

As Nietzsche observes, philosophy subsequently becomes a degeneration of thinking. One cannot, however, overcome this degeneration by reversing the hierarchy between the world of becoming and the world of being. If the solution were such a reversal, madness or death would have been privileged, since they have mostly been associated with the body and the world of becoming. However, since we do not intend to engage in such a reversal, madness and death have to be understood in terms of a "neither/nor" with respect to the distinction between the sensuous and suprasensuous worlds. This indecidability designates our contemporary relationship to the philosophical tradition. Philosophical concepts (for example, madness and death, even if they are not regarded as "proper" philosophical concepts) can neither be abandoned nor preserved, neither condemned nor emancipated. One cannot be for or against madness or death. By the same token, one cannot simply condemn or embrace philosophical rationality either. Most importantly, one cannot simply oppose the philosophical tradition, since the terms of oppositionality have already been determined by rational thinking. I believe this is what the power of Hegel's thought teaches us. To oppose the philosophical tradition requires that one be able to delimit philosophical thought; it presupposes that one can separate philosophical thought from what remains outside of it, and thereby render a voice to the other. Yet all these operations in their fundamental honesty remain philosophical operations. This predicament does not mean, however, that one cannot continue to think. It requires us to understand the philosophical tradition not in terms that oppose this tradition, but in those that may potentially disrupt philosophical thinking. This work contends that madness and death are terms that may potentially disrupt philosophical thinking, but it also recognizes the possibility of this contention having already been taken up by the philosophical vocabulary.

Philosophical approaches to madness are ambiguous, and the power of philosophical discourse does to a certain extent emerge from this ambiguity. Madness has always been that which is the other of philosophy (of *logos*, of reason). Plato considers madness to be that which is associated with the body, the sensuous world of the particulars, and the world of becoming. Thus, to restore the dignity of madness would be nothing other than to restore the dignity of the world in which we live. Yet would this task go against Plato? Plato also designates philosophy as a kind of madness, a divine inspiration. Thus, that reading which condemns madness as bodily, sensuous, and mortal is also one that claims to be madness itself (philosophical madness). How can we oppose Plato without accepting these terms? It is true that Plato appeals to a distinction within the notion of madness, which underlies all the subsequent conceptions of madness. Plato believes that philosophical madness is the "proper" madness. Proper madness is not a-logical (that is, it is not against *logos*) but an extreme form of *logos*, the language of the forms (beings as they are). If one would agree with Nietzsche that Platonism is the origin of nihilism, one could claim that we need to rehabilitate the other form of madness, namely the bodily, the sensuous, the mortal (disease, madness of human origin) in order to overcome nihilism. Yet how are we to do that without accepting all the characteristics attributed to this type of madness by Plato? What would it mean to dignify this type of madness other than to claim that it is not really madness, but rather a profound insight? Does not this attempt simply affirm the Platonic opposition as well as the Platonic strategy of dignifying madness by making it other than madness, that is, by turning it into rationality? In light of this problem, our aim should not be to understand just madness, but rather philosophical rationality through a study of madness. What we designate here as "understanding" necessitates an attempt to rethink the nature of philosophy itself and the way in which it articulates itself. This is because in the very operation of defining any possible understanding of madness one also defines the possibilities of understanding philosophy itself. Thus, in the attempt to understand the philosophical concept of madness, we have to rethink the way in which we understand philosophy itself.

In a sense, death exemplifies a more radical relationship of philosophy to negativity. In death the continuity of thinking seems to be potentially interrupted beyond any possibility of recuperation. Yet philosophy has incorporated the possibility of death into its own discourse and thereby secured the continuity of thinking beyond death. Death here obviously does not refer to the death of an individual, but to a general concept. Philosophy incorporates death into the life of philosophy in the same way it incorporates madness into rational discourse. We can observe this incorporation both in Plato and Hegel. The fact that death and madness do not belong to an individual points to an important issue between Hegel and Heidegger. According to Heidegger, Hegel's thinking remains committed to the philosophical notion of subjectivity, not because Hegel presupposes the subject as the ground of thinking, but because Hegel constructs philosophical discourse in the shape of subjectivity. For Heidegger, subjectivity means that the philosophical discourse is a self-restoring identity that incorporates difference in the form of opposition. Heidegger attempts to question and displace this very notion of subjectivity rather than the individual subject, which is already sublated in Hegel's thinking.

MADNESS AND MENTAL ILLNESS

This work is philosophical and does not approach the question of madness from a medical point of view. Yet one has to explain the difference between madness and mental illness. Philosophers often speak about madness without explicitly articulating its relationship to mental illness. From a medical perspective, this may be explained by saying that philosophers do not sufficiently know medical "facts" concerning mental illness; what they designate as "madness" are variations of mental illness. My aim is to displace this objection to philosophy on several grounds. First of all, some philosophers do know a great deal about mental illness and the physical and somatic aspects of madness. Secondly, even within the medical traditions of the past and the present there is not a unified conception of what madness really is. Hence, it may be misleading to separate different interpretations of madness and designate one as closer to "reality" as understood from a scientific perspective. Thirdly, and perhaps most importantly, every conception of madness already presupposes or bases itself upon, knowingly or unknowingly, philosophical determinations of what it means to *be* a human, what it means to know, what it means to be rational, and so on. Hence, in and through this work I will try to suggest that our understanding of mental illness in the Western world is grounded upon philosophy. This suggestion does not deny that there might be an organic basis of madness, but it does require a rethinking of the conception of body and organism. I am not going to be able to carry out all this "rethinking" that I suggest. However, I will expose the most basic presuppositions of theories of mental illness, namely, that such theories are based upon a subjectivist view of the human being, and a scientific-objectivist view of the world. By exposing the difficulties of these views, I will not suggest that they are simply wrong, but rather that their presuppositions are to be grounded in a more fundamental understanding of the human being and the world.

The aim of this work is not to explain madness and death, but to show how philosophy relies on these notions to articulate itself. Therefore, this work does not discuss any of the "mad philosophers" (Nietzsche, Kierkegaard, Hölderlin, etc.) or "mad artists" (again Hölderlin, Nerval, Artaud, etc.). The reason for this is that I do not want to give the impression of relying on any "authority" that is considered to be mad. Instead I will discuss perhaps the "most rational" philosophers: Plato, Hegel, Heidegger, Foucault, and Derrida. These thinkers are not generally considered to be mad. The philosophers I discuss wrote on madness and death as explicit and constructive themes of philosophy, and we can reconstruct their thinking, at least partially, on the basis of these themes. Also, without totalizing the history of philosophy, I argue that these thinkers articulate a fundamental tendency within philosophy with respect to its relationship to negativity. Plato and Hegel construct philosophy in relation to madness and death. Heidegger and Foucault question philosophy on the basis of its relationship to these concepts. Hence, madness and death not only constitute philosophy, but also by this very constitution problematize philosophical discourse. Heidegger and Foucault articulate this problem of philosophy without relying on a proximity to madness.

This work does not pretend, therefore, to display a "proximity" to madness. It is inevitably a rational endeavor. Yet it is also ex-centric, or rather bi-centric. The two centers of this work are Hegel and Heidegger. These two thinkers represent two different conceptions of madness, two different tendencies toward negativity. Hegel regards negativity as the necessary "capital" of philosophy. He articulates the power of rationality in its assimilation of madness. Therefore, under a Hegelian law, every discourse on madness inadvertently benefits rationality. Heidegger, by contrast, questions this "power" of philosophical rationality. For Heidegger, there is a fundamental "finitude" of philosophical discursivity that undermines its purported power. Heidegger is also quite aware that the very thematization of this finitude is in danger of undermining itself and of contributing to philosophical discourse. The present work will remain within this tension. However, this tension does not simply represent an "either/or" in its articulation of madness. I argue that this tension transforms philosophy, or rather reconfigures philosophical discourse. I will try to show that philosophical discourse is no longer able to justify itself in terms of its correspondence to what it claims to be about. Between Hegel and Heidegger, a significant transformation takes place within philosophy (perhaps for Heidegger we should not call this discourse philosophy anymore). In Heidegger's reading of Hegel, philosophy no longer remains a rational or cognitive activity. For Heidegger, the overcoming of philosophical subjectivity, the subjectivity that reached its culmination in Hegel, requires a rethinking of the notions of madness and death and thereby a different way of thinking, one where the principle of contradiction is not the criterion for truth, where the human being is not a rational animal, and, finally where the self-referentiality of thinking does not recuperate its own ground. The themes of madness and death illustrate this transformation.

THE WORK

For the most part, this work consists of close readings of a number of texts. My primary aim is to explicate what Plato, Hegel, Heidegger, and Foucault write on madness and death. However, mere explication is not sufficient to see what is at stake in the constitution of philosophical discourse. Heidegger and Foucault also engage in a certain performance of negativity in their respective discourses. This performance cannot be reduced to the content of what they write. Therefore, my interpretation will also try to explicate this performativity. I believe this performance becomes a way of manifesting negativity in a text without simply becoming caught up in a contradiction. Finally, my text will also try to be sensitive to its own limitations.

Philosophically, I will approach madness and death as "instances" of negativity. We will not encounter this terminology of negativity until we read Hegel. However, in terms of what negativity stands for, it is not simply a designation of an operation that emerges with Hegel. For Plato, negativity stands for both the transient nature of the world of becoming as well as the "absence" to which only the human mind has access. Therefore, negativity, since the inception of philosophy, stands for both something to be overcome, and something that is desired. I will connect this ambiguous necessity to the question of the metaphysics of presence as instituted, according to some, by Plato. The very same operation of a simultaneous overcoming and accommodation will also be crucial in the institution of subjectivity as the locus of philosophical thinking. The figure of Hegel represents the most extreme possibility of subjectivity. For Hegel, subjectivity is not opposed to objectivity, and does not rely on interpreting the human being as an individual subject. Subjectivity designates a fundamental operation of philosophical thinking.

The first chapter consists of a close reading of Plato's *Phaedo* and *Phaedrus*. I try to demonstrate that Plato inaugurates the philosophical relationship to negativity. Plato initially understands philosophy in terms of a question of engagement. The necessity of engagement arising from the question of absence in the world of becoming, however, is circumvented by the constitution of an intellectual presence to the forms. Plato delimits the possibilities of addressing negativity in general, and madness and death in particular, within a philosophical discourse. Therefore, every subsequent attempt to address the question of negativity philosophically has to take Plato into account. Plato also connects the question of madness to the question of truth. Consequently, all subsequent chapters address the connection between truth and madness.

The second chapter articulates Hegel's thinking as one of the centers of this work. I present a reading of Hegel's discussion of madness in the *Encyclopaedia*, and try to connect this discussion to the question of death in the *Phenomenology of Spirit*. In Hegel, we observe that madness and death, as instances of negativity, secure the continuity of the dialectical movement. However, this continuity (especially in the case of madness) depends on a specific interpretation of these themes in terms of the question of truth. I argue that Hegel transforms the locus of the question of truth from our access to a suprasensuous world to the *continuity* of the dialectic. I will argue that the problem of the continuity of the dialectic pervades Hegel's entire system. Hegel argues that thinking can proceed without any presuppositions because he formulates the relationship to negativity as a "cognitive" problem.[4] I will challenge Hegel's consignment of madness and death to a cognitive problem. My reading of Hegel is already informed by and anticipates Heidegger's interpretation and response to Hegel.

The third and the fourth chapters concern the second center of this work, and thereby show the ex-centric nature of the question of negativity. Here I will explicate Heidegger's insights not against (in opposition to) Hegel, but *after* Hegel. That is to say, if Heidegger's philosophy were simply in opposition to Hegel, Hegel would have a dialectical defense. I will argue that Heidegger's philosophy is not simply in oppositon to Hegel, but tries to deconstruct the very logic of the dialectic of opposition. Even though I do not compare and contrast Hegel and Heidegger in every respect, I do raise the question of whether Heidegger articulates a different relationship to negativity than Hegel.

The third chapter presents an interpretation of *Being and Time* in terms of the question of negativity. In *Being and Time,* this question manifests itself in terms of the figure of being-towards-death. I read *Being and Time* with an eye toward the possibility that a Hegelian response would complicate its aims. I contend that *Being and Time* is a *staging of a failure.* Heidegger stages *Being and Time* such that if it is read as a constructivist discourse, it undermines itself. *Being and Time* is a necessary path to be followed in order to question the limits of "description" in philosophy and the scope of subjectivity.

The fourth chapter is an attempt to reconstruct Heidegger's later philosophy as a response to the difficulties raised in *Being and Time.* Here I raise the question of the relationship between Hegel and Heidegger explicitly and interpret a number of Heidegger's texts as a response to Hegel. I configure this relationship in terms of the question of subjectivity in its connections to the themes of truth and historicity. I conclude this chapter with a close reading of Heidegger's texts: "The Anaximander Fragment" and "Language in the Poem." My claim here is that Heidegger's interpretation of madness demonstrates a different relationship to negativity than that of Hegel. It might not be adequate to designate Heidegger's interpretations of madness and death as negativity, since this term presupposes and remains within the limits of a structure of opposition (in relation to positivity). Heidegger uses the terms of nothingness, nihilation, or absencing in characterizing madness and death. Yet he also uses the term negativity. Therefore, I will continue to use the term negativity while emphasizing that it means something different for Heidegger, something that is neither rational nor cognitive.

The fifth chapter focuses on the debate between Foucault and Derrida concerning Foucault's *Histoire de la folie*. I connect the problems arising in this debate to the questions arising from the confrontation between Hegel and Heidegger. Hence, the debate between Foucault and Derrida is not an afterthought, but addresses the very same question concerning the possibility of interpreting negativity (madness). I show a connection between the "late" Heidegger and the "early" Foucault concerning the relation between truth and madness and their relationship to the Greeks.

Between the fourth and fifth chapters, the figure of Derrida emerges as what can be described figuratively as a "ghost." I do not explicitly deal with Derrida's own texts in terms of their possible contribution to the question of madness. Yet I do discuss his texts on Heidegger (*Of Spirit*) and Foucault ("Cogito and the History of Madness"). At times I treat Derrida as a "ghost" of Hegel, complicating and questioning Heidegger and Foucault. I have to acknowledge, however, that Derrida, in his own way, attempts to think the limitations of a Hegelian law. Yet Derrida's deconstruction (at least in his reading of Heidegger and Foucault) at times seems to attribute a certain integrity and set of "rules" of formation to philosophical discourse that has to be questioned.

Even though the theme of death has been a philosophical topic throughout the history of philosophy, it has mostly either assumed a religious connotation or been regarded as an existential problem. No doubt the latter is true for Heidegger. However, in this work I contend that for Heidegger death also transfigures philosophy rather than grounding it existentially. Death, in this precise sense of negativity, has not been the focus of philosophical reflection. This is also true for madness. Madness has not even been considered a proper philosophical problem. Even Plato's claims that philosophy is a kind of madness have mostly been understood either in a divine-religious sense or as an idiosyncrasy of a philosopher. My treatment of madness and death as instances of negativity attempts to explain the historical and conceptual configuration of philosophy, which almost always has been a self-grounding discourse. While philosophy grounds, that is, justifies itself in relation to its other, it also produces, interprets, and incorporates its other. In fact, philosophy has always justified itself on the basis of this fundamental ability to incorporate its other by performing better what its other proclaims to do. Hence madness and death, as well as the relationship of philosophy to these notions, are not peripheral questions in philosophy, but rather concern and question the very essence of philosophical discourse.

ONE

Plato

Death and Madness in the *Phaedo* and *Phaedrus*

Immortal mortals, mortal immortals, living their death and dying their life.
—Heraclitus

Why should we not call madness death, seeing that by it mind dies, the noblest part of us?
—Philo

READERS OF PLATO'S dialogues would recognize a constantly renewed desire to define philosophy and to distinguish it from sophistry, rhetoric, poetry, etc.[1] One suspects that this attempt to delimit philosophy as a discourse is itself what philosophizing is. In Plato, reflexivity is already inscribed into the nature of philosophical activity. The *Phaedo* and the *Phaedrus* are two of Plato's dialogues where philosophical activity is presented as a questioning of what philosophy is. In the *Phaedo*, Plato claims that philosophy is a practice for dying and death, whereas in the *Phaedrus* philosophy is described as a kind of madness. Through these two characterizations of philosophy, Plato determines the subsequent attempts to think philosophy, as well as to think philosophically about the themes of madness and death. After Plato, madness and death become deeply connected to the way in which philosophy interprets itself. Therefore, to the extent that philosophy is considered to be, among other things, the activity of asking what philosophy is, madness and death emerge as two themes that can help us understand this activity. To say that philosophy is an activity of asking what philosophy itself is does not suggest

13

that all philosophical activity explicitly asks this question. Historically, the question of what philosophy is has not always been explicitly posed. However, every philosophical questioning does in fact bring together an implicit understanding of what philosophy is. Martin Heidegger expresses this conviction in *What is Philosophy?*[2] and "What is Metaphysics?"[3] These two works not only connect the question of what philosophy is to philosophical activity itself, but also articulate this activity in terms of a certain engagement.[4] Philosophy, according to Heidegger, is a question of a fundamental attunement *(Stimmung)* where philosophy "concerns us, touches us in our very nature."[5] In "What is Metaphysics?" Heidegger expresses the same conviction in terms of metaphysical questions: ". . . every metaphysical question can be asked only in such a way that the questioner as such is also there within the question, that is, is placed in question."[6] Plato shares the conviction that philosophy is a matter of engagement. In the *Phaedo* this engagement is characterized in terms of death.[7] Socrates states that Evenus, who is otherwise indistinguishable from a philosopher, ought to follow him to death if he (Evenus) is a real philosopher. Yet Evenus's alleged unwillingness to do this "surprises" Socrates and leads him to question whether Evenus is actually a philosopher. Evenus is only *believed* to be a philosopher. Is there a criterion to distinguish a philosopher from a sophist? It seems that philosophy and sophistry speak about the same thing to a large extent. What distinguishes philosophical activity is an engagement with not only what is said, but also with that which speaks to us. The response to being *(ousia)* is a response to what a moment presents.

Yet what is philosophical activity as opposed to sophistry? Where does philosophy begin? What, if any, is the mark of the moment where philosophy is not a matter of content, but a desire for engagement?[8] At this point one must not simply ask the historical question as to when philosophy started, or who the first philosopher was. Even when we raise this historical question we realize that our answer depends upon the way in which we understand what philosophy is. Hence, the question of the beginning of philosophy is itself a philosophical question, not only because beginning is a philosophical problem, but also because we need to raise the question of what philosophy is, that is, *the* philosophical question of *ti to estin?* (what is . . . ?). We often take it for granted that the philosophical (rather than the historical) beginning of philosophy is wonder *(thaumazein)*.[9] Yet we must emphasize that wonder is not the origin of philosophy in the sense of a beginning, which is left behind. In *What is Philosophy?*, Heidegger claims that *arche* is both the beginning and the principle of (that which rules) philosophy.[10] Hence, *thaumazein* is not simply the mood one is in before starting to philosophize, but it is an attunement between the questioner and the world. In this sense of the word "beginning," there are in fact multiple beginnings of philosophy, and perhaps wonder is one of them. In Plato we find two

different origins (archai) or definitions of philosophy: philosophy as a practice of death, and philosophy as a kind of madness.

In what follows I will discuss the Phaedo and the Phaedrus. My guiding
topic in these discussions will be the following: For Plato philosophy, defined
as a kind of madness and as a preparation for death, is, in the first instance, a
relationship to absence. To the extent that one is called to understand the
world around oneself, one is called to respond philosophically to the being of
things, and thereby one is transported to a realm of absence. Death characterizes this experience of transport, which is not simply an experience in
time, but an archaic experience, perhaps an experience of that which,
according to Plato, has never been present. Hence, the willingness to die, or
to assume a different relationship to death, is what distinguishes the philosopher from the sophist. However, this understanding of absence is displaced in
and through Plato's text once he adopts the language of forms (ideas). The
theory of ideas (or even the lack of such a theory) is Plato's response to the
philosophical question of absence.[11] Plato articulates this absence as that
which accounts for (grounds and causes) things that are present. Things
themselves are constituted in terms of archai that are not present, in fact
those that are always absent. Philosophy, therefore, is an attempt to speak of
that which is absent, that which is the ground of what is present. For Plato,
death and madness give "access" to this absence. Yet this possibility of access
also transforms absence into presence. This transformation enables us to
understand Heidegger's claim that the Greeks think being always as presence.
This is not to say that the Greeks did not think of absence, but that Greeks
had a particular understanding of absence derived from presence. Therefore,
Plato institutes a conceptual continuity between presence and absence, that
is, absence is understood as a modification of presence within a conceptually
homogenous field.[12]

PHAEDO

In terms of the dramatic structure of the dialogue, the question of philosophy
as a preparation for death emerges in the context of Socrates' impending
death. We tend to think that the dialogue introduces the question of death
because it concerns Socrates' death. Yet this question is introduced in a seemingly accidental manner. Socrates says that Evenus has to follow him to death
if he (Evenus) is a real philosopher. The puzzle this advice causes leads
Socrates to explain why "those who are touched[13] by philosophy in the proper
manner (orthos)[14] practice dying and death." There is, therefore, an improper
way of practicing philosophy, as well as an improper way of understanding
death.[15] Philosophy is a practice for death only when philosophy and death
are understood in the proper manner. Socrates articulates this distinction in
response to Simmias's statement that there are people who think that

philosophers desire death and well deserve it too. Socrates answers that these people speak the truth, but "they do not know in what way they [philosophers] deserve death, nor what kind of death it is" (64b).

What, then is the improper manner of practicing philosophy? Is an improper practice of philosophy still philosophy, or does it become some other activity? Socrates formulates his answer on the basis of philosophical engagement rather than on content. What distinguishes proper philosophy from improper and perhaps even non-philosophy is not the presence of a certain content in the philosophical discourse. It is not as if philosophers think about certain issues, as opposed to nonphilosophers who do not know anything about these issues. What makes a certain activity philosophy, according to Plato, is the way in which someone is engaged with this activity. Philosophy is not the knowledge of certain principles, or content, but a particular engagement with *logos*. Yet one does not simply enter into a philosophical engagement at will.[16] Even though the philosophical engagement manifests itself as a willingness to die, one does not engage with philosophy merely by willing to die, for example, by committing suicide. Socrates articulates the distinction between suicide and the philosophical conception of death in terms of his response to Cebes' question concerning the incompatibility of Socrates' claims that Evenus should follow him to death, and that suicide is not permitted. Socrates answers that one should not escape life to the extent that one is the property of the gods, but one can, through the practice of philosophy, join "other wise and good gods." A mere willingness to die, to end one's life, does not guarantee proper philosophical activity. Thus, philosophical engagement requires a displacement of the ordinary understanding of death. Since philosophy articulates itself in terms of a different understanding of death, it has to delimit itself with regard to other activities by raising the question of what it itself is. The accompaniment of this questioning and reflective attitude concerning philosophy itself is what makes a question a philosophical question. This seems to be a characteristic that Heidegger attributes to metaphysics: ". . . every metaphysical question always encompasses the whole range of metaphysical problems. Each question is itself always the whole."[17]

Plato understands this engagement with/of "the whole" in terms of death.[18] Yet what does it mean to say philosophy is a preparation for death? Socrates establishes what death is quite unproblematically, without any resistance from his interlocutors.[19] "Do we think there is such a thing as death?" The answer is an unequivocal "yes." There *is* such a thing. Socrates continues: "we believe, do we not, that death is the separation of the soul from the body, and that the state of being dead is the state in which the body is separated from the soul and exists alone by itself and the soul is separated from the body and exists alone by itself?" (64c). The word for separation, *apallagen*, can also mean "deliverance," "release," or "departure." According to this definition of death, not only the soul, but also the body has a separate existence, that is, it can also exist by itself. Yet what kind of existence can one attribute to the body by itself? Is the body not dead once separated from the soul? Isn't the body precisely that which cannot exist by itself?[20] This understanding of death as a separation is the most important aspect of the dialogue, since the subsequent discussion in its entirety follows from this understanding of death.[21] Moreover, this definition of death is particularly important for subsequent interpretations of Plato's philosophy. Obviously, there is a metaphysical difficulty in this definition, since it implies the separability, and consequently the potentially independent existence, of the body and the soul.[22] Philosophically, it is difficult to accept this conclusion. However, one has to distinguish the question of the independent existence of the body and the soul from the question of their separation in death. Even if one says that the soul and the body cannot exist separately, one still has to explain why Plato defines death as their separation, and why he introduces this understanding of death in a few lines without any apparent complication.

Socrates' explanation of why philosophy is a preparation for death and dying starts out with a description of the philosopher. The philosopher, according to Socrates, is not concerned with the pleasures of the body. People would think that someone who is not concerned with the pleasures of the body "does not deserve to live, and that one who cares nothing for the pleasures of the body is about as good as dead" (65a). Initially it appears that Socrates associates life with the bodily functions. Yet this is what most people think, and not necessarily a proper understanding of life. This poses a special difficulty in understanding the role of the soul for life. The soul is said to be the cause (aitia) of life. It is also that which is related to death in that its separation from the body leads to death. Socrates leaves the description of the philosopher with respect to the bodily pleasures and moves on to the acquisition of knowledge. The body is also said to be a hindrance in gaining knowledge, as the body's sources (the senses) do not yield accurate knowledge. In other words, both in everyday life, as well as in the pursuit of knowledge, the philosopher tries to dissociate him/herself from the body. Yet Socrates' discussion up to this point does not provide a proper explanation of how philosophy is a practice for the separation of the soul and the body. One cannot understand this separation by simply observing or describing the philosopher. As we see in the next argument, true understanding is not to be accomplished in terms of things we observe, but in terms of principles that are not immediately present. At this point the content of Socrates' argument converges with the way in which he designs his argument, that is, Plato articulates the necessity of looking away from the sensuous by himself looking away from what is given to the senses.

Socrates changes his line of questioning by asking whether we think that there is such a thing as the just itself. By admitting that there are such things as beauty itself, goodness itself, justice itself, Socrates' interlocutor is forced to look away from the realm of the sensuous to that which is not sensuously present.[23] Socrates claims that these forms are the underlying being of everything. To know what lies before us, one must look *away* from that thing. It requires a certain kind of access to something that is absent, yet which constitutes the underlying being of that which is in front of us. This look away is not a voluntary action that results from a decision, but a condition for the possibility of perceptual knowledge. As Plato demonstrates in his argument that knowledge is recollection, a prior knowledge of forms, such as the knowledge of equality, is necessary in order to be able to perceive any two things resembling each other (i.e., falling short of equality) (73c–75c). The knowledge of these forms cannot be reached through the senses. The senses only give access to things that are physically present. Yet their ground, cause, or underlying being (*ousia*) is not present (65e). These grounds can only be accessed through thinking detached from the senses, that is, through the soul "separated" from the body. Hence the body is said to be the cause of the evil that distracts the soul from its pursuit of truth. The foolishness of the body keeps one away from this pursuit. Since pure knowledge is impossible to the extent that the body intervenes in this pursuit, it can only be gained at the moment of a complete separation of the soul from the body. Yet this does not mean that there is nothing to do while the body is still with the soul, namely, while one is alive. The philosopher engages in a kind of purification in order to collect and bring the soul together from all parts of the body as much as possible, that is, he or she tries to separate the soul from the body. Hence, it would be absurd for the philosopher to be afraid of death once this separation is finalized. Once death is understood properly, then the fear of death is circumvented, and once this fear is circumvented, there is nothing more to be afraid of in life.

Socrates' response to Cebes' concern that people still fear that the soul does not exist after death makes explicit what has been implicitly the underlying theme of the dialogue, namely, the relationship between the opposites. Plato had already intimated the structure of oppositions at the beginning of the dialogue. Opposites are related to each other in such a way that one cannot experience or even comprehend one of the opposites without the other; for example, there is no pleasure without pain, as Socrates suggests when he is freed from his shackles. In response to Cebes, Socrates argues that opposites come from each other; death comes from life just as life comes from death. The move from death to life is necessary for existence in general to continue, and is possible only through the soul being immortal. Our souls exist in another world when we are dead. Hence "the living are generated from the dead, just as much as the dead is from the living . . . it seems . . . to be a sufficient proof that the souls of the dead exist somewhere, whence they come back to life" (72a).

According to the dialogue, this structure of opposites not only establishes that the souls of the dead in fact survive death, but also shows that knowledge is recollection.[24] Socrates establishes that knowledge is recollection through demonstrating that the concept of equality cannot be derived from the things that we observe, since no two things exhibit perfect equality. This proof seems to be similar to the one in the *Meno,* in that both demonstrate the impossibility of arriving at the "itself" through things that we can observe. However, the argument in the *Phaedo* demonstrates the additional point that this knowledge of equality as such is necessary in order to perceive two things as similar.[25] The requirement of the form of equality connects the conviction that things in the world are what they are through the forms with the claim that we cannot even perceive and understand things in the world without an access to forms.[26] Since the knowledge of forms must have been with us prior to any perception, it can only be explained as being in our soul prior to having any experience, that is, prior to birth.

Yet, according to Simmias, the childish fear of death in us is not satisfied by this argument. The proof only shows that the soul existed before we were born, but not after we die. As a response to this difficulty, Socrates connects the being of the soul with the being of things.[27] The soul knows the being of things because it is akin to such being, unchanging, divine, deathless, intelligible, and invisible. Therefore, we should understand the soul in terms of the characteristics of the forms. Yet how is the knowledge of the soul possible? If the soul is itself invisible and absent in any given presence, what is it that knows the soul? The answer seems to suggest that the soul has a circular relationship to itself.[28] It has to know itself. Within the Platonic framework, the knowledge of the soul is only possible with regard to its form.[29] That is to say, we can only know one, unchanging, immortal soul. Therefore, the relationship between the being of the soul and individual souls seem to have a similar character to the relationship between equality itself, and equal things. Socrates explains this relationship in terms of his response to Cebes' objection that the soul may live longer than the body, but that this does not prove that it is immortal. Socrates' response first establishes that forms, that are invisible, are the causes of things that are visible. The individual things are what they are in virtue of their participation in the universals. Accordingly the soul, considered as a universal, is that which gives life, as well as that which does not accept its opposite, namely death. This response is intended to explain the relationship of the soul to the body, but not the relationship between the being (form) of the soul and the individual souls. The question remains as to how one can distinguish individual souls from each other. To the extent that the soul is united with the body it can be said to be individuated, but what is it that individuates the soul after its separation from the body?[30] The soul is that which gives life to the body, but without the body it is impossible to understand the identity of the individual soul. The soul is not only inaccessible to the senses, but it is not a "thing" that can exist independently of the body and still be individuated.

The soul in a body is that which gives access to what is absent. It has access to things that are not immediately present. Yet the presence of the things that are present is constituted (caused) by things that are themselves not present, namely, forms. On the other hand, since the soul is no*thing*, but rather is that which provides access to (perceives and understands) the presence of things that are present, it can be read as the unity of presence, just as forms constitute the unity of particulars. In the dialogue Socrates refers to this unity in terms of the individual soul "collecting and bringing itself together" (67c). Yet this unity is already presupposed since it cannot be first constituted from the things that are present. Since this unity is also the presupposition for any perception, Plato attributes this unity to a time before birth. The soul is said to exist before we were born. The soul, therefore, has to be understood as that which is absent, yet constitutes the presence of the things that are present. To the extent that it can be known it is one, and the multiplicity of individual souls can only be understood in terms of the multiplicity of bodies.

To say that the soul is immortal is to say that there *is* a unity of presence, and individuals participate in this unity. The soul is the cause of life. Yet what does it mean to say that the individual is dead? If the soul is that which causes life and if the body is alive to the extent that it is united with the soul, human life is a unity of life and death. Therefore, death is not the simple opposite of life as people generally think, taking it to be the end of ordinary life, but it already *is* in and through life. But which part of human existence represents life and which part represents death? Plato's response to this question is complicated.[31] First of all, we have to reiterate that death is that which provides access to beings in themselves, as well as that which makes human perception in life possible. The soul is the part, which represents both of these aspects. Furthermore, the soul is that which knows death the least, because it is said to be immortal. Hence, by displacing the ordinary understanding of death, Plato associates the soul with life and the body with death.[32] People, who think that philosophers are as good as dead because philosophers deny bodily pleasures are wrong in thinking that life is to be associated with the body. Plato's strategy does not simply reverse the terms of the body and the soul with respect to life and death, but complicates the opposition between life and death while carrying over the opposition to one between body and soul. As a result, that which represents absence (the soul) emerges as that which is the prime presence. This is to say that even though Plato initially articulates the nature of the soul in terms of absence (i.e., in terms of "things" that are not present), he displaces this explanation by attributing a full presence of these things to the soul after death. The soul (that which practices philosophy properly) is going to be fully present to forms, just as they are going to be fully present to the soul.

Death for Plato provides an access to forms that are not present. However, death (i.e., a certain type of absence within presence) is already presupposed in order to be able to perceive anything. Plato demonstrates this presupposition in his argument that learning is recollection. It is this confrontation with death that Plato sees as an engagement of philosophy. "I do not believe anyone who heard us *now* . . . would say that I am chattering and talking about things which do not concern me" (70c, my emphasis). The "now" Socrates is referring to is the moment of confrontation with death, where philosophy is not an activity that is to be justified in terms of its content, but in terms of being touched. It is precisely the same touch that Plato articulates in the *Phaedrus* as madness.

PHAEDRUS

In the *Phaedrus*, madness plays a similar role to that played by death in the *Phaedo*. A special kind of madness, just like the particular understanding of death we have just considered, is said to provide access to the forms that are not present in front of us. This transition from death to madness is especially important between the *Phaedo* and the *Phaedrus*, because Plato refers to the contamination of the soul by the body as a kind of foolishness. Yet this conception of madness (referred to as "of human origin" in the *Phaedrus*) has to be distinguished from divine madness, just as the ordinary death of the body has to be distinguished from death as the separation of the soul from the body. Madness is a peculiar configuration of death in life, and plays the same role as death in delimiting philosophy as a peculiar engagement.

Socrates' speech developing philosophy as a kind of madness follows two speeches, Lysias's speech read by Phaedrus, and Socrates' own speech attempting to surpass the former. The dialogue starts out with Socrates meeting Phaedrus who is on his way to take a walk outside the city walls. Socrates has already been lured outside the city, to unfamiliar domains. Yet Socrates immediately displaces the unfamiliarity of the country outside the city walls by locating exactly where Boreas is said to have carried off Orethyia, just as he is going to circumvent the unfamiliarity of madness through philosophy. Phaedrus has spent the entire night with Lysias who was in the city, and promises to tell Socrates Lysias's speech about love. Phaedrus says that this is particularly fitting for Socrates, as he claims to be a lover. Lysias's speech argues that favors should be granted to the one who is not in love rather than to the lover.

Lysias's speech is predicated upon the assumption that the lover is insane (*nosein*) rather than being in his or her right mind (*sophronein*). This assumption accompanies all the advantages Lysias claims the nonlover has over the lover. He argues that the "beloved," who is assumed to be acting according to his or her self-interest, should choose the nonlover over the lover, as the nonlover will serve this self-interest better. Socrates finds Lysias's speech repetitious and not well organized. Yet there seems to be a more fundamental problem with the speech, namely that even though it represents the virtues of granting favors to the nonlover, Lysias actually becomes a lover, and demonstrates all the qualities of the "lover." In other words, in order to gain the favors of the "beloved," the nonlover appeals to all the advantages that can equally originate from a lover. That is to say that since Lysias does not proceed from a definition of love, he is not in a position to distinguish the lover from a nonlover. Thus Lysias does not have knowledge of himself, and is not in a position to preserve his identity as non-lover throughout the speech.[33] Socrates' response and his subsequent speech underscore this problem. Socrates delivers the speech as a lover disguised as a nonlover. Moreover, Socrates indicates the difficulty of distinguishing the lover from a nonlover because they both have desires (epithumiai).

Socrates claims that it is possible to deliver a better speech than Lysias's. In fact his breast is full, and the speech is forcing itself outside. Thereby, Socrates gives the first indication that he is not going to be responsible for the speech. In addition, he covers his head, and qualifies his speech as a lover disguised as a non-lover in order to win over the beloved. These qualifications move Socrates further away from being the origin of the discourse he is about to deliver. Yet Socrates admits that he cannot surpass Lysias's speech in every aspect; this is something that would not even happen to the worst speaker. Phaedrus agrees and allows Socrates to retain the premise that the lover is more insane (nosein) than the non-lover. Therefore, both speeches share the same assumption: love is a kind of insanity. This assumption will not be entirely denied in Socrates' second speech, although it will be modified.

Socrates starts his speech with a definition of love. Yet this definition is already qualified by the phrase "everybody knows."[34] Evidently love is going to be different than what everybody thinks it is. Everybody thinks that love is a kind of desire. But nonlovers also have desires for what is beautiful. So the definition is not proper to distinguish lovers from nonlovers. Socrates proceeds to distinguish two ruling and leading principles in human beings, the innate desire for pleasures, and the acquired opinion that strives for the best. When the opinion leads through reason its power is called self-restraint, but when desire irrationally leads human beings toward pleasure it is called excess (hubris) (237d–e). Love, accordingly, is a particular kind of excess where desires overcome rational opinion and lead one away toward the enjoyment of beauty (238c). The important point to underline in this definition is Socrates' dissociation of love and logos. Love, as hubris of a specific kind, is without logos, an opposition that Socrates will later dissolve, and join love with logos.[35] Philosophical madness combined with logos will be excess of logos, rather than of irrational desire. The rest of Socrates' speech follows from this definition of love. Someone who is overcome by this particular excess (the lover) prefers the beloved to resist as little as possible in order to satisfy his desires. The lover would thus try to make the beloved intellectually inferior, physically weaker, and prefer that the beloved would not have any possessions. Yet this excess of being overcome by the desire for the enjoyment of beauty is necessarily transient. The lover, having made various promises while in love, will be governed by different principles, once his love has ceased. Sense and reason are going to replace love and madness (mania). The beloved may think that he is speaking to the same person, but this is not the case. Socrates' indication of this change refers to the difficulty in Lysias's speech. The lover cannot preserve an identity without knowing what love is. Once love is articulated in terms of transient bodily desires for pleasure, we cannot distinguish the lover from the nonlover; even the "lover" himself cannot do this. The problem of opposites is also at issue here, just as it was in the *Phaedo*, albeit in a different context. The lover cannot be identified by simply observing the behavior of a person. To understand love one has to look away from what is present ("the lover"). One can understand what is present only after one determines what love is. This structure is similar to the one in the *Phaedo* where Socrates looks away from the philosopher in order to understand how the philosopher practices death. In fact, the structure is not just similar, but is identical to the extent that the philosopher is a lover. Love cannot be comprehended in terms of transient human desires; one has to introduce *logos* into love in order to account for its permanent nature, which in turn will provide the identity of the individual. This transformation requires a different interpretation, as well as a "rationalization" of madness.

After Socrates finishes his speech prematurely, he attempts to leave in order to escape any further compulsion Phaedrus may put upon him. He is unwilling to complete his speech. Phaedrus is surprised that Socrates delivered only half of the speech, as he did not talk about the advantages of the nonlover, but only the disadvantages of the lover for the beloved. Socrates proposes to simply read all the disadvantages of the lover as the advantages of the nonlover. Yet could one do this? Does this not presuppose that one can already distinguish the lover from the nonlover? Socrates does not continue because he cannot say that the nonlover will make the beloved intellectually superior, physically stronger. The nonlover cannot be said to be the opposite of the lover, because the former also has a desire (otherwise he would not even deliver a speech in order to win over the "beloved"). Socrates' speech is problematic in two aspects. First, the lover, by trying to make the beloved less resistant, destroys the object of his love (the beloved), and consequently his love itself. He thereby undermines his identity as a lover. Secondly, the nonlover is in exactly the same position as the lover, and it can be said that he will do exactly what the lover would do because he also has bodily desires. The difficulties Plato underlines indicate the necessity of rethinking love, and require an appeal to the being of love, rather than an observation of what is present. What is present ("the lover") cannot be comprehended by the senses. The lover cannot even *be* who he or she is without knowing what love is.

As Socrates is about to leave, he claims to be stopped by his *daimon*. Socrates attributes this to his being a seer *(mantis)*.[36] He is aware that he has offended the god of love, the son of Aphrodite, and he has to engage in a kind of purification in order to avoid punishment, for example, the blindness which Homer could not avoid but Stesichorus could. The purification is the same as in the *Phaedo*, a cleansing from the bodily aspects of existence, that is, articulating love not in terms of what we physically see as bodily pleasures, but as the way in which one is possessed by the gods. Socrates does not want to lose his prophetic power (as a *mantis*, a seer), a power which protects itself as a power (of seeing) by making Socrates aware of the danger of blindness.

In his second speech Socrates puts into question the fundamental assumption that love is a kind of madness, and that it is harmful for the beloved. More precisely, he does not displace the fact that love is a kind of madness, but he transforms the ordinary understanding of madness as the absence of *logos*. Proper madness has to be understood differently, specifically as of divine origin; as such, madness is not evil, but on the contrary the greatest goods come through madness if sent as gift of the gods (244a). The immediate example Socrates gives is the prophetess of Delphi, the oracle associated with Apollo that delivered the prophecy that Socrates is the wisest of men. It is clear that Plato now has a positive conception of madness. However, it would be premature to claim that Plato endorses madness uncritically. Love as madness has to be thought together with *logos*, or, to be more precise, as a peculiar manifestation of *logos* rather than as its absence.

According to the *Phaedrus*, there are four kinds of madness of divine origin that provide goods for human beings. Therefore, it is clear at the outset that Socrates distinguishes madness of human origin (a disease) from madness as a gift from gods. As Socrates later indicates while reflecting on the structure of his speech, madness of human origin is a disease (*nosematon*, the same word both he and Phaedrus used to describe madness as an excess of desire).[37] Therefore, Socrates does indeed leave a certain kind of madness intact, but he distinguishes this type of madness from the proper kind of madness, just as he distinguishes the death of the body from the proper conception of death in the *Phaedo*.

The first kind of madness is that which is related to prophecy, the noble art of foretelling the future. The *mantic* art, according to Socrates is in fact the same as *mania*, a word that was later modified with an addition of the letter "t" (244c). This kind of madness is a gift from Apollo (265c). To the extent that Socrates sees his philosophical activity as an investigation of the statement that he is the wisest man, he associates philosophy with the type of madness given by Apollo.[38] However, prophetic madness will be only one of the mad origins of philosophy, as all the other three types of madness seem to be within philosophical activity. Socrates already incorporated this type of madness by saying that he was a seer (*mantis*), a claim that led to this speech in the first place.

The second type of madness deals with purifications (*katharmos*) and sacred rites. Purification is the same notion Socrates uses to describe the practice of death in the *Phaedo*. Socrates describes the benefits of this type of madness in the following manner: ". . . when diseases and the greatest troubles have been visited upon certain families through some ancient guilt, madness has entered in and by oracular power has found a way of release [*apallagen*] for those in need . . ." (244d–e). These greatest troubles seem to be related to bodily existence, as the diseases (*noson*) referred to here are bodily diseases. The release from these troubles seems to be possible only through a kind of madness.[39] The word for "release" (*apallagen*) is the same word that Socrates uses to describe the separation of the soul from the body in his definition of death in the *Phaedo*. The second type of madness is related to the god Dionysus, and is also exemplified by Socrates, as he is engaged in an act of purification in order to dissolve the possible punishment for offending the god of love.

The third kind of madness comes from the Muses.[40] It inspires the souls it possesses to songs and poetry. The poetic madness is what Socrates has appealed to while delivering his first speech. However, there is a definite irony associated with Socrates' description of himself as inspired. It is important to note that all four types of madness are related to philosophy.[41]

The first three types of madness already establish that god-sent madness is far superior to any self-restraint of human origin. Therefore, the nonlover is not to be preferred to the lover. Socrates moves to the discussion of the fourth type of madness by implicitly raising the question of how the gods send madness to humans.[42] In order to understand how madness is sent to the soul of the human being, Socrates claims, one has to understand the truth about the human and divine soul. At this stage, it is established that madness concerns the soul rather than the body. It is, therefore, necessary to know the nature of the soul. Socrates seems to suggest that we can do this by observing how the soul acts and is acted upon. Evidently this is not to be an "observation" at all. We are faced with the same problem as in the *Phaedo*: how is it possible for the soul to know itself? This question does not concern, according to Socrates, the immortality of the soul, but rather its form (*idea*). He claims that to describe the soul "would require a very long account, and is a task for a god" (246a). It is not clear whether this task is at all possible for the human being. In any case, Socrates claims that it is possible to describe it briefly in a figure (in what it is like, *eoiken*). This appeal to *eoiken*, we must emphasize, does not solve the problem of the soul describing itself. As we said in the context of the *Phaedo*, this knowledge can only be of the being of the soul, rather than of an individual soul.

The soul, Socrates continues, can be likened to a pair of winged horses and a charioteer. This appeal to a mythic story suggests that the soul has to know itself through something other than through what Socrates claims to be its proper activity of contemplation.[43] The division within the soul (the different actors involved) implies that there is a multiplicity in the soul, the very unity of which is in question. Socrates continues to describe different forces within the soul in terms of the characters of the horses. One horse is of good breeding and the other one is the opposite. What distinguishes the soul of a mortal being from that of an immortal one is the fact that an immortal soul has a constant unity among the different parts, whereas unity is something elusive that mortal souls must constantly achieve. The wings of the horses suggest that the story describes the movement of the soul, which is said to be self-moving, hence immortal. The wings allow the soul to accompany the divine, which is beauty, wisdom, and the good. The ability to continue to accompany the gods in their procession around the heavens depends on the possibility of sustaining the dominance of the good horse, which is nurtured by the good and the beautiful. Socrates continues to describe what is to be seen beyond the heavens and thereby seems to be going beyond the self-imposed modesty of appealing to an image. What is there above the heavens is *ousia ontos ousa*.[44] The phrase is very difficult to translate.[45] I will leave it simply as being(s). It seems that Socrates is referring to beings like absolute justice, temperance, knowledge, and so on.[46] These beings are constantly accessible to the gods, as they preserve the unity of their souls. As the souls of mortal beings attempt to behold these beings by preserving the unity of their souls, they inevitably fail, because they have a negative dimension to their souls, which represents their bodily aspects. The degree to which the soul sees these beings along with the gods creates a hierarchy among them once they are born. The soul of the philosopher is the one that had seen being(s) the longest time before it was born. However, the difference between the soul of a philosopher and others is only a matter of degree. Socrates states:

> For the soul which has never seen the truth can never pass into human form. For a human being must understand according to a form [*eidos*] of what is said [*legomenon*] formed by collecting many perceptions of the senses into a unity [one, *hen*]; and this is a recollection of those things which our soul once beheld, when it journeyed with god, and looking down upon the things which now we suppose to be, gazed up to being as such [*to on ontos*].[47]

This passage complements the argument concerning equality in the *Phaedo*. A prior access to beings is the precondition for having a meaningful experience.[48] In other words, the beings Plato refers to are not simply to be contemplated after one is dead, but they also underlie the structure of human existence, and human perception. As Heidegger notes:

If we did not know what difference and equality were, we could never encounter different things, that is, we could never encounter things at all. If we did not know what sameness and setting-against were, we could never comport ourselves toward ourselves as selfsame in each case; we would never be alongside ourselves, we would never *be* ourselves. Nor could we experience something, something that stands over against us, something that is other than ourselves.[49]

Plato predicates the possibility of gathering perceptions of things that are present, indeed the possibility of perception in general, upon the "existence" of these beings. I believe this predication is more important than whether Plato regards them as unchanging forms or not, because he opens the possibility of reading absence within the structure of things that are present in terms of *presence*, that is, the presence of beings to thought.[50] The claim that such beings are necessary in order to have a meaningful experience changes the concern about the theory of forms.[51] It also underscores the necessary structure of absence in sensible presence.[52] Therefore, Plato can be said to understand sensible absence in terms of intelligible presence, but he also circumvents a more radical understanding of absence.[53]

Plato explains the fourth kind of madness in terms of a memory of forms:

> Now a man who employs such memories rightly (*orthos*)[54] is always being initiated into perfect mysteries and he alone becomes truly perfect; but since he separates himself from human interests and turns his attention toward the divine, he is rebuked by the vulgar, who consider him mad, and do not know that he is inspired (*enthousiazon*). (249c–d)

This explanation of madness is also the coincidence of madness with what is most rational. The person who remembers being(s) is *considered* to be mad. As a philosopher he is engaged in the maddest, and at the same time the most rational activity. For the outside observer, the philosopher is mad. However, the observer does not know the true cause or nature of this madness, just as for the observer the philosopher is just as good as dead, although for completely different reasons. *The madness of the philosopher is the presence of death in life.* Socrates' explanation does not imply the existence of a different realm of ideas completely separate from the sensuous world. In fact his subsequent discussion exhibits the intimate relation between the two realms. The one who sees beauty in the world remembers the being of beauty, and the soul develops wings to reach that beauty. Therefore, the one who is in love with a beautiful person is reminded of the being of beauty. He or she is really in love with the person as such only to the extent that the person reminds him or her of the being of beauty. What distinguishes this type of madness from other kinds is that the mad one loves the beautiful, and is called a lover, and this is the best and the highest origin (249d–e). Beauty has a privilege among other beings such as justice and temperance because "in the appearances of justice and temperance and other ideas which are precious to the soul there is no light, but only a few approaching the images through the darkling organs of sense" (250b). But beauty is the most radiant, and also the most enchanting *(host ekphanestaton einai kai erasmiotaton)* (250d).[55] What distinguishes beauty from other forms is its shining forth in the realm of appearances. It is clear that Plato attributes great significance to the relation of being(s) to the sensuous world. Beauty is the most visible of the being(s), the one in which the relation between presence and absence takes the most complicated form. On the one hand, love is a desire for something that is forgotten and absent. On the other hand, love is also triggered by what is most present of the being(s) that are absent. Beauty as the true object of love snatches one away from the world of human affairs, yet also demands the most intensified preoccupation with what is present, namely the beloved. Beauty is the proof (exhibition, brilliance) of being(s) in the world.[56] Socrates concludes his speech by further explaining love as a kind of madness. The soul of the lover is reminded of the god that it followed and tries to treat the beloved as if he were a god. Since the lover also tries to liken the beloved to the image of a god, he or she always makes the beloved better, contrary to what is suggested in Lysias's and Socrates' first speeches. Thereby, Socrates demonstrates that Lysias's speech that claimed that the nonlover would make the beloved better was misguided in that he did not know himself as a lover or a nonlover. However, Socrates is careful to preserve the purity of love and the soul of the philosopher by attributing the highest rank to the souls that followed Zeus, and by claiming that they are of a philosophical nature (252d). These (philosophical) lovers practice a philosophical life of wisdom and prudence, in which their souls preserve the power to reach the heavens. The beloved, by contrast, is seized by the image of himself reflected from the lover, and in a sense falls in love with himself through the lover, enclosing the narcissistic circuit of love. Love as a type of madness is also beneficial for the beloved in that he or she is improved as a person provided that madness is restricted to the soul, rather than the body.

Socrates' speech is an explanation of the way in which the gods send madness to human souls. God-sent madness is united with *logos*. Plato also thereby inscribes an opposition between *logos* and a different type of madness, namely, a madness of human origin. This madness seems to be associated with everything that is related to embodied existence: the senses, desires, and so on. If madness is to be praised in terms of any positive aspect, then it can only be done within this oppositional structure that Plato articulates. The very attempt to simply restore the dignity of madness, of the bodily and the sensuous, that is, to read one Plato against another Plato, will already take place within a certain kind of Platonism. Therefore, madness is already a philosophical term in Plato, both as a "definition" of philosophy where the mad-

dest is also the most rational, and as that which is "excluded" from philosophical activity, namely all things associated with the sensuous world.

Plato's relationship to madness is ambivalent. Even though he appears to
be restoring madness, or indicating the inevitable crossings between madness
and reason (logos), he also solidifies the opposition between madness and reason by incorporating a particular definition of madness while excluding
another one. I do not claim that the opposition between life and death, or
madness and reason, is a privileged opposition in terms of which every other
opposition can be understood. However, taking Heidegger's claim that every
metaphysical question contains the entirety of metaphysics as a point of
departure, I claim the opposition of madness and reason as the inscription of
oppositionality in general. Admittedly my reading of the Phaedrus is influ-
enced by Derrida's interpretation in "Plato's Pharmacy." I do not claim, however, that madness can be substituted for pharmakon, even though such substitution is in principle possible.[57] Indeed, such a possibility would be
troublesome for Derrida's deconstruction. Reason is that which inscribes
oppositions. Yet reason has to situate itself on one side of an opposition.
Thus, there is a difficulty, one has to acknowledge, in situating reason both
as one side of the opposition, and at the inception of oppositionality in general. This difficulty forces us to think madness not as a positive experience,
nor as a negative accessory, but as pointing to the "between" of madness and
reason, the neighborhood in which the oppositionality comes to be inscribed.
This inscription takes place both at a textual and an experiential level. To
read this inscription as a relation to absence, and, fundamentally, to death is
not to attempt to describe, nor to explain madness, but rather to underline
the need to rethink philosophy not as a series of formal delimitations, but as
a risky engagement with what is not present in and through what is present.

TWO

Hegel

The Madness of the Soul and the Death of the Spirit

The constant solicitation of madness is the indispensable requirement of the active living understanding. Where there is no madness there is, of course, also no proper, actual and living understanding.

—F. W. J. Schelling

But truly to escape Hegel involves an exact appreciation of the price we have to pay to detach ourselves from him. It assumes that we are aware of the extent to which, insidiously perhaps, he is close to us; it implies a knowledge in that which permits us to think against Hegel, of that which remains Hegelian. We have to determine the extent to which our anti-Hegelianism is possibly one of his tricks directed against us, at the end of which he stands, motionless, waiting for us.

—Michel Foucault

Whether we know it, or like it, or not most of us are Hegelians and quite orthodox ones at that.

—Paul de Man

Before allowing Hegel's dismissal to dismiss the problem, one should remember that, in a truly dialectical system such as Hegel's, what appears to be inferior and enslaved (*untergeordnet*) may well turn out to be the master.

—Paul de Man

WHY WOULD ONE concentrate on Hegel in a study about the history of the philosophical conceptions of madness? Why do we not concentrate on

31

Hölderlin and Nietzsche, who themselves were considered to be mad, in order to understand the fate of madness in modernity? Hegel, despite the fact that he was not generally considered to be mad, occupies a unique position within the historical understanding of madness and death. First of all, Hegel both adopts and yet significantly modifies Plato's conception of madness. With Hegel madness becomes a question of the subject and interiority. For Plato madness (even madness of human origin) does not necessarily arise within the human mind but is related to exteriority.[1] Hegel is also a turning point in the history of the philosophical conception of madness, as subsequent interpretations of the question of madness inevitably relate themselves to Hegel. Initially, Hegel represents the triumph of reason over its other. Madness is overcome, and thereby is seemingly excluded from the domain of Spirit. In this respect Hegel's philosophy prefigures the questions concerning alterity in twentieth century philosophy. Many of the twentieth century philosophers, including Heidegger and Derrida, attempt to disentangle themselves from Hegelian thought in different ways. Hegel's discussion of madness is radical in that he attributes a special place to it in the dialectic. Hegel does not simply exclude and exile madness, but disarms it by incorporating it within the movement from the soul to the spirit. Derrida expresses this sentiment when he writes:

> Concerning dialectic and alienation of madness—concerning *everything*, in fact that happens in the circulation of this "anthropological circle" wherein psychoanalysis is caught up or held—one should, and I myself would have liked to have done this given more time, pause a bit longer than Foucault did on a passage from *Encyclopaedia*. I am referring to the Remark of 408 in which Hegel situates and deduces madness as a contradiction of the subject between the particular determination of self-feeling and the network of mediations that is called consciousness.[2]

Derrida sees the necessity of pausing because Hegel is not simply someone to be overcome, or to be regarded as representing the oppressive nature of rationality. Hegel disarms any subsequent attempt to restore the dignity of madness, and to expose the limitations of reason. The way Hegel does this is to incorporate and domesticate madness rather than exclude it. The result of this strategy is that the radical nature of madness is already included within reason. One of Hegel's interpreters formulates this problem in the following manner:

> Hegel makes the phenomenon of negation the central element of his system so that any attempt to stand outside it becomes an indirect way of being imprisoned within it. As [Hegel] expresses the point in both the *Phenomenology* and the *Logic*, the kind of negation, opposition, and difference that appears to be external to the system is included in it as the moving principle that allows thought to become a living unity.[3]

However, there still may be a certain understanding of negativity that cannot be swallowed by positivity.[4] Perhaps such a conception of negativity (which is other than Hegel's conception) can be articulated in terms of Hegel's discussion of madness in the "Anthropology." Yet such a conception of negativity cannot be restricted to anthropology, but will affect the entire system, the question of subjectivity in Hegel's system.[5] Therefore, the question of subjectivity concerns not just an understanding of human existence as a subject, or the presence of a *human* subject. Since, for Hegel, the question of subjectivity concerns not the human being, but being itself,[6] a proper understanding of this subjectivity has to move beyond anthropology. In Hegel's thinking, madness will allow us to understand the nature of the *logos* through which human beings are formed as subjects.

Hegel's main discussion of madness appears in section 408 of the third part of the *Encyclopaedia of the Philosophical Sciences*[7] and the substantial part of this discussion is provided in the oral *Zusatz* to this section. For Hegel, the question of madness is a problem of anthropology, specifically of the feeling soul. My aim in this chapter is to question the possibility of restricting madness to this domain. Hegel's own discussion of madness leads to the suspicion that madness becomes a problem of phenomenology, and even logic.[8] In other words, Hegel's discussion of madness prepares the possibility of continuing the dialectical movement from anthropology to phenomenology. I will argue, however, that the question of madness affects the entirety of Hegel's philosophical thinking. I will raise this question not simply in order to make the claim that madness as a topic has far more significance than Hegel attributes to it, but also in order to draw attention to an abyssal dimension within thinking that can be characterized in terms of madness. Hegel would probably never concede that there is such a radical abyss within thinking that cannot be mediated through dialectic. Indeed, a certain confrontation with *Abgrund* is the very first moment of the *Logic*. Yet, for Hegel, the possibility of a disruption of the dialectical movement is always a contingent possibility. My claim is that with madness we observe that there is conceptual necessity for the dialectic to come to a halt. Such a rupture occurs when there is a difference without opposition or contradiction. Such a rupture is a true negativity, that is, the difference between reason and madness cannot be dialectically sublated since they are not opposites, nor do they contradict each other, nor are they the same.[9]

I recognize that the question of negativity is a methodological issue for Hegel, whereas madness is one of content. One of Hegel's interpreters explains the relationship between madness and negativity as follows:

> Self-feeling is the moment of the feeling soul's particularization (*Besonderung*), in which negativity will make its appearance in the strongest and most acute form thus far encountered in the soul's development. The negativity here is the

"first negation," which is necessary to all determinations. This moment, therefore, is essential to the soul's actualization as controlling power in its substantial being. For the particular finite subjectivity, however, the negativity can
also mean a schism in which the very selfhood is rent asunder. This takes place
in extreme form of insanity (Verrücktheit).[10]

I will analyze madness as one of the places (hence, contents) where the
methodological question of negativity manifests itself. My argument is that
we can infer some fundamental insights into the structure of negativity from
Hegel's discussions of madness.[11] The most significant insight is that madness
as "the negative" of the soul is overcome by being reduced to the question of
truth. Unlike Hegel, I contend that the problem of the mad person cannot
be understood with respect to the question of truth. There is something fundamentally more enigmatic in madness that complicates not only Hegel's
treatment of madness but also his understanding of system. Madness, once
separated from the question of truth, is a possible break, in the dialectic
process. In order to show this possibility, Hegel's interpretation of madness
must be resisted. I will resist Hegel's interpretation, not simply by being
against or in contradiction to Hegel, but with the tools that are already *in
Hegel's thinking*. It would be a misunderstanding of my argument to claim
that I ignore the fact that madness concerns the sentient soul, the individual subject, whereas Hegel's phenomenology and logic take place precisely
in and through a sublation of this understanding of the subject. Therefore,
one might claim that to elevate a question concerning the individual subject to the level of phenomenology and logic is a misunderstanding of
Hegel's thinking. Hegel's phenomenology and logic are precisely domains
where the question of subject is overcome. I agree with this observation, but
not with the objection as such. The question of subjectivity in Hegel is not
a question of whether phenomenology and logic have to be thought, or even
undergone by a subject. The problem of subjectivity in Hegel concerns the
way in which the dialectical movement takes place. Subjectivity is the
nature of the movement of spirit and of thinking. Specifically, subjectivity is
the very possibility of the continuity of this movement, and the possibility
of movement is the very nature of the dialectic. Once the question of subjectivity is displaced to this level, one can also see the problem of madness
at the same level. Hence, by reformulating what is at stake in the question
of madness, I will show that Hegel's methodological treatment of negativity
at the level of phenomenology and logic is committed to the same *form* that
it is committed to in his treatment of madness. What is at stake in madness
will prove to have implications that are beyond the domain that Hegel
reserves for it. Consequently, madness will be an "index" (a content) to
themes that concern the continuity of the dialectic, namely contradiction
and negation.

THE MADNESS OF THE SOUL

Hegel's discussion of madness (*Verrücktheit*) is situated within his treatment of the feeling soul, which in turn is located between the description of the physical and the actual soul. The discussion of the soul constitutes the "Anthropology," the first subsection of "Subjective Spirit." Hegel clearly indicates that the subjective spirit, as in itself (*an sich*) or immediate (*unmittelbar*), is the soul or natural spirit, and hence the object of anthropology. This designation is important because spirit *is* the soul even though it is not mediated. The relationship between the soul and spirit is important in assessing the status of different phases of the dialectical movement in general, and that of madness in particular.[12] Madness is a necessary stage in the development of the soul. As Hegel puts it, "madness is the second of the three developmental stages that the feeling soul has to go through in order to overcome the immediacy of its substantial content to raise itself to the self-related simple subjectivity present in the 'I,' whereby it becomes completely self-possessed and conscious of itself" (Enz., 163, 124). What is the distinguishing mark of this stage, and how does it differ from the first stage, namely, the stage where the soul is "entangled in the dreaming way and dim presaging of its concrete natural life is still in immediate, undifferentiated unity with its objectivity" (Enz., 121, 92)?[13]

Madness, according to Hegel, consists of the opposition between the totality systematized in the consciousness of the subject and the single phase or fixed idea of the subject. This single phase or fixed idea is a result of the soul still being bound up with immediacy, which is a consequence of corporeality. In immediate self-feeling (the first stage of the feeling soul), however, there is no contradiction but a mere difference, because in this phase there is no sense of totality that is systematized. Regardless of whether the mad person is aware of it or not, his or her madness requires the presence of fully developed consciousness as well as of the immediacy of self-feeling. "In considering madness, the fully formed rational consciousness is to be anticipated, the subject of which is at the same time the natural self of self-feeling" (Enz., 161, 123). This requirement, however, is only necessary from the perspective of the insane, because *"the spirit (Geist) is free, and therefore for itself it is not susceptible to this disease"* (Enz., 161, 123, my emphasis). This statement is important since Hegel is trying to remove the possibility of madness from the domain of spirit. This exclusion is possible only if one accepts the claim that madness is necessarily tied to immediacy and corporeality, because spirit's freedom in this context is freedom from corporeality. Hegel, therefore, limits madness to the domain of the subject, not the concrete subject as this will emerge as a result of mediation, but the subject that is embodied and bound up with corporeality, that is, the *human* subject. Spirit requires the sacrifice of this subject. Hegel justifies his claim that spirit is not susceptible to madness on the basis of his distinction between the soul and the spirit. The distinction Hegel makes is that the spirit is not a thing whereas the soul is. Hegel writes: ". . . in older metaphysics it [spirit] was treated as a soul, as a thing *(Ding)*; and it is only as a thing, i.e., as natural and existent, that it is liable to insanity—the settled fixture of some finite element in it" (Enz., 161, 123). How exactly does Hegel's interpretation of spirit and soul differ from that of older metaphysics? By stating that spirit is to be separated from the soul, because the latter is a thing whereas the former is not, Hegel agrees with older metaphysics that the soul is indeed a thing. Consequently, Hegel does not simply disregard this belief of older metaphysics; he accepts it, but also claims that spirit is not reducible to a thing. The distinction between the soul and the spirit within Hegel's anthropology is justified only because the soul is transformed into a thing from the perspective of spirit. Spirit executes this transformation by separating the unity of the soul with the world from itself, and only then can the soul be said to be a thing.[14] This strategy is our first clue in understanding the nature of the dialectical movement; it proceeds by objectifying its previous stage. This clue, however, will not yield the crude criticism of Hegel that his thought objectifies everything. It will lead to an understanding of the relationship of the subject to itself, that for Hegel this relationship is a cognitive[15] one, one that takes the negativity proper to an earlier stage to be the content of a later stage. I will argue to the contrary that this confrontation with negativity, namely, being conscious of the negativity as negativity is in fact *not* a confrontation. The movement of spirit is not necessarily cognitive, because a confrontation with negativity does not have to be cognitive.[16]

Since spirit is that which designates the soul as a thing that is entangled with corporeality, madness, the result of this corporeality, can only be designated as such from the perspective that already includes the potential overcoming of madness. What distinguishes madness from the first stage of the feeling soul, namely magnetic somnambulism, is a different configuration between the psychical element in the soul and the objective consciousness. In madness there is a contradiction between the soul and the external world. However, Hegel does not exactly formulate madness in terms of this opposition, but rather in terms of a contradiction between objective and subjective consciousness. Madness is a split within consciousness. The relationship of the psychical element to the objective consciousness is not one of mere difference *(bloss verschieden)*, but of direct opposition *(direkt entgegengesetzt)*, and therefore the physical element is not mixed with this consciousness (Enz., 164, 125). Yet this opposition may appear to be a contingent event, as would seem to be consistent with the corporeality of the soul. In this case, madness would be a merely accidental disease. In a sense, madness is an accident in that it is, like a crime, an extreme. Not every soul has to go through the condition of extreme dismemberment *(äußerste Zerrissenheit)*.[17] Nevertheless, madness for Hegel is a necessary stage that the soul has to go through in its struggle with the immediacy of its substantial content. Therefore, Hegel claims that there is a *necessary* and rational progress from the magnetic states to insanity. Madness does not simply concern the corporeality, naturalness, and immediacy of the soul. These qualities, in themselves, do not lead to madness, as they are present in every soul. The necessity of madness, that is, the necessity of going through the stage of madness, is due to the fact that "the soul is already *in itself* the contradiction of being an *individual*, a *singular*, and yet at the same time immediately identical with the *universal* natural soul, with its substance" (Enz., 164, 125). There is, therefore, a necessary transition from madness to truly objective intellectual and rational consciousness. The presence of a contradiction in the soul shows that madness and reason share the same structures[18] in this respect: "insanity is not an abstract *loss* of reason (neither from the side of intelligence nor of will and its responsibility), but only derangement (*Verrücktheit*), only a contradiction in a still present reason" (Enz., 163, 124). According to Hegel, in madness the contradiction[19] between the individual soul, and the natural soul (substance) is made explicit as an opposition. What leads to madness is not the absence of a unity, but the fact that this unity is a merely subjective unity that raises itself to the level of a veritable unity of the subjective and objective unity (Enz., 164, 125). Thus, madness is a false unity, where the "evil genius" (the evil in the heart) of a man gains the upper hand (Enz., 162, 124).[20] Madness is a content that perfectly demonstrates how negativity as methodological structure works in Hegel.[21] Madness is opposed to and contradicts reason. Yet madness is, for that very reason, one configuration of necessary difference or contradiction that constitutes the identity of reason. It is a stage incorporated into the movement of rational consciousness. Yet the unity present in madness is a static unity, as proper madness is defined by Hegel as being fixed to a single idea. Madness is thus also opposed to the rational consciousness, whose only difference at this point is that it continues to move forward. The unity of madness is different from the unity of fully formed consciousness because the unity of madness is an imperfect one. Rational thinking, on the other hand, requires not only a subjective unity, but also a separation from the unity of the subjective and the objective, and must set this unity against itself as an objective unity,[22] "in doing this not only freeing itself from its Other but at the same time discharging this Other from its immediate identity with the feeling soul" (Enz., 164, 125).[23] In "genuine madness" (*in der eigentlichen Verrücktheit*), two modes of finite mind—rational consciousness with its objective world, and the world of inner feeling, which clings to itself and has its objectivity within it—are developed into a separately existing totality, into a separate personality (Enz., 165, 126). Therefore, madness is not only a static phase within the development of the soul, but also a struggle between two stages.[24] This struggle may indeed be true of all the phases of the development of spirit, as well as of the soul, that is, such a struggle may manifest itself through the dialectical movement. Hegel expresses the claim that madness consists of a struggle between two stages of the soul in terms of two states: "in genuine madness . . . two personalities are not two different states but are in one and the same state, so that these *negatively* related personalities—the psychical and the intellectual consciousness—have mutual contact and are aware of each other. The insane subject is therefore alongside itself in the negative of itself [*Das verrückte Subjekt ist daher in dem Negativen seiner selber bei sich]*" (Enz., 165, 126).[25] In madness the subject cannot achieve the unity of these two personalities, and one is, therefore, considered to be mad.[26]

Being alongside oneself in the negative is not only a problem that emerges in madness, but it is also the driving force of the dialectical movement. How is madness, then, to be identified? Hegel recognizes part of this problem in acknowledging that "in the concrete it is often difficult to say where it [error] begins to be madness" (Enz., 162, 123). However, I believe the problem is much graver than being limited to the concrete, unless Hegel refers to "the concrete" in its proper dialectical sense, that is, as the moment when consciousness goes beyond madness or beyond the place to which Hegel restricts madness, and proceeds through mediations. Hegel first appears to restrict the question of the identification of madness to the context of errors. However, Hegel also admits the difficulty of such an identification:

> I can be mistaken not only about the outer world but also about myself. Unintelligent individuals have empty, subjective ideas, unrealizable desires, which all the same they hope to realize in the future. . . . But this narrow-mindedness and this error are still not madness if these persons at the same time know that their subjective idea does not as yet have an objective existence. Error and folly only become madness when the individual believes his merely subjective idea to be objectively present to him and clings to it in the face of the actual objectivity, which contradicts it. . . . When addressing a madman one must therefore always begin by reminding him of all the facts and circumstances of his situation, of his concrete actual world. Then, if in spite of being made aware of this objective interrelated whole he still sticks to his false idea, there can be no doubt that such a person is insane.[27] (Enz., 167, 128)

Madness is not an occasional error, but a belief one clings to even when it is contradicted by the objective world. This identification can mean one of two things: either the insane person is not aware of his or her mistakes, in which case one has the problem of distinguishing long term mistakes from madness, or the insane person may cling to a fixed idea even if he or she is aware of its falsehood, in which case one cannot distinguish madness from imagining the world differently and changing it accordingly.[28] Madness cannot be identified in terms of errors if error is an empirical question. The truth of madness has to be thought as truth is thought in general in Hegel, namely, as a movement to the next stage of the dialectic. The truth of madness, even though it is different from the question of whether the mad person has true or false beliefs, still relies on the fact that madness is a question of truth or falsehood. The problem of the mad is that it refuses to move to this stage,[29] but instead disrupts and prevents the possibility of reaching its own truth, yet thereby also displays its truth for the rational consciousness. This disruption is possible because, in madness, the subject is alongside itself in its negative. Why, then, is madness a problem of the soul, but not a possibility in every stage of the dialectic? It is, according to Hegel, a state in which "spirit (Geist) is shut up within itself, has sunk into itself, whose peculiarity . . . consists in its being no longer in immediate contact with actuality but in having positively separated itself from it" (Enz., 171, 131). Therefore, it is interesting that Hegel discusses "habit" (die Gewohnheit) in the context of his explanation of how the soul moves to the truly objective intellectual and rational consciousness. First of all, there is a necessity of the dialectical progress from insanity to habit (Enz., 187, 143). In habit "we come to a being-for-self of the soul that has been brought into being by the notion of soul which has overcome the inner contradiction of mind present in insanity, has put an end to the complete dismemberment (Zerrissenheit) of the self" (Enz., 188, 144). Habit overcomes the negative being alongside itself of insanity, because habit (Gewohnheit) is "being-alongside-oneself (Beisichselbersein)." Hegel uses the word Gewohnheit presupposing its connotations of dwelling (wohnen, as in Wohnheim). Therefore, habit, although repetitive, does not have a pejorative connotation. Indeed, since in insanity the moral being of the individual is still present, habit through work (which Hegel sees as a fundamental dimension of the cure for madness) has the power to cure the mad person. The implication of the fact that Gewohnheit is the stage that follows insanity is that in madness one is not at home. However, there is a unity in madness, albeit a false unity, that is, a unity that cannot sustain itself, and is destined to dissolve. The negativity of madness is overcome by the "at-home" of Gewohnheit. However, being at home is not necessarily a positive designation for Hegel. Being-at-home and not taking the risk of going through negativity is precisely a dimension of thinking that Hegel criticizes. How does this negativity in the case of madness differ from negativity as structured at different stages of the system? Or more precisely, does Hegel's treatment of the negativity in the case of madness give us a clue to understanding his attitude towards negativity in general?[30]

The difficulty of distinguishing Hegel's *conceptual* understanding of madness from negativity in general lends legitimacy to Hyppolite's claim that "the essence of man is to be mad, that is to be himself in the other, to be himself by this very otherness."[31] Hyppolite detects a certain kind of madness within the structure of consciousness precisely because consciousness relates to itself as other, that is, in the negative. The significant question at this point is not whether it is legitimate to label this negativity madness or not, but how to understand the nature of this negativity.[32] The Ego, according to Hyppolite's interpretation of Hegel, is constituted as a relationship between the I and the other. Hegel's discovery is that there can be no sense of speaking of an Ego outside of this relationship. Doubling ("duplication," according to Hegel) is essential in self-consciousness. Hyppolite reads this doubling as an indication of madness. Obviously he does not mean by this that we all are mad; rather, he states that madness manifests the dialectical relationship between the self and the other. Initially self-consciousness appears to have "fallen back upon itself . . . to a certain extent it has made otherness disappear. It is the *unhappy consciousness*" (HPP, 63). "But the mirror play of self-consciousness does not come to a dead end" (HPP, 64). Therefore, Hyppolite regards the necessity of madness precisely within the possibility of continuing with the dialectical movement. Consequently, not only is rational consciousness the presupposition of madness, but madness is also the presupposition of rational consciousness. Hyppolite articulates this presupposition in his discussion of the law of the heart, where the relationship between subjective enjoyment and desire is displaced in and through the confrontation with the world. The subject "fails to recognize himself in the man that *he becomes in others and for others*. And this drama is the beginning of a madness through which man is unable not to pass (as a man) . . . the fundamental thing here is that consciousness is deranged within itself" (HPP, 66). While Hyppolite describes a fundamental aspect of madness in Hegel, he does not push the question to the point where a recoil within the dialectic may be shown to be a problem not of the individual, but of the dialectic itself. He concludes that "the emergence of the 'we' may still suffer an ultimate failure—a frightful failure due to what might be called the death instinct of him who does not wish to be cured, that is, who does not wish to speak anymore" (HPP, 70). Yet the question remains: what if this death instinct were not of an individual, but of the dialectic, what if the dialectic came to a halt at that place where it discovers not an opposition or a contradiction, but rather a difference which would not allow itself to be transformed into an opposition, that is, would not allow itself to be sublated?[33]

Hyppolite observes that in Hegel "the notion of truth as revelation is established by the intercommunication of human self-consciousness, by mutual recognition . . ." (HPP, 58). This observation is crucial to the extent that Hegel appeals to truth and falsehood in identifying madness. Yet if truth consists of this intercommunication between reason and madness, it cannot be the place from which madness can be identified. Therefore, the place at which rational consciousness and madness are to be distinguished cannot be rational consciousness, especially if rational consciousness presupposes madness. If one argues that madness can only be properly designated retrospec-tively, this amounts to admitting that the difficulty concerning the relation-ship between madness and rational consciousness is present in other phases of Hegel's dialectical movement. However, if this is true, then the dialectical movement is always threatened, not by an insane individual who may disrupt it, but by a possibility of disruption that is inherent in it. I believe Hegel would admit to this possibility, but he would not admit that this could under-mine "the perfect unity of thought and being" (Enz., 169, 129). This unity would be impossible to achieve, however, if there were no contradiction and opposition between the subjective and the objective, which determines the opposition between madness and concrete objective consciousness.

Hegel's conception of madness is inserted into the relationship between the individual and the universal. This is due to the fact that the soul is already within itself a contradiction: it is "an individual, a singular, and yet at the same time immediately identical with the universal natural soul, with its substance" (Enz., 164, 125). The significant words in this statement are "immediately identical." This means that this identity is a finite identity, not one that has gone through necessary mediations. Therefore, on the one hand, madness is a necessary stage that the soul has to go through. On the other hand, madness concerns the access to the universal. In this respect Hegel's understanding of madness is close to that of Plato. However, for Hegel this access cannot be immediate, because it is precisely the overcom-ing of this immediacy that leads to the proper universal. Madness, therefore, also constitutes the possibility of not reaching the universal to the extent that it is a result of the soul's being incapable of overcoming its immediacy, naturalness, and corporeality. Therefore, Hegel agrees with Plato in this respect as well: madness concerns that which is related to the sensuous, to the corporeal, and is therefore a disease. Yet in Hegel madness becomes a question of interiority in two ways; first, as he admits, it concerns the inter-nal structure of the human soul. And secondly, as I argued, madness also concerns the internal structure of the dialectical movement in general. The discussion of madness reveals a tendency in Hegel's philosophy, namely that the question of alterity becomes a question that is internal to self-con-sciousness. The question of madness concerns the movement of the dialec-tic, the actualization of the absolute. Hegel and Plato agree on this point. For Plato, madness provides an access to the universal, just as for Hegel the actualization, concretion, or mediation of the substance is nothing other than the universal subject itself.[34] For Hegel, the true absolute and universal is not simply a product, but the process of moving toward it. Therefore, the presence of the product depends on the possibility of the movement of the process. The possibility of the disruption of the process, consequently, amounts to the absence of the product. Hegel secures the possibility of this process by attributing a dialectical structure to the process. For Hegel this movement is fundamentally subjectivist, not because there is a subject undergoing this process (in fact the individual subject is absent from, or rather sublated within this process), but because the movement that takes place as the substance of the movement is alongside itself *(bei sich)*. In this sense Hegel's philosophy is committed to subjectivity, and this is the level at which the question of subjectivity is to be encountered.[35]

THE DEATH OF SPIRIT

The intimation that the question of madness, which I take to be an index of negativity, concerns subjectivity at the level of dialectical movement can be observed in Hegel's remarks in the Preface to the *Phenomenology of Spirit*.[36] In arguing against a formalistic approach to the absolute, Hegel claims that "in my view, which can be justified only by the exposition of the system itself, everything turns on grasping and expressing the true, not only as *substance*, but equally as subject" (Phen., 23, 10). It is clear that Hegel does not see the problem of the subject as a question of that which underlies *(hypokeimenon)* the dialectical movement. The subject is not a simple identity that remains the same through actuality, but rather its identity is constituted in and through difference. In this respect, the subject for Hegel cannot simply be understood as the human agent that has to undergo the process of thinking.

Yet what is the subject, and how does it relate to dialectical movement? The subject *is* the dialectical movement in that it is actualized in and through this movement. For Hegel negativity is at the heart of this actualization, because negativity "produces" the nonactuality that is necessary for the dialectical movement to continue. In this context "[d]eath is the revelation of absolute negativity, because man, as pure self-consciousness, exists as this nothingness *[existe ce néant]*."[37]

Thus, negativity is not an addition or accessory aspect that Hegel has to incorporate into the movement of spirit, but rather an absolutely necessary dimension of this movement. The relationship to the negative, be it madness or death, is not an accidental characteristic of philosophy that reason may or may not choose to deal with. The relationship to negativity distinguishes Hegel's conception of substance from that of Spinoza,[38] because substance, for Hegel, is not an abstract unity beyond and above otherness, that is, it is not a dead principle, or a static absolute at the beginning of philosophical think-ing. Dialectic demonstrates that substance is subject, not a "thing," but a movement. Therefore, the result of philosophy is not simply that which lies outside of the movement of consciousness; rather the movement itself is the result: "For the real issue is not exhausted by stating it as an aim, but by car-rying it out, nor is the result the actual whole, but rather the result together with the process through which it came about" (Phen., 13, 2). Therefore, dialectic embraces negativity, because "the power of spirit is only as great as its expression, its depth only as deep as it dares to spread out and lose itself in its exposition" (Phen., 18, 6).

The essential character of the dialectic is articulated in Hegel's claim that spirit is "never at rest but always engaged in moving forward" (Phen., 13, 6). This character of substance, namely, that it is at the same time subject, distinguishes Hegel's conception of subject from an abstract, immediate, pure, and hence, dead one:

> The living substance is being which is in truth subject, or, what is the same, is in truth actual only insofar as it is the movement of positing itself, or is the mediation of its self-othering with itself. This substance is, as subject, pure *simple negativity*, and is for this very reason the bifurcation of the simple; it is the doubling which sets up opposition, and then again the negation of this indifferent diversity and of its anti-thesis [the immediate simplicity]. Only this self-*restoring* sameness, or this reflection in otherness within itself—not an original or immediate unity as such—is the True. (Phen., 23, 10)

It is true that an important dimension of this movement is a self-restoring, and this happens in and through recognizing the negative as negative and overcoming it, not by excluding it but by incorporating it into the movement of spirit:

> Thus the life of God and divine cognition may well be spoken of as a disporting of Love with itself; but this idea sinks into mere edification, and even insipidity, if it lacks the seriousness, the suffering, the patience, and the labor of the negative. *In itself*, that life is indeed one of untroubled equality and unity with itself, for which otherness and alienation, and the overcoming of alienation, are not serious matters.[39] But this *in-itself* is abstract universality, in which the nature of the divine life *to be for itself*, and so too the self-movement of the form, are altogether left out of account. (Phen., 23, 10)

The dialectical movement does not simply incorporate negativity or otherness in order to be able to account for it, rather negativity provides for the possibility of movement, and consequently for the possibility of truth. Truth is the entirety of this movement rather than its result or its *telos* in isolation.

> The true is the whole, but the whole is nothing other than the essence consummating itself through its development. Of the absolute it must be said that it is essentially a *result*, that only in the *end* is it what it truly is; and that precisely in this consists its nature, viz. to be actual, subject, the spontaneous becoming of itself. Though it may seem contradictory that the absolute should be conceived essentially as a result, it needs little pondering to set this show of contradiction in its true light. The beginning, the principle, or the absolute, as at first immediately enunciated, is only the universal. (Phen., 24, 11)

The dialectical movement is a movement of mediation, "for mediation is nothing beyond self-moving selfsameness, or is reflection into self, the moment of the I which is for itself pure negativity, or, when reduced to its pure abstraction, *simple becoming*" (Phen., 25, 11). There is therefore a "purpose" to reason, but this end, or *telos* does not remain outside of the activity itself. "Reason is *purposive activity*" (Phen., 26, 12), and its purpose is the activity itself. The result or purpose of the dialectical movement coincides with the beginning of the movement, precisely because substance is subject. Its [the subject's] power, taken abstractly, is *being-for-self* or pure negativity. The result is the same as the beginning, only because the immediate, as purpose, contains the self or pure actuality within itself (Phen., 26, 12).

It is the presence of this negativity within the movement of spirit that renders knowledge possible only as a system. "Knowledge is system. . . . The refutation would properly consist in the further development of the principle, and in thus remedying the defectiveness, if it did not mistakenly pay attention solely to its *negative* action, without awareness of its progress and result on their *positive* side too" (Phen., 28, 13). Therefore, to be against Hegel, to criticize the system from the outside is not only doomed to failure, but renders the very system that is criticized stronger. This implication is possible on the basis of the pivotal role that negativity plays within the system. At this point, we see another aspect of the dialectical movement, namely, the fact that the presentation of the system is not different than what is presented. This aspect is connected with Hegel's claim that the dialectical movement in its entirety rather than in its results in isolation constitutes the true nature of the absolute.[40] The coincidence of presentation and presented renders the external critique of the system elliptical. The position that claims to situate itself outside the system recoils back onto itself and displaces itself *into* the system. Therefore, for Hegel, the negativity of criticism coincides with the positivity of pushing the system further, which is nothing but this pulsing forward; that is, its power is not the power of exclusion of different views. Rather, it has the structure of incorporating its opposite as its driving force. The presence of these negativities constitutes (or rather *is*) the life of spirit:

> Quite generally, the familiar, just because it is familiar is not cognitively understood. . . . The *analysis* of an idea, as it used to be carried out, was in fact, nothing else than ridding it of the form in which it had become familiar. . . . This analysis, to be sure, only arrives at *thoughts* which are themselves familiar, fixed, and inert determinations. But what is thus *separated* and non-actual is an essential moment; for it is only because the concrete does divide itself, and make itself into something non-actual, that it is self-moving. The activity of dissolution is the power and the work of the *Understanding*, the most astonishing and mightiest of powers, or rather the absolute power. The *circle* that remains self-enclosed and, like substance,

holds its moments together, is an immediate relationship, one therefore which has nothing astonishing about it. But that an accident as such, detached from what circumscribes it, what is bound and is actual in its context with others, should attain an existence of its own and a separate freedom—this is the tremendous power of the negative; it is the energy of thought, of the pure 'I.' Death, if that is what we want to call this non-actuality, is of all things the most dreadful, and to hold fast what is dead requires the greatest strength. Lacking strength, Beauty hates the Understanding for asking of her what it cannot do. But the life of the spirit is not the life that shrinks from death and keeps itself untouched by devastation, but rather the life that endures it and maintains itself in it. It wins its truth only when, in utter dismemberment (Zerrissenheit), it finds itself. It is this power, not as something positive, which closes its eyes to the negative, as when we say of something that it is nothing or is false, and then, having done with it, turn away and pass on to something else; on the contrary, spirit is this power only by looking the negative in the face, and tarrying with it. This tarrying with the negative is the magical power that converts it into being. This power is identical with what we earlier called the subject. . . . (Phen., 35–36, 18–19)

The preceding lines bring together a number of themes that constitute my argument. First of all, it connects the themes of madness and death as instances of negativity; both share a similar function of contributing to (or constituting) the power of the dialectic. Just as the soul embraces madness, spirit embraces death in order to ascertain its "magical power." Hegel uses the same word "dismemberment" (Zerrissenheit) to characterize the effect of death on spirit,[41] as he used for the effect of madness on the soul. Philosophy achieves its aim, not by excluding madness and death from the life of spirit, or from system, but rather by incorporating them into interiority. The nonactuality of death and madness is a necessary dimension of the dialectical movement. The necessity of nonactuality is an inner necessity that renders the movement of actualization possible, just as difference is necessary for identity.

And yet, the passage above also betrays the fundamental structure of this dialectical movement, namely, how it transforms the most unfamiliar into the familiar through cognitive understanding.[42] This movement constitutes a circle in that the content of a previous stage is preserved and transformed into "the circle that remains self-enclosed."

Pure self-recognition in absolute otherness, this Aether as such, is the ground and soil of Science or knowledge in general. The beginning of philosophy presupposes or requires that consciousness should dwell in this element. But this element itself achieves its own perfection and transparency only through the movement of its becoming. (Phen., 29, 14)

The power of the spirit to go through negativity is asserted by a number of related presuppositions. First of all, it is necessary for the relationship between different stages to be cognitive. Secondly, the movement has to transform the previous stage into an object, as well as into a content. Finally, this tendency to transform the negativity of a particular stage, which is initially a way of relating to otherness, into a content allows the possibility of recollection that is necessary for the life of spirit:

> That the true is actual only as system, or that substance is essentially subject, is expressed in the representation of the absolute as *spirit*—the most sublime Notion and the one which belongs to the modern age and its religion. The spiritual alone is the *actual*; it is essence, or that which has *being in itself*; it is that which *relates itself to itself* and is *determinate*, it is *other-being* and *being-for-self*, and in this determinateness, or in its self-externality, abides within itself; in other words, it is *in and for itself*.—But this being-in-and-for-itself is at first only for us, or *in itself*, it is spiritual *substance*. It must also be this *for itself*, it must be the knowledge of the spiritual, and the knowledge of itself as spirit, i.e., it must be an *object* to itself, but just as immediately a sublated object, reflected into itself. (Phen., 28, 14)

The transformation of spirit into knowledge of itself is possible on the condition that the dialectical movement proceeds as mediation. "The need to represent the absolute as *subject* has found expression in the propositions: God is eternal, the moral world-order, love and so on. In such propositions the True is only posited *immediately* as subject, but is not represented as the movement of reflecting itself into itself" (Phen., 26, 12). This nature of the dialectic supports the claim I have made above with regard to the relationship between soul and spirit, and its implication for the nature of the dialectical movement. Hegel criticizes the tendency to take the subject as a fixed point and a content: "[t]he subject is assumed as a fixed point to which, as their support, the predicates are affixed by a movement belonging to the knower of this subject, and which is not regarded as belonging to the fixed point itself; yet, it is only through this movement that the content could be represented as subject . . . the actuality is self-movement (Phen. 27, 13). Hegel criticizes this tendency, but does not dismiss it entirely. Just as he claimed in the *Encyclopaedia* that the soul is a thing from the perspective of spirit, which implies that spirit is not a thing, he states that the truth of the subject as a fixed point is revealed at a later stage and thereby justifies the legitimacy of the dialectical movement. The subjectivity of Hegel's system, therefore, consists precisely in the fact that it objectifies its life.

Yet what does it mean to say that subjectivity has to be questioned at the level of dialectical discourse? Is it a critique of Hegel to claim that he is still committed to a variation of subjectivity? Does not a discourse progressing like a subject displace the problems of understanding the human being as subject?

Even if one agrees with Hegel that the individual subject is not needed for the dialectical process, one can still claim that Hegel relies on subjectivity.

My argument accepts Hegel's displacement of the human subject. I have also accepted the fact that one cannot object to or criticize Hegel from a perspective that has the possibility of being incorporated into Hegelian logic. My aim here is to lay out the commitments of this logic. Hegel's dialectic is committed to a notion of subjectivity. There is an operation of subjectivity in Hegel that is beyond the designations of subjective and objective spirit. This type of subjectivity can only be overcome if the dialectical process is interrupted, where spirit might never come back to "itself" and might not restore itself. Such an interruption is possible if one does not define the relationship to negativity as a cognitive problem, and resists the idea that the notion of alterity at a given stage of the dialectic can become the content of the next stage. Such a radical negativity cannot be incorporated into the system. This negativity must be thought otherwise than dialectically. We have to observe that, for Hegel, the possibility of overcoming negativity in the life of spirit depends on a specific understanding of the relationship of spirit to itself. I do not mean a specific understanding of the relation of human being to the world, but of spirit to itself. This relation, according to Hegel, is one of cognition. Now this is not the same claim as the one that states that for Hegel the fundamental human attunement is cognition. One has to recognize that for Hegel the movement of spirit does not exclusively concern the human relation to the world, even though this is a necessary relation within the dialectical process. Spirit knows itself, is conscious of itself, and thereby overcomes negativity, even by incorporating unintelligibility through thought. Yet there is, I suggest, a possibility that spirit may not overcome its own negativity, that is, a possibility that spirit might not relate to itself exclusively through cognition. The negativity of the subject may be otherwise than the finitude of human knowledge and thought. If, as I said, the question of madness concerns the relation of spirit to itself in its movement, then madness is neither an experience nor a concept. It is not a concept because if it were it would be incorporated into the structure of rationality, and would not be madness anymore. However, madness does not designate a pure, unmediated experience either, because such an experience can only be designated and understood as experience if mediated by consciousness.

What does it mean to say that spirit's relation to itself is not necessarily cognitive? Does this not render philosophical activity mute? Philosophy has always been an activity of knowing and comprehending the world. At this point one has to recognize another dimension of philosophy, namely, that it is not only a question of cognition, but also of engagement. Philosophy is not simply a question of knowing, an activity of scholarly argumentation, nor is it solely a matter of experience and artistic enthusiasm. Philosophy lies precisely in between these two. It is neither simply a matter of conceptual investigation, nor an aesthetic sensibility. I believe that Hegel's philosophy makes room for such an engagement. Just like Plato, Hegel situates death and madness in the very beginning of philosophy. The beginning, however, is also the movement and the end of philosophical thinking for Hegel.

My suggestion here, therefore, is that the knowledge of finitude is not the same as a confrontation with finitude. Finitude cannot be overcome through thinking if thinking is making oneself the content of one's own thought. Negativity is not overcome by being recognized, precisely because the confrontation with negativity is not in the first instance cognitive. Also, within Hegel's system different stages of development have different conceptions of negativity. For Hegel, these different conceptions are all preserved within the movement of the dialectic. This preservation is possible only to the extent that the subject knows them, because they are part of the subject. Different contents in which negativity works become contents of absolute knowledge. Being a content is a necessity for knowledge. Within this system, the subject recollects previous stages as contents, that is, it transforms them into contents and thereby preserves these stages by transforming them. The possibility of preservation is dependent upon this transformation. Negativity, however, is a way of relating to the other rather than a content. The problem arises when the negativity specific to a stage (and there are specific characters of negativity at every stage) is reduced to a content, becomes a different negativity. The negativity, which is specific to the feeling soul, namely madness, is different in phenomenology, in the life of spirit. However, just because madness, for example, can be known as madness does not mean that it can be sublated. Heidegger's critique of Hegel makes this point. Heidegger's critique does not say that there is a precognitive relationship to the world; but rather it points to a noncognitive relationship of the self to itself, which does not yield a perfectly circular recoil where negativity is preserved by being sublated.

I would like to connect this argument to the issue of engagement that I discussed in the previous chapter on Plato. The philosophical engagement, which is necessitated by negativity, cannot be known. It cannot be transformed into a content and taught or distributed. This engagement does not appeal to the notion of immediacy that the Hegelian system has sublated. Even if one accepts the sublation of immediacy of the individual subject, there is a dimension of philosophy that cannot be reduced. The question of the confrontation with negativity concerns spirit's movement. Even though "philosophy moves essentially in the element of universality," according to Hegel, there is a sense in which the movement of spirit is also a particular movement. This particularity is different from immediacy. In the cases of madness and death there is a possibility of thinking an engagement with negativity that cannot be sublated within a system. Hegel's system operates like Plato's recollection of forms in that by incorporating madness and death, philosophy becomes madder than madness, and spirit becomes the most radical articulation of death. Yet everything depends on realizing that what is at stake in madness may not be an individual human being.

As I said above, a number of twentieth century thinkers try to escape Hegelianism. One must ask why this is the case. Why should one try to escape, if Hegel allows madness and death to be incorporated into the system so forcefully? The only motivation for a desire to escape Hegel is the thought that philosophy is not exclusively an intellectual activity. The oppressiveness associated with philosophy is not that it excludes the other (e.g., madness) from its domain, but that it incorporates it. Therefore, escaping Hegel does not mean criticizing him in order to restore the dignity of madness. To escape Hegel means, in a sense, to recognize the power of the negative that Hegel attributes to the power of the intellect, and to think the relationship to negativity otherwise than as power of exclusion. One has to think a different relationship to negativity whereby it is not overcome or reduced to a content of intellectual thought. One must also realize that one cannot articulate this relationship in terms of immediacy, corporeality, or individuality. And despite all these attempts to escape Hegel, one has to remember Foucault's words: "we have to determine the extent to which our anti-Hegelianism is possibly one of his tricks directed against us, at the end of which he stands, motionless, waiting for us." To escape Hegel, therefore, is an enterprise that is perhaps ultimately doomed to failure, just as the attempt to lend a voice to madness may ultimately become a betrayal of madness.

THREE

Heidegger

Death as Negativity

HEIDEGGER'S CONTRIBUTION TO the question of madness has to be understood in the context of the role of negativity in his thinking. As in the case of Hegel, the themes of madness and death are related to the question of negativity for Heidegger. The underlying question of the following two chapters is whether Heidegger articulates a different conception of negativity than that of Hegel. "Negativity" does not appear to be a part Heidegger's common vocabulary.[1] It would be difficult to assess Heidegger's relation to Hegel in terms of negativity if Heidegger had not even used this word. However, Heidegger does indeed use the word "negativity" in relation to Hegel in his treatise *Negativität: Eine Auseinandersetzung mit Hegel aus dem Ansatz in der Negativität*.[2] In this work, Heidegger claims that negativity is the only notion that allows us to confront Hegel without becoming caught up in the dilemma between the outside or inside of Hegel's thinking. In addition, my contention is that Heidegger, throughout his career, confronts Hegel's thinking, and that Heidegger's own thinking can be reconstructed in part as a response to Hegel. Even though the term negativity might not be explicitly present, the problem of negativity is pervasive in Heidegger's writings. The value of such a reconstruction is that it clarifies and strengthens Heidegger's critique of subjectivity. Hegel is the thinker who most challenges Heidegger's thinking in the sense that we find resources in Hegel's thinking that can answer some of the claims of Heidegger's critique of the metaphysics of presence and subjectivity. Therefore, reading Heidegger against the backdrop of Hegel allows us to understand how we can think about negativity.[3] My aim here is to articulate Heidegger's understanding of negativity and to try to show why it is perhaps the single most important issue in understanding the relationship between Hegel and Heidegger.[4] Once again, madness and death are the themes that will enable us to think negativity in specific contexts.

In Heidegger's corpus negativity emerges in several contexts. In the context of *Being and Time*, death, (or more specifically *being*-towards-death) represents negativity. After *Being and Time*, Heidegger continues to think the finitude of being, which is a negativity in and of being by designating it as concealment, absencing, or *Enteignis*. For Heidegger, the question concerning the finitude of being is a question of negativity.[5] However, our confrontation with the nothingness of existence is not a cognitive limitation. In *Being and Time* this confrontation is understood in terms of attunement and mood. Later in his career, Heidegger also characterizes this confrontation in terms of madness (*Wahnsinn, Verrücktheit*). With this thought, Heidegger displaces an important dimension of the traditional way of understanding madness. The philosophical conception of madness has almost always been associated with the notion of error. Madness is considered to be a particular configuration of error. From Plato to Hegel, this conviction remains relatively constant, even though the notions of truth and error undergo significant modifications. By displacing the traditional understanding of truth, Heidegger also articulates a different understanding of madness than the one traditionally understood. I will explain this conception of truth specifically in relation to Hegel's dialectic.

Does the question of being (*Seinsfrage*) which is considered to be the single theme of Heidegger's thinking, have anything to contribute to the question of madness? Heidegger did write about madness, both as a psychiatric problem and otherwise. My discussion of Heidegger and madness will demonstrate how Heidegger's understanding of madness is closely related to his displacement of the metaphysics of presence and his critique of subjectivity. I will connect his discussion of madness to his understanding of the notion of death, and the way in which they characterize a similar experience. A corollary to this connection will be a discussion of Heidegger's *Zollikon* Seminars[6] where he speaks explicitly about what it means to be "mentally ill," and how this question presupposes an understanding of human existence in terms of temporality. Within the context of these seminars, Heidegger goes back to his treatment of time in *Basic Problems of Phenomenology*.[7] His understanding of human existence is always bound to the question of time. Hence, the question of temporality will be the domain where madness and death come together.

Heidegger discusses different experiences in different contexts which may all be translated as "madness," yet are designated by different German words such as *Raserei, Verrücktheit, Wahnsinn*, or *zerbrochen* (shattered), referring to Schiller, Hölderlin, Kierkegaard, van Gogh, and Nietzsche.[8] No doubt translating all these words as "madness" is problematic. Yet I believe there is a unitary phenomenon that Heidegger has in mind when he uses these terms.

In this chapter I will articulate this phenomenon in terms of *Being and Time*, and in the next chapter I will turn to Heidegger's later texts including "Language in the Poem: A Placing of Georg Trakl's Poem" and "The Anaximander Fragment."

BEING AND TIME

In *Being and Time*, the question of negativity is not articulated in terms of madness but in terms of death. This is not to say, however, that the question of madness does not have any relevance for *Being and Time*. I will try to develop the argument that as a text *Being and Time* has to be read as the performance of a failure, which can be designated as madness understood in a Hegelian sense. Heidegger's critique of subjectivity is not a simple dismissal of the possibility of subjectivity, but a performance of the groundlessness of the discourse of subjectivity. In order to accomplish that, *Being and Time* proceeds through the presuppositions of subjectivity and thereby tries to demonstrate subjectivity's closure. The negativity of death is the substantial part or the "content" of this performance, whereas madness is its style, or form. I will interpret *Being and Time* in terms of the issue that was raised in my previous chapter on Hegel. I will demonstrate that *Being and Time* stages, or illustrates how the notion of death speaks to a *radical break, or discontinuity* within existence and thinking, which is much more radical than any break within the dialectical movement of thinking. In other words, I argue that whereas the incorporation of death leads to the continuity of the life of spirit for Hegel, Heidegger's discussion of death demonstrates that death is a radical disruption of existence and thinking beyond any possibility of recuperation.

Heidegger's attempt to read absence within being is expressed in terms of the question of death. The nothingness primordially dominant in the being of Dasein is revealed to it in authentic being-towards-death. This revelation of being-towards-death is also the way in which Heidegger answers the question of the unity of the existential structures of being-in-the-world. Therefore, in terms of what it accomplishes, namely, allowing a self-revelation of Dasein, death may seem to be a reinterpretation of Plato's insights as we outlined them in the first chapter. However, Heidegger's interpretation of death is also a response to Hegel's conception of death in the *Phenomenology of Spirit*, as well as a subversion of both of these conceptions. Heidegger's understanding of death is neither an appeal to a suprasensuous world, nor a recuperable event within thinking (dialectical or otherwise). Death indicates an absence "within" being that requires a new interpretation of the sensuous as well as of thinking. Even though Heidegger does not explicitly speak of madness within the context of *Being and Time*, his analysis of Dasein's care structure tries to bring out a phenomenon that Heidegger subsequently interprets as madness. This phenomenon is already presupposed by

reflection or by self-consciousness, that is, it is a more primordial phenomenon than cognitive self-consciousness, according to Heidegger.

The relationship of the self to itself is the starting point of *Being and
Time*. Heidegger declares the aim of his work as the investigation of the question of being. Since being is always the being of an entity, Heidegger identifies Dasein as that entity which may possibly provide an access (*Zugang*) to
the question of being.[9] The reason that Dasein is this privileged entity is due
to the fact that Dasein is the only entity that raises this question.[10] In the
Introduction of *Being and Time*, the only distinguishing feature Heidegger
attributes to Dasein is that Dasein is the questioner.[11]

Dasein is the questioner that raises the question of its own being. However, Dasein's being is not only a theoretical question for Dasein, but also a
concern. Hence, for Heidegger, the fundamental human relationship to the
world is not a cognitive one. This is not to say that this relationship is a practical one, or that there is a relationship between two separate entities. Human
existence *is* relationality.[12] Heidegger characterizes Dasein in terms of a double
determination: 1) the essence (*Wesen*) of this being lies in its to be (*in seinem
Zu-sein*). This is to say that the essence of Dasein lies in its existence. 2) The
being (*Sein*) which this being (*Seiendes*) is concerned about in its being is in
each case mine. This is what Heidegger calls *Jemeinigkeit* (SZ, 42). These two
determinations of Dasein should be understood with respect to the relationship between Dasein and being. One of the most significant and obscure
aspects of *Being and Time* is the relationship between the being of Dasein and
being. This question is a complicated one, because a straightforward designation of Dasein as the site of disclosure of being has the potential implication
of treating Dasein as a *foundational* relation or even as an entity.[13] In other
words, the designation that Dasein is the site of disclosure of being is problematic if Dasein is not understood in a proper way. At the very beginning of
Being and Time, Heidegger explicitly distinguishes being (*Sein*) from beings
(*Seiendes*), a distinction he later calls the ontological difference. Consequently, it is clear that Dasein (as a way of being as well as as an entity) is not
the same as being itself. There is a multiplicity within being understood as the
totality (*Ganzheit*) of beings. Yet the source of the difference that comprises
multiplicity cannot be articulated in terms of a multiplicity of entities. The
reason for this is not simply internal to Heidegger's vocabulary and thinking,
namely, to his claim that being cannot be explained in terms of beings themselves, but lies within the phenomenon itself. Even outside of a Heideggerian
context we can assert that not every entity displays a peculiar and unique way
of being. Heidegger tries to explain the difference and multiplicity within
being in terms of Dasein's relation to it and to the world. This is a significant
point to emphasize, because the reason Heidegger appeals to Dasein, a particular way of being, is not to privilege one entity over others, but in order to
articulate the difference and negativity within the structure of being.

THE PROBLEM OF *BEI SICH* AND
DASEIN'S DIFFERENCE FROM OTHER ENTITIES

Heidegger designates the basic constitution of Dasein as being-in-the-world. From the beginning of his discussion of being-in-the-world, Heidegger insists that it is a unitary phenomenon. Yet Heidegger starts out by dividing this unitary phenomenon into its three components: "the worldliness of the world," "the who," and "to be in." In order to articulate being-in-the-world one has to 1) clarify the ontological structure of the world, 2) inquire into the "who" of being-in-the-world, and 3) explicate the ontological constitution of being-in. Heidegger continues with a discussion of "being-in." Being-in does not signify a present-at-hand occurrence of Dasein among other innerworldly entities. Dasein's being-in-the-world is an *existential*. Heidegger states that being-in has to be understood as "*innan, wohnen, habitare, sich aufhalten*, I am accustomed to, familiar with, I am *(Ich bin)* in the world" (SZ, 54). At this point Heidegger indicates the relationship between the first person conjugation of the verb "to be," *bin* (am), and the proposition *bei* (alongside). Dasein *is alongside* the world, the explication of which will lead to a discussion of ecstatic temporality. Dasein is not in the world in the same way as other entities precisely because Dasein does not share the same temporality as other things in the world, even though other beings are drawn into the world through Dasein. Therefore, Heidegger's discussion of Dasein does not attribute a positive description to Dasein, but articulates it in terms of a kind of negativity.

Heidegger starts his discussion of being-in-the-world by designating it, in the first instance, as an absorption. Dasein is not present-at-hand in the world, even though Heidegger writes that the presence-at-hand proper to innerworldly entities should not be confused with Dasein's genuine way of being present-at-hand. Heidegger relates Dasein's presence-at-hand to facticity: "The concept of facticity implies that an innerworldly being has being-in-the-world in such a way that it can understand itself as bound up (*verhaftet*) in its destiny with the being of those entities which it encounters within its world" (SZ, 56). How is this notion of destiny to be understood? And why does Dasein understand itself at first in terms of innerworldly entities? This second question ties Heidegger's discussion to his confrontation with the metaphysics of subjectivity.

If being-in-the-world is a unitary phenomenon, and the meaning of being is to be related to this phenomenon in terms of questioning, it is also legitimate to say that Dasein is in a sense also alongside itself *(bei sich)* to the extent that it is alongside the world. As I indicated above, earlier in *Being and Time* Heidegger justifies the existential analytic in terms of Dasein's relationship to being. Even though being is not a being (the ontological difference between being and beings), being is always the being of an entity, and the investigation of being has to start from an analysis of a being. As we have mentioned, the reason why we investigate Dasein as the entity whose being will provide access to the meaning of being is because, for Dasein, its own being is a question. Dasein is the only entity that raises the question of the meaning of its own being. That which is questioned is being, yet that which is interrogated is Dasein (that which is asked about, *das Befragte*). Questioning *(Fragen)* is the comportment of a being that has its own character of being (SZ, 5). Therefore, not only does Dasein question itself in order to reach the meaning of being, but the questioning of its being characterizes the positive character of Dasein. There is, therefore, a certain reflexivity inscribed into the question of the meaning of being. However, Heidegger does not explicitly formulate this reflexivity in terms of being-alongside-oneself *(bei sich)*, which is the most significant trait of the subject according to German Idealism. This is because Heidegger does not want to reduce being to the being of a questioning subject. Yet the problem he tries to avoid is precisely that which illuminates his project. As we have seen for Hegel, to be alongside oneself *(bei sich)* is the character of the subject. This character makes the movement of spirit possible. The movement of spirit is actuality. Actuality is an actualization from the nonactual (negative). Therefore, spirit not only needs to be alongside itself in and through negativity, but it *is* this negativity. For Heidegger, negativity cannot be understood in this way, because it cannot be reduced to negativity within the structure of spirit's movement. This, in turn, is because spirit is not alongside itself in a cognitive way, or rather the confrontation with negativity is not cognitive. Heidegger's appeal to disposition *(Befindlichkeit)* and to attunement (or mood: *Stimmung)* is an attempt to understand negativity as irreducible to a split within spirit.

Immediately after articulating being-in-the-world in terms of being alongside, Heidegger states that this phenomenon is prior to any cognition between two beings, the world and the soul (SZ, 59). Being-in-the world is not to be understood in terms of a subject knowing an object. "Subject and object are not the same as Dasein and world" (SZ, 60).[14] In section thirteen, Heidegger presents explicitly how the cognition of the world *(Welterkennen)* is a founded mode of being-in-the-world. The main claim of this section is that cognition is a derivative mode of being of Dasein as being-in-the-world. Phenomenologically, one can assert that "cognition itself is grounded beforehand in a being-already-alongside-the-world which essentially constitutes the being of Dasein" (SZ, 61). For our purposes it is important to note that cognition as a founded mode concerns not only the relationship of Dasein to the world, but also Dasein's relationship to itself. In fact, Dasein is nothing but this relation. Thus, ". . . Dasein does not first go outside of the inner sphere in which it is initially encapsulated, but, rather in its primary kind of being, it is always already 'outside' alongside some being encountered in the world that is already discovered" (SZ, 62). This primary familiarity with the world (being-alongside) is the precondition of encountering entities within the world. Heidegger explains this relationship in section eighteen of *Being and Time* entitled "Involvement (or Relevance: *Bewandtnis*) and Significance: The Worldhood of the World." Heidegger first indicates that readiness-to-hand is a mode of the being of beings. Readiness-to-hand is only possible on the basis of a world. Ready-at-hand entities can only be encountered in a world. Heidegger's next move is to explain a difference within the being of innerworldly beings (readiness-to-hand and presence-at-hand) on the basis of Dasein's relationship to the world. The first step in this move is to establish that ready-at-hand entities constitute an interconnected whole with reference to each other.

> The being of the ready-to-hand has the structure of reference. A being is discovered as the being it is when it has been referred to something. With any such being there is an involvement (*Bewenden*), which it has in (*bei*) something. The character of being of ready-to-hand is involvement (*Bewandtnis*). (SZ, 84)

Hence, involvement constitutes the being of certain innerworldly beings for which they are always already freed. In other words, involvement in and with is the ontological determination of the being of these beings. Consequently, such innerworldly entities are encountered on the basis of a totality of involvements (*Bewandtnisganzheit*), which is "earlier" than any single entity in the world. This totality of involvements is made possible by a primary "for the sake of." The totality of involvements leads to a "for the sake of" (*Wozu*) where there is no more involvement, that is, to a being that does not have the character of being ready-to-hand. This being is Dasein, whose being is determined as being-in-the-world. At this point it is clear that Heidegger traces the being of entities and more importantly the differentiations within the being of beings back to Dasein's relationship to the world. The primary "for the sake of" is Dasein's being, whose being is an issue for itself. The totality of involvements can only be understood on the basis of Dasein's a priori letting-something-be-involved (*Bewendenlassen*). Heidegger writes: "This 'a priori' letting-something-be-involved is the condition for the possibility of encountering anything ready-to-hand. . . . To have always already let something be freed for involvement is an *a priori perfect*, which characterizes the kind of being of Dasein itself" (SZ, 85). In a marginal note to this sentence, Heidegger refers to Aristotle's notion of *to ti en einai* (what already was; what always already has presenced in advance, what has been, *Gewesen*, the perfect). The *a priori* perfect is not something ontically in the past, but something always ontologically earlier. Therefore, it could also be called the ontological or transcendental perfect. This is the way Heidegger interprets Kant's doctrine of schematism (SZ, 441–442). Heidegger proceeds to connect this *a priori* letting-something-be-involved with Dasein's understanding of being. Consequently, since Dasein understands the primary for-the sake-of in terms of its own being, beings in the world are also understood and differentiated on the basis of Dasein's being.

> Previous letting something be involved in *(bei)* . . . with . . . is grounded in an understanding of something like letting-be-involved *(Bewendenlassen)*, as well as the in-which and with-which of involvement. . . . *As that for which it lets beings be encountered in the kind of being of involvement, the wherein of self-referential understanding is the phenomenon of the world.* (SZ, 86)

The world is that which is understood beforehand, before encountering any particular entity in it. Or more precisely, an understanding of the world is the condition for the possibility of encountering any being in the world. This *a priori* understanding is more like a familiarity than a theoretical transparency. The ontological understanding of the world amounts to an understanding of being. This connection between the world and being ties Dasein's understanding of its own being in with the understanding of beings in the world, which Heidegger earlier referred to as Dasein's "being bound up with the being of beings it encounters within its own world" (SZ, 56). The connection also indicates that a differentiation of the "regions" of being ("readiness-to-hand" and "presence-at-hand") is only possible on the basis of Dasein's being.

Heidegger's discussion of the *a priori* nature of the world is the initial step he takes in articulating his reinterpretation of ideas, or universals. As we have seen in chapter one on Plato, a prior understanding of ideas (forms) is a precondition of perception. In Heidegger's discussion of involvement, we see that a notion of totality understood in terms of the *world* plays a role comparable to that of ideas. Thereby, Heidegger responds to the necessity of something prior to perception while avoiding an appeal to a suprasensuous world. The world is not something to be observed sensuously or cognitively. It is not something to be theoretically accessed either, because the possibility of a theoretical access reduces being to intellectual (non-sensuous) presence. Heidegger resists reducing the world to formal relations (to a functional system of relations) precisely because such a reduction transforms these relations into cognitive ones and strips away the phenomenal structure of the world.

After his initial characterization of being-in in section twelve, Heidegger returns to this theme in chapter five, section twenty-eight. He declares explicitly that investigating being-in as such in a more penetrating fashion will "pave the way to grasping the primordial being of Dasein itself, care *(Sorge)*" (SZ, 131). Heidegger once again emphasizes that being-in has to be distinguished from a subject-object relationship. However, this time he intimates that being-in-the-world has something to say about the being of the subject:

Being-in is distinct from the present-at-hand insideness of something present-at-hand in something else. Being-in is not a characteristic that is
effected, or even just elicited, in a present-at-hand subject by the world's
being present-at-hand; being-in is rather an essential kind of being of this
entity itself. But then what else presents itself with this phenomenon
other than the *commercium* between a present-at-hand subject and a present-at-hand object? This interpretation would come closer to the phenomenal content if it were to state that Dasein is the being of this
"between." (SZ, 132)

Nevertheless, "this interpretation" is inadequate as well, since it suggests that
there are two entities in terms of which a "between" can be articulated. Heidegger's problem here is how to articulate the unitary structure of the phenomenon of being-in-the-world without dividing this phenomenon into theoretically present-at-hand "objects" of inquiry. In more general philosophical
terms, the same problem can be articulated as the difficulty of understanding
human existence other than as a subject relating to a totality of objects. The
scope of this problem is not limited to a "correct description" of what is phe-
nomenally there to be described, but rather the description itself is a part of
the phenomenon in the sense that there is a danger of reducing the phenomenon to something to be described without paying attention to how the
description itself transforms the phenomenon. This circularity is based upon
Heidegger's initial conviction that an understanding of being belongs to and
in part constitutes Dasein's own being. When Heidegger states that being-in
can be understood as the being of "the between," he wants to give a description of what could traditionally be understood as the being of the subject. Yet
the consequence of this description is that the being of Dasein, even though
it is the being *of* Dasein, does not *belong* to it in the sense that it would belong
to a subject that could appropriate its being as its own through a cognitive
transparency and description. Therefore, the desire to articulate the *being* of
the subject has the dangerous potential of restoring the unity of the subject
rather than explaining its dissolution.

DISPOSITION AND ANXIETY

Dasein's being-in is to be understood in terms of disposition (*Befindlichkeit*).[15]
Disposition is the ontological counterpart of attunement (moods). Heidegger
claims that "the possibilities of disclosure belonging to cognition fall short of
the primordial disclosure of moods in which Dasein is brought before its being
as the there" (SZ, 134). Heidegger points to a more originary relationship to
the world than cognition ("Disclosed does not, as such, mean to be known"
(SZ, 134). What is disclosed to Dasein in moods is its own being. So moods
reveal, not only the ontological structure of the world, but also Dasein's own

being. It is clear at this point that the world and Dasein have to be understood as one and the same ontological phenomenon. Heidegger defends his
understanding of facticity in terms of thrownness into being-in-the-world
against the charge of not being certain, or theoretically evident:

> Phenomenally, *what* attunement discloses and *how* it discloses would be
> completely misunderstood if what has been disclosed were conflated with
> that which disposed Dasein "at the same time" is acquainted with, knows,
> and believes. Even when Dasein is "sure" of its "whither" in faith or thinks
> it knows about its whence in rational enlightenment, all of this makes no
> difference in the face of the phenomenal fact that moods bring Dasein
> before the that of its there, which stares at it with the inexorability of an
> enigma. Existential-ontologically there is not the slightest justification for
> minimizing the "evidence" of disposition by measuring it against the apod-
> ictic certainty of the theoretical cognition of something, which is purely
> present-at-hand. However the phenomena are no less falsified when they
> are banished to the sanctuary of the irrational. When irrationalism, as the
> counterpart of rationalism, talks about the things to which rationalism is
> blind, it does so only with a squint. (SZ, 135–136)

This is a rare reference to irrationalism in *Being and Time*. One can observe
Heidegger's desire to displace the opposition between rationalism and irrationalism in understanding human existence in the world. It is also a
response to a potential Hegelian criticism of disposition, which would state
that the pre-rational character of disposition could only be articulated in
and through a dialectical mediation and rationalization. Heidegger's characterization of disposition does not rely on the immediacy of an experience.
Heidegger is very clear in distinguishing disposition and attunement from
an onlooking to the world (theoretical or sensuous). Referring back to his
discussion of the totality of involvements in section eighteen, Heidegger
writes: "We said earlier that the world already disclosed lets innerworldly
beings be encountered. This prior disclosedness of the world, which belongs
to being-in, is also constituted by disposition. Letting something be
encountered is primarily *circumspective*, not just a sensation or staring out
at something" (SZ, 137). The relationship to the world in disposition is not
a sensation or experience that can or should be reduced to thinking or consciousness. This passage also makes it clear that *"attunement has always
already disclosed being-in-the-world as a whole and first makes possible directing
oneself toward something"* (SZ, 137). Hence, already in his discussion of disposition and attunement, Heidegger raises the question of the unity of
being-in-the-world.

Heidegger deals with the issue of the primordial totality of the structural whole of Dasein in section thirty-nine. The question of structural
totality is the same question as the unity of being. Since innerworldly enti-

ties are freed (let be) in terms of the referential totality organized "for the sake of" Dasein, the question of Dasein's structural totality is Heidegger's way of understanding the unity of the presence of beings. Heidegger finds the existential-ontological possibility of the question of totality in what he calls "a fundamental attunement" (*Grundstimmung*). It is important to note that even in the question of unity there is already a multiplicity involved. Heidegger writes:

> When we see the 'world' in an unsteady and wavering way in accordance with our attunement, what is ready-to-hand shows itself in its specific worldliness, which is never the same on any given day. Theoretical look-ing at the world has always already flattened it down to the uniformity of what is purely present-at-hand, although, evidently, a new abundance of what can be discovered in pure determination lies within that uniformity. (SZ, 138)

Unlike the theoretical-cognitive understanding of the world, attunement does not explain the multiplicity within the being of beings in terms of the multiplicity of entities. Even though there is a unity of presence and a struc-tural totality of Dasein, this is never a unity that can be reduced to a primal element. In articulating the structural unity of Dasein's being, Heidegger con-siders two different points of view. The first is the perspective of the phe-nomenologist, namely, the philosophical perspective from which one articu-lates this unity. The second is the perspective of Dasein: How can its unity be recognized, and be available to Dasein? In other words, how can this unity be accessible to Dasein existentially? Ultimately, for Heidegger, these different points of view will converge. Heidegger will not rely exclusively on the per-spective of a phenomenologist observing Dasein in the world. This desire is already clear in Heidegger's formulation of the question of unity in terms of an understanding of being. An understanding of being belongs to the onto-logical structure of Dasein. Beings are disclosed to Dasein in its being. Dis-position, discourse, and understanding constitute the manner of being of this disclosedness. Is there, then, an understanding disposition in Dasein in which it is disclosed to itself in a distinctive way?

The unity of Dasein's existential structures is disclosed not in theoretical cognition, but in a fundamental disposition, namely anxiety: "Anxiety pro-vides the phenomenal basis for explicitly grasping the primordial totality of the being of Dasein. Its being reveals itself as care" (SZ, 182). Heidegger articulates the notion of anxiety in contrast to the average everydayness of Dasein. In its everyday absorption in the world Dasein is "in flight" from its own existence. This flight is not from a specific object in the world, as in the case of fear, but rather an escape from anxiety itself. Dasein is in flight from this fundamental disposition, and the public domain of average everydayness is constituted on the basis of this flight.

Thus *anxiety* takes away from Dasein the possibility of understanding itself,
falling, in terms of the "world" and the public way of being interpreted. It
throws Dasein back upon that for which it is anxious, its authentic poten-
tiality-for-being-in-the-world. *Anxiety* individuates Dasein to its ownmost
being-in-the-world, which, as understanding, projects itself upon possibilities. (SZ, 187–188)

In its disappearance from public understanding, anxiety reveals the totality
of Dasein's being-in-the-world. *"That about which one has anxiety is being-in-
the-world as such"* (SZ, 186). Heidegger situates the disclosiveness of anxiety
in contrast to the totality of involvements discussed in section eighteen of
Being and Time, as well as the phenomenon of being-in in terms of familiarity in section twelve: "What anxiety is about is not an innerworldly being.
Therefore, essentially it cannot have an involvement *(Bewandtnis)*. . . .
What anxiety is about is completely indefinite" (SZ, 186). As we will see in
the context of the connection between anxiety and death, Heidegger's
understanding of the negativity associated with the possibility of the disclosure of Dasein's existential structures has to be understood in terms of this
indefinite nature of anxiety. Heidegger does not simply state that Dasein does
not know what it is anxious about. If indefiniteness were simply a problem
of knowledge, the very articulation of it in the context of *Being and Time*
would transform the nature of this indefiniteness. That is to say, the very
intervention of the phenomenological "description" would transform the
indefiniteness of anxiety into something definite. Therefore, the movement
of *Being and Time* has to be thought otherwise than as a descriptive gesture
of determination, as seems to be the case for Hegel's description of the movement of the spirit.

At this point it may be useful to distinguish Heidegger's notion of anxiety from that of Hegel. One can discern a similarity between Heidegger's discussion of anxiety and Hegel's discussion of the master-slave dialectic. Hegel
writes in the *Phenomenology of Spirit*: "For this consciousness [the consciousness of the slave] has been anxious not about this or that particular thing, or
for this or that particular moment, but about his whole being, because it has
sensed the fear of death, the absolute master."[16] Even though both Hegel and
Heidegger seem to be speaking of a similar phenomenon, their understanding
of this phenomenon is quite different. For Hegel, anxiety, despite the fact
that it concerns the entirety of being, is ultimately a relational concept. It is
articulated in the context of the dialectical relationship between master and
slave. This relationality is in contrast to Heidegger's understanding of death
as nonrelational, as we see in the context of his discussion of death in con-
junction with anxiety. For Heidegger, any determination of anxiety, not only
of what Dasein is anxious about but of the attunement of anxiety itself, is
only possible in a public space of Dasein's average everydayness. By insisting

that anxiety "fetches Dasein back out of its entangled absorption in the 'world'" (SZ, 189), Heidegger dissociates the confrontation with death from a relational context. This dissociation is important because the negativity of death can only be overcome through its relationality. As Hegel writes: "the pure, universal movement, that absolute melting-away of everything stable (*alles Bestehen*) is however the simple being of self-consciousness, the absolute negativity, *the pure being-for-itself*, which consequently is implicit in this consciousness" (Phen., 153, 117). Heidegger resists this conclusion, because absolute negativity cannot be reduced to a determination of consciousness. Therefore, Heidegger will claim that Dasein's being as a movement is different from the movement of self-consciousness.

Heidegger articulates the indefiniteness of anxiety in terms of "uncanniness." "In anxiety it is *uncanny* for one" (*In der Angst ist einem* 'unheimlich') (SZ, 188). The word *unheimlich* literally means, "not being at home." Hence, Heidegger contrasts the "dwelling alongside" and "being familiar with" of being-in with the disposition of anxiety. Once everyday familiarity collapses in anxiety, being-in enters the existential "mode" of not-being-at-home. For Heidegger, not-being-at-home is a more primordial phenomenon than the familiarity of average everydayness. The nature of this primordiality is important to question, because it will ultimately illuminate Heidegger's conviction of the priority of negativity, or of absence over presence. In a later marginal note to "not-being-at-home," Heidegger indicates that this phenomenon can be understood as *"Enteignis"* (expropriation) (SZ, 443). Ex-appropriation is a cognate of Heidegger's term "event of appropriation" (*Ereignis*) and illuminates the negativity implied in this term.

How does anxiety reveal Dasein's being as a whole? Heidegger takes up this question in section forty-one, where he explicitly designates Dasein's being as care. The connection between anxiety and care has to be thought in terms of the fact that there are two dimensions that are revealed in anxiety: thrownness and the potentiality for being-in-the-world. Dasein's being is constituted through a noncognitive concern. This concern is revealed in anxiety as an understanding in self-projection in terms of Dasein's ownmost potentiality-for-being. It is important to underline that this potentiality of being is not a "fact" that is revealed to Dasein ontically. In anxiety, a *structural* dimension of Dasein's being is revealed, namely, that it is always already *ahead* of itself. This dimension is for the most part covered over by being reduced to the notion of willing. Heidegger calls this covering over a modification of Dasein's potentiality-for-being. The being-ahead-of-itself of Dasein is not the isolated tendency of a subject. Being-ahead-of-itself (*sich-vorweg-sein*) is based upon Dasein's already being-in-the-world. Therefore, it is not to be reduced to a concern about the future, but is characteristic of Dasein's existence. The way to distinguish the two is once again to emphasize that concern is not something that Dasein thinks, wishes, or plans, but is a way for Dasein to exist that is not to be understood cognitively. The being-ahead-of-itself of Dasein is already a being-alongside entities encountered within the world.

Anxiety reveals Dasein's existence as ahead-of-itself. Being-ahead characterizes a sense of freedom from the presence of entities. Heidegger claims that anxiety in the face of being-in-the-world as anxiety in the face of death also individuates Dasein. It is important not to reduce this individuation to the uniqueness of a subject as opposed to other subjects. The nonpublic dimension of anxiety is not that one "I" feels anxiety as opposed to another "I," but that the noncommunicable nature of anxiety undermines the very possibility of an "I" that is said to "have" anxiety. Therefore, individuation does not designate the integrity of an individual, but a moment of Dasein's being, which undermines the possibility of any constitution of subjectivity. Being-ahead-of-itself is also a structural dimension of Dasein that is other than "rational." Dasein's concern is a noncognitive existence, and the possibility revealed in anxiety is noncommunicable in a radical sense. It undermines the self-communication that is necessary for the constitution of subjectivity.

DASEIN'S BEING: CARE AND BEING-AHEAD

In the second division of *Being and Time*, Heidegger raises the question of the unity of Dasein's existential structures. Grasping the totality of Dasein's existential structures seems to be impossible precisely because Dasein's being is care. The primary implication of care is that Dasein is always "ahead of itself" (*sich-vorweg*). Being-ahead-of-itself is the structure in which Dasein exists for the sake of itself, which is also the condition for the possibility of the world as the horizon according to which beings are revealed. Yet if Dasein is always a "not yet" that is already implicated in the determination of its essence as existence, then it is impossible to grasp it in its totality. There is always something outstanding (*Ausstand*) in Dasein. The problem is that as long as Dasein exists, it cannot be grasped in its totality, and its totality can only be grasped when Dasein has already lost the world. That is to say, being-in-the-world as a totality can be grasped only when Dasein has ended. The "end" of being-in-the-world is death. Heidegger's notion of death as an end has a double signification. First, death is *not* the end of being-in-the-world if "end" is understood as the last event of a series or of a movement. Such an understanding of end would regard Dasein's existence as a present-at-hand occurrence, or a motion that can be understood over and against an observer that describes it. Secondly, death *is* the end of Dasein to the extent that it is understood as a particular relationship of Dasein to its own existence, that is, as a relation to negativity. Heidegger designates this relationship as *"being-towards-death."* Being-towards-death is ultimately the ground of Dasein's being-ahead-of-itself (sich-vorweg). Therefore, that which makes the expla-nation of totality impossible under a present-at-hand description of Dasein is the only way of understanding Dasein's totality. This totality that is Dasein's being is indeed revealed only on the basis of the being of nonbeing (Sein des Nichtseins) (SZ, 444). Dasein's being cannot be revealed in a descriptive mode because in that mode Dasein is always "not yet something," but it can be understood if it is regarded from the perspective of an authentic poten-tiality-for-being-a-whole (eigentliche Ganzseinkönnen). The ultimate ground of being-in-the-world is nothingness or negativity, which can be understood in terms of temporality.

Heidegger explicitly distinguishes the contradiction between care and the possibility of attaining wholeness from an imperfection of "our cognitive faculties" (SZ, 236). Dasein's existence can never be reduced to a particular constituted presence, because Dasein is always ahead of this presence. In any given being-alongside beings, Dasein is always already absent. This irre-ducibility reveals itself phenomenologically in any given presence (as a con-figuration of time). In any involvement with entities Dasein is already given over to another possibility, already absent. This absence constitutes Dasein's being as care, and it is for this reason that Dasein's existence cannot legiti-mately be reduced to presence-at-hand. However, Dasein is not to be under-stood as something that is not yet present-at-hand either. In other words, Dasein's existence should not be regarded as being secured through the con-tinuity of a movement.[17] Heidegger's understanding of Dasein's existence as a movement is different from that of Hegel in this respect. The absolute nega-tivity or absolute restlessness that constitutes the movement of spirit would only be a particular understanding of Dasein's existence, which is not pri-mordial for Heidegger. Dasein's movement, for Heidegger, is not a movement of spirit, precisely because the relationship to negativity undermines the pos-sibility of a "cognitive" movement. In order to understand Dasein's relation-ship to death as an instance of negativity we must concentrate on Heidegger's discussion of death.

Heidegger distinguishes the existential notion of death from the experi-ence of the death of others in grasping the whole of Dasein. Heidegger's dis-cussion has two dimensions: First, he distinguishes the existential notion of death from an experience of death in the world. The death of others is com-monly regarded as an event to be experienced and is thereby necessary to pro-vide the wholeness of Dasein's being. The experience, however, presupposes that death is an end in the sense of being the last phase of a series of events. This understanding, however, makes death a transition from being to non-being in the sense of an arrival of something not-yet. Such a notion of death, however, is not only inaccessible through the death of others, but is also denied to Dasein in relation to itself. Secondly, in denying that death is inac-cessible through others, Heidegger does not undermine an ethical relationship to others, such as the one articulated by Derrida and Levinas. What Heidegger emphasizes is that the death of others, or of a Dasein, is not a communicable event. The mineness of death does not simply mean that my death essentially belongs to me as a person as opposed to other persons, but that death has a radical mineness in the sense that it undermines the possibility of communication and representation by undermining the possibility of being-in-the-world. What is at stake in articulating death as a relation to negativity is a displacement of the formal understanding of phenomenology. This is a task Heidegger describes as "deformalizing the formal concept of phenomenon into the phenomenological one" (SZ, 35). The formal understanding of death as a phenomenon has now to be understood phenomenologically, which requires a different interpretation of the notion of end than as a phase in a present-at-hand entity or process. That which is outstanding in Dasein's being is not something that is simply "not-yet" in the sense of not yet present. "Dasein always exists in such a way that its not-yet belongs to it" (SZ, 243). Heidegger connects this problem of "not-yet" to the question of being and nonbeing. Therefore the not-yet character of Dasein is not to be understood in terms of the question of progress, completion (finishedness), and fulfilling. By undermining the notion of completion in Dasein's being Heidegger also implies that death is not something to be overcome. For Heidegger, the finitude that is expressed in the figure of the death of an individual being cannot be overcome in and through a discourse that subsumes the individual under the movement of spirit. Heidegger relates the possibility of such an understanding of death as a sacrifice to its public communicability, which ultimately undermines its radical alterity. Dasein's being-towards-death is a way to be rather than something it encounters in the world. Death is something to which Dasein relates in its being. But how exactly is this relationship to be understood?

Death is the possibility of no-longer-being-able-to-be-there (Nicht-mehr-dasein-können). Heidegger writes:

> When Dasein is imminent to itself as this possibility, it is completely thrown back upon its ownmost potentiality-of-being. Thus imminent to itself, all relations to other Dasein are dissolved in it. This non-relational ownmost possibility is at the same time the most extreme one. As a potentiality of being Dasein is unable to overcome (überholen) the possibility of death. Death is the possibility of the absolute impossibility of Dasein. Thus death reveals itself as the *ownmost nonrelational possibility that cannot be overcome.* (SZ, 250)

One could read this passage as a phenomenological description of an individual's relationship to his or her own death. One could say that death isolates the individual from the others, that it cannot be avoided, and that it is one's most proper belonging to. Under this interpretation, however, death would be regarded as a problem of the individual, and the negativity of death could be swallowed by the positivity of a universal discourse. The absence pertaining to death could be subsumed under the presence of the movement of a universal spirit. Such an understanding, however, misses the point of Heidegger's discussion of death, as well as of the entire thrust of *Being and Time*. For Heidegger, death is not an event that happens to an individual in the sense that Dasein owns its death. Death is a particular configuration of temporality that concerns not simply the individual Dasein as a present-at-hand entity, but the movement of being-in-the-world as such.[18] Death does not reveal itself in a theoretical discourse about death as a cognition, but rather in a disposition (anxiety). "What anxiety is about is being-in-the-world itself. . . . Anxiety about death must not be confused with a fear of one's demise" (SZ, 251). Death is ownmost because it cannot be communicated in a language to others. Heidegger implies that death is nonrelational not because it belongs to one entity as opposed to others. Heidegger's insistence on the nonrelational character of death is the result of his resistance to the idea of overcoming death in its relationality. Death is not to be subsumed under a universal motion by being understood as negativity inserted into the self-relation of a universal subject. Heidegger does not undermine the possibility of this motion by insisting on the individuality of Dasein, but by displacing the nature of the movement that produces universal subjectivity. It is not simply that there is an individual who owns his or her death, and the individual cannot overcome death; rather the relationship to death undermines the possibility of the movement of subjectivity by emphasizing the concretion of subjectivity in a moment (*Augenblick*). This concretion, which is not the concreteness of an individual being, but rather the concretion of temporality as such, makes it impossible to subsume the negativity of death under the absolute restlessness of spirit. Heidegger resists a "communicative" interpretation of death because the subsumption of death under a universal movement of spirit is only possible in and through its expression as a "public" discourse. Heidegger is quite explicit on this point. Immediately after his explanation of death he moves on to the everydayness of Dasein.

In this discussion Heidegger points out that the publicness of everydayness knows death as a "constantly occurring event." Thereby death becomes the topic of idle talk (*Gerede*), which reduces the relationship to death to a matter of indifference. Heidegger states that everydayness veils two factors belonging to death: that it is nonrelational, and that it cannot be overcome. The fundamental attitude toward death in public discourse becomes a constant tranquillization about death (*ständige Beruhigung über den Tod*) (SZ, 254). There are once again two ways of interpreting the role of public everydayness. One could understand the role of everydayness as simply the way in which people speak about death. This interpretation is consistent with what Heidegger designates as a "constant flight from death." However, one could also understand everydayness as a generalized realm of communication. In this respect everydayness is not simply a phenomenological description of what we observe, but is rather the ground of a philosophical understanding of death and its possible overcoming. Only on the basis of this untroubled indifference of everydayness is a cognitive relationship to death possible. In everydayness death is regarded as certain. The mode of this certainty is conviction (*Überzeugung*). Since death is regarded as being the death of someone else, it is an undeniable "fact of experience." Heidegger's most explicit formulation of the relationship to the negativity of death is expressed in the following lines: "One knows about the certainty of death, and yet 'is' not really certain about it" (SZ, 258). The question of death, therefore, can never be entirely reduced to the indifference of cognition, and death cannot be treated as a problem to be overcome. Neither can the negativity of death be used as the certain ground that makes the movement of spirit possible. Heidegger writes that through "idle thinking about death . . . death is postponed to sometime later by relying on the so-called general estimation. Thus 'the they' covers over what is peculiar to the certainty of death, *that it is possible in every moment*" (SZ, 258). Heidegger is not simply inviting us to the necessity of "thinking about" death in every moment, nor is he claiming that death is possible for someone in every single moment. In this passage Heidegger uses the word *Augenblick* for the first time in the sense of the concretion of temporality, in the sense of the temporalization of temporality, which is different from the movement of a subject. Death, accordingly, far from being the property of an individual Dasein, is an individuation of time, which is the ground of Dasein's being in the first place.

We explained above the irreducibility of Dasein to any given presence. In line with Heidegger's discussion of death, this irreducibility is not to be understood on the basis of Dasein's thinking of the future (a "not-yet"), but rather on the basis of Dasein's existence as being-towards-death. Dasein is never fully present as such because of its relation to absence (death). Heidegger articulates this relation in terms of possibility. Dasein's existence as care is a relation to possibility "not in thematic-theoretical regarding of the possible, or even with regard to its possibility as such, but rather in such a way that it circumspectly looks *away* from the possible to what it is possible for" (SZ, 261). Thereby, Heidegger displaces a certain understanding of actuality and possibility. Dasein's "being-toward-death is not meant as an actualization of death, neither can it mean to dwell near the end in its possibility. . . . As something possible death is supposed to show as little as possible of its possibility" (SZ, 261). Dasein's authentic relation to death is not an expectation of the occurrence of an event but a running ahead (anticipation, *Vorlaufen*) that preserves death as a possibility that cannot be understood from the perspective of the actual, because death undermines being-in-the-world as the ground of any sense of actuality. This anticipation frees

Dasein for its possibilities. Therefore, Heidegger designates authentic being-towards-death as "freedom-toward-death." Authentic freedom is an understanding of being in terms of nothingness and reveals itself not in and through cognition, but in anxiety. Being-towards-death is essentially anxiety: "In anxiety Dasein is faced with the nothingness of the possible impossibility of its existence" (SZ, 266). Therefore, ultimately, being-in-the-world, that is, Dasein's existence, is to be understood in terms of nothingness or negativity. There is no present ground underlying Dasein's existence. Dasein's authentic understanding of death implies a kind of certainty. Yet we have to emphasize two points in this context. Dasein's understanding is not a cognitive apprehension of a *meaning*. Heidegger writes: "we must remember that understanding does not primarily mean staring at a meaning *[Sinn]*, but understanding oneself in the potentiality-of-being that reveals itself in the project *[Entwurf]*" (SZ, 263). This notion of understanding transforms Dasein's relationship to the meaning of being, because even the possibility as to whether there *is* a meaning of being (*der Sinn des Seins*) is questionable. The second point is that being certain with respect to death is *indefinite*. The designation of the "indefinite" nature of certainty is important because it underlines Heidegger's desire to understand the negativity of Dasein's being as a movement that is different from the movement of determinate negation. Overcoming death as negativity is only possible on the basis of reducing negativity to the movement of the negation of negation. This is a fundamental difference Heidegger sees between his understanding of temporality and that of Hegel.[19]

At this point the question still remains as to whether Heidegger ultimately articulates an opposition between an authentic and inauthentic understanding of death. Such an articulation would imply that his discussion of authenticity ultimately betrays a metaphysical desire for a "correct" description of the phenomenon, which would signify a desire for presence. This suspicion can be answered at two different levels. First, it is clear that Heidegger does not articulate authentic and inauthentic being-towards-death as instances of correct or incorrect ways of being. It is true that the authentic anticipation of death reveals Dasein's finitude, yet there is absolutely nothing that is communicated in and through this anticipation. In fact, this anticipation implies the perversion of the place of communication, the space where philosophical discourse itself has its place, namely, being-in-the-world. In this respect, Heidegger does not try to overcome negativity in and through his description of the phenomenon of death. Secondly, the question concerns the role of *Being and Time* with respect to the phenomenon of death. Is it not the case that *Being and Time* as a discourse still makes present a dimension of negativity that ultimately is communicated in and through the text? This question concerns the status of a text with respect to its "object" of study. Is one not implicated in the content of what one writes in such a way that the very act of writing can undermine the possibility of articulating what it is "about"? I contend that a certain staging of this inevitable "failure" is what Heidegger has in mind in *Being and Time*. To articulate Dasein's existence as an insurmountable negativity, Heidegger has to move through the way in which the subject constitutes itself in and through negativity. Yet this movement of Heidegger's text is never merely a formal description (even though to a certain extent all description is bound to be formal, as Heidegger himself admits) of a "subject matter." The movement, or rather the ultimate failure of the movement of the text, "performs" the very dilemma Heidegger tries to articulate in Dasein's being. This performance does not come back to itself in the sense of still moving forward through its failure, but performs this very noncognitive relation to negativity in and through the text. The text "speaks" with an alien voice, which Heidegger designates the call of conscience. Thus, Heidegger's text can be said to be the performance of a certain kind of madness, as understood in a Hegelian sense. Yet madness is not performed as something to be overcome within the movement of a discourse about, and of, spirit. The finitude of Dasein means a finitude of the temporality of a discourse concerning being in which the finitude is not overcome by the sacrifice of the individual because the finitude does not belong to nor is even accessed by, the individual. Finitude is the finitude of the temporalizing of temporality, that is, of the movement of something like spirit itself.

CONSCIENCE AND THE IMPOSSIBILITY OF COMMUNICATION

Heidegger's discussion of conscience is a part of his attempt to deformalize phenomenology[20] by articulating it in terms of ontic attestation (*Bezeugung*). Conscience (*Gewissen*) is the way Heidegger reformulates the question of the certainty (*Gewißheit*) of death, and the attestation of conscience (*Bezeugung*) is his way of reformulating the conviction (*Überzeugung*) concerning the certainty of death. In conscience, Dasein is called back to its ownmost potentiality-for-being. Heidegger says "the call addresses Dasein as guilty" (SZ, 281). However, being guilty is not a result of a lack, which would ultimately be a moral or ethical understanding of conscience.[21] With the call of conscience Heidegger performs the way in which the constitution of subjectivity is undermined in and through the discourse of *Being and Time*. The call of conscience, far from constituting the subjectivity of the subject, undermines the discourse in and through which this subjectivity is constituted. Heidegger states that the call of conscience is still discourse, that is, it is not prediscursive in so far as it can still be taken up into public discourse. In the call to the self (rather than to the subject), the they-self (*das Man*) collapses. Yet there is nothing *spoken* in this discourse. Heidegger asks "*what* does conscience call to the one summoned?" and answers: "Strictly speaking nothing. The call does not say anything . . . has nothing to tell. Least of all does it strive to open a 'conversation with itself' in the self which has been summoned" (SZ, 273). This last sentence changes the emphasis of the discussion. The call of conscience does not individualize a subject as opposed to others in the world, but undermines the possibility of the self, communicating itself in the negative. The movement that is secured by a subject's being alongside itself *(bei sich)* in a relation to itself through its other and consequently the possibility of subjectivity as such is undermined. Therefore, when Heidegger says that *"conscience speaks solely and constantly in the mode of silence"* (SZ, 273), he does not simply mean that a confrontation with negativity cannot be communicated to others, but that it cannot even be communicated to Dasein itself. It remains in indefiniteness, resisting the movement of discourse and the possibility of overcoming negativity. The voice of conscience manifests itself as an alien power entering Dasein *(hereinragenden fremden Macht)*, as an alien voice *(eine fremde Stimme)* (SZ, 277).[22] The nothingness of Dasein does not arise from interiority, but enters Dasein as an attunement *(Stimmung)*. In anxiety Dasein is thrown back to its thrownness, to the negativity of its ground. Heidegger writes:

> The self, which as such has to lay the ground of itself, can *never* gain power over that ground, and yet it has to take over being the ground in existing. . . . Being the ground, that is, existing as thrown, Dasein constantly lags behind its possibilities. It is never existent *before* its ground, but only *from it* and *as it.* Thus being the ground means *never* to gain power over one's ownmost being from the ground up. This *not* belongs to the existential meaning of thrownness. Being the ground, it itself *is* a nothingness *(Nichtigkeit)* of itself. Nothingness by no means signifies not being objectively present or not subsisting, but means a 'not' that constitutes this *being* of Dasein, its thrownness. . . . Dasein is not itself the ground of its being, because the ground first arises from its own project, but as a self, it is the *being* of its ground. (SZ, 285)

This relationship to the ground as nothingness constitutes the not-being-home character of Dasein *(Unheimlichkeit)*, the "naked 'that' in the nothingness of the world" (SZ, 276). This in turn is revealed in anxiety, as Dasein finds itself "faced with the nothingness of the possible impossibility of its existence" (SZ, 266). The absolute nothingness of being-in-the-world, therefore, undermines the possibility of a philosophical discourse that can articulate this nothingness as the positive ground of the movement toward an absolute knowledge. Yet this is still not a nondiscursive phenomenon, but an essential possibility of discourse itself. Heidegger articulates this implication in terms of "willing to have a conscience," or as willing to *be* certain of the nothingness of death. "The mode of articulative discourse belonging to willing to have a conscience is reticence [*Verschwiegenheit*], consequently silence [*Schweigen*] [that is, the character of the call of conscience which says *nothing*] is an essential possibility of discourse" (SZ, 296). Silence corresponds to the nonrelational nature of death, which implies that the nothingness of being cannot be overcome or covered over in and through a philosophical discourse. Reticence is precisely that which resists a movement of spirit as overcoming negativity. For Heidegger the question of negativity concerns the movement of philosophical discourse, a perversion of this discourse that cannot be assimilated into the movement of the subject. As Heidegger puts it, Dasein's openness to this negativity in running ahead is not "a way out fabricated for the purpose of overcoming death . . ." (SZ, 310).

The unity of the existential structures of Dasein is care. Dasein's being-ahead-of-itself (*sich vorweg*), when understood authentically, manifests itself in running ahead (*vorlaufen*). Yet this authentic understanding is possible in anxiety only as a confrontation with death. Death as the possibility of the impossibility of existence reveals the absolute nothingness of Dasein. As Heidegger puts it: "As care Dasein is the thrown (that is null) ground of its death. The nothingness primordially dominant in the being of Dasein is revealed to it in authentic being-towards-death" (SZ, 306). Yet how exactly does Dasein relate to its death?

As we have indicated, Dasein is never reducible to a particular presence. That is to say, Dasein's being is never exhausted in a particular moment. In any given moment Dasein is already outside of the presence of the things that it is alongside. Indeed, this very being-alongside (*sein-bei*) of beings is made possible by Dasein's being *away*. This necessity is difficult to articulate in terms of a conception of time as a succession of now points. Any meaningful experience that is said to happen in time is to be comprehended in terms of a unity of temporality. No event can be meaningfully experienced, or rather experienced at all, without a holding together of the past, present, and future. Yet for Heidegger this holding together is not a cognitive activity, an act of consciousness, but the way Dasein exists. Dasein makes beings present, draws them into presence, that is, allows them to be, not through consciousness, but through its being. Therefore, in being alongside beings, Dasein is also alongside itself (*bei-sich*). Beings are drawn into presence in terms of significance and involvement, that is, they are organized around and "for the sake of" Dasein's own being. However, in authentic being-towards-death Dasein comes face to face with the nothingness of being-in-the-world that is with the negativity of its own existence. Thus the being-ahead of Dasein is ultimately grounded in its groundlessness, in death, rather than in the "always to come" characteristic of the succession of nows. When Heidegger states that Dasein's being is for the most part bound up with innerworldly entities, he does not simply mean that Dasein understands itself as a thing or entity. Dasein's fate is also bound up with innerworldly beings in the sense that Dasein understands the movement of presencing as a succession of contents. In other words, Dasein constructs the movement of its existence in terms of the succession of the content of what comes to presence. Dasein thereby understands its existence as a movement that can ultimately be thought, represented, or brought to presence in a discourse. Is this not precisely what Heidegger is doing as well? Heidegger does indeed present a phenomenology of Dasein's existence as a movement. Even though this movement cannot be represented without rendering the movement itself present-at-hand, Heidegger articulates this movement ultimately, I believe, in such a way as to render it impossible, and to show how the discourse itself undermines its own constitution. Accordingly, Dasein's existence as a movement is fundamentally different from a constitution of subjectivity. Indeed, Dasein's existence complicates the very continuity of its own movement that could (mistakenly) be interpreted as the movement of subjectivity (in a Hegelian sense). Yet Dasein's existence is still connected to the question of the self. Heidegger tries to explain this connection by introducing the question of temporality as the ontological meaning of care through a discussion of care and selfhood.

SELFHOOD AND TEMPORALITY

The question of the self for Heidegger is not to be understood in terms of an "I" that holds together the totality of the structural whole. Indeed, there is *nothing* in the unity of Dasein's existence. Dasein is neither a substance nor a subject. The primordial self-constancy of Dasein is only possible on the basis of holding itself as possible, that is, as outside of the actual configuration of beings and presence of beings and consequently outside the actuality and presence of itself. This possibility is grounded in running-ahead-in resoluteness toward death, and only on the basis of this futural existence can Dasein come back to itself as a unity: "Dasein *can* come toward itself *at all* in its ownmost possibility and perdure the possibility as possibility in this letting-itself-come-toward-itself . . ." (SZ, 325). In authentic running-ahead Dasein comes back to its thrownness, that is, to its "having-been." In other words, the negativity of Dasein's being not only designates a finitude with respect to the present-at-hand future (Dasein will die in the future), but also the groundlessness of its having-been, its past as well as its being-ahead. Dasein is finite in this radical sense, and the limitation of the present has to be understood in terms of this finitude. Only finitude allows entities to be drawn into the world, only a finite being can make the meaning of being accessible, because "meaning signifies that upon which the primary project is projected, that in terms of which something can be conceived in its possibility as what it is" (SZ, 324). The finitude of Dasein is not the physical and temporal limitedness of a present-at-hand entity. Dasein's being as care is grounded in temporality itself: "The unified phenomenon of the future that makes present in the process of having been [is] *temporality*. . . . Temporality reveals itself as the meaning of authentic care" (SZ, 326). Dasein for the most part understands itself in terms of entities that it makes present. This is because temporality is fundamentally understood with respect to the present. The present is, and the future is not yet, and the past is not anymore. In this very articulation one can discern that the future and the past are themselves understood in terms of the present, and being is understood in terms of presence. Finitude, according to this understanding, is a limited lingering in the present. Finitude, in this respect, is thought out of its opposition to infinity, or rather as a derivative of the infinite. For Heidegger, however, "primordial time is finite" and it is only because of this that derivative time can "temporalize as infinite." Time does not have the structure of a continuum, but is primordially "outside of itself" in and for itself. Time is ecstatic, which implies that it is not simply non-static, but also that its movement is not linear. Indeed, every designation of "is" remains problematic in describing the ecstatic unity of temporality. Time "moves" finitely. Even though the finitude of time is not a stopping, this finitude undermines the movement of an ever-moving consciousness or spirit, because it undermines the conception of time that is assumed to be always yet to come, as well as the completion of a particular segment in this movement. The movement of time is not the movement of the "now," but the authentic concretion of the "Moment" (*Augenblick*), which ultimately suggests that the finitude of Dasein does not belong to it, but is grounded in the Moment, in the temporalizing of temporality itself.

Heidegger continues to explain how ecstatic temporality is the ground of everydayness. Understanding, disposition, and falling are made possible by the ecstatic unity of temporality. For our purposes the important point to underline is the connection between the character of death as "the ownmost nonrelational possibility that cannot be overcome" and temporality. Death as an instance of negativity is not to be overcome, according to Heidegger. The possibility of covering it over in everydayness is based upon a particular understanding of time in terms of the present. The temporal sense of presence is also related to presence in the sense of presentation to others. The nonrelational character of death means that it cannot be presented or represented to someone else, or even to Dasein itself. Thereby the possibility of overcoming death as negativity is undermined. The question, however, still appears to be legitimate: Is not death the death of a being? Why should it be the focus on the basis of which time is to be understood? Time encompasses every being, after all, not simply Dasein. Why should Dasein's death be critical? These questions presuppose that death *belongs* to Dasein. However, as a form of negativity, death does not belong to Dasein. Indeed, Heidegger's conception of death undermines the very possibility of belonging in that it undermines the subject to which anything can belong to.[23] In the history of philosophy time has been thought in relation to the soul and to the spirit. Thinking human existence in terms of time answers the question concerning the differentiation and difference within being that we raised at the very beginning of this chapter. As we have seen, the differentiation in the being of beings (e.g., presence-at-hand, readiness-to-hand) has to be understood in terms of Dasein, and temporality is the ground of this differentiation. Dasein, existing finitely, is the focus of the differentiation of the being of entities. Therefore, the question of death ultimately is a question of temporality. The non-cognitive confrontation with death in anxiety is the way in which Dasein renders time as outside itself into nothingness, and the very unity of being is "constituted" in this nothingness.

HEGEL IN *BEING AND TIME*

Throughout this chapter I have tried to develop Heidegger's notion of negativity in contrast to that of Hegel.[24] The last chapter of *Being and Time* is a response to Hegel's understanding of the relationship between time and spirit. Even though Heidegger explicitly writes about Hegel in section eighty-three, sections seventy-eight to eighty-two have Hegel as their background. Heidegger criticizes Hegel's understanding of the relation between time and spirit as based upon a "vulgar" concept of time. Yet Hegel's concept of time is not the only issue here. Heidegger tries to show that Hegel's conception of time is based upon a natural interpretation of time, but he does not think that Hegel understands time naturally as a being within nature. For Heidegger, the important question concerning Hegel's notion of time is how time has to be understood for this movement of the spirit to be possible. In explaining how ecstatic temporality is transformed into a vulgar concept of time as an infinite succession of nows, Heidegger designates three characteristics of Dasein's relation to time: it is datable *(datierbar)*, spanned *(gespannt)*, and public *(öffentlich)*. These characteristics explain how being-in-the-world is constituted on the basis of temporality. In reckoning with time, Dasein makes present the beings that it is alongside. However, together with beings, time itself comes to be regarded as something present. Presence, in this sense, has to be understood both in a temporal sense and as a presentation, as we indicated above. Hence, primordial time itself becomes "public." Ultimately, through this publicness, time comes to be seen as something present, something to be present to everybody in the same way as a uniform continuum of a succession of now points. Public time interprets Dasein's being as "within time." The "forgetting" of the ontological difference between being and beings (within time) is made possible on the basis of a transformation of the primordial ecstatic unity of temporality into public time. This transformation is parallel to the structure that dominates

Dasein's relationship to death. The negativity of death is also overcome in being transformed into public everydayness. As we indicated above, by designating death as nonrelational and not to be overcome, Heidegger resists making negativity and finitude a cognitive problem and a property of Dasein. Time itself, that is, the ecstatic unity of temporality (the movement of existence) happens in such a way that it undermines the possibility of the movement of spirit *through* this negativity, but at the same time "explains" the possibility of the unity of Dasein's existence. Hence, Heidegger does not undermine subjectivity by simply objecting to it or by insisting that Dasein is not a subject, but rather by explaining the way in which the movement of subjectivity undermines itself in the negativity of finitude. Heidegger's response to Hegel in this context is not that Hegel first thought time as infinite and articulated spirit's movement accordingly. Rather, the relational understanding of negativity and time renders spirit's movement as sublating negativity possible. Hegel defines time as the negation of negation, as the "now" turning into "not yet," as the movement from one now to the other. Time as intuited becoming signifies "the transition from being to nothingness and from nothingness to being" (SZ, 431). The movement of spirit is also based on the negation of negation. Heidegger writes:

> The essence of spirit is the *concept* . . . by this Hegel understands . . . the form of the very thinking that thinks itself: conceiving *itself as grasping* the non-I. Since grasping the *non*-I presents a differentiation, there lies in the pure concept, as the grasping of *this* differentiation, a differentiation of the difference. Thus Hegel can define the essence of spirit formally and apophantically as the negation of negation. This 'absolute negativity' gives a logically formalized interpretation of Descartes' *cogito me cogitare rem* wherein he sees the essence of *conscientia*. Thus the concept is the conceivedness of the self-conceiving itself, the way the self is authentically as it can be, that is, *free*. 'The I is the pure concept itself that has come to existence as the concept.' 'But the I is this *first* pure unity relating itself to itself, not directly, but rather, in abstracting from all determinateness and content and going back to the limitless identity with itself.' Thus the 'I' is *'universality,'* but it is 'individuality' *just as* immediately. This negating of negation is both the 'absolute unrest' of spirit and also its *self-revelation*, which belongs to its essence. The 'progression' of spirit actualizing itself in history contains a 'principle of exclusion.' However, in this exclusion what is excluded does not get detached from the spirit, it gets surmounted (*Überwindung*). Making itself free in overcoming, and at the same time supporting characterizes the freedom of the spirit. (SZ, 433–434)

The formal identity between time and spirit is Hegel's way of securing the movement of spirit as "falling into time." Therefore, for Hegel, the possibility of the movement of spirit is predicated upon the succession of "nows."

Finitude is understood as the finitude of a particular "now" or a series of "nows." For Hegel *the movement* of finitude is infinite. For Heidegger, however, the movement that Hegel designates as infinite is itself finite. Finite movement does not mean that the movement continues for a time and then stops. It means that the very possibility of movement is its finitude. "Spirit," according to Heidegger, does not first fall into time, but *exists as* the primordial *temporalizing* of temporality (SZ, 436).

Heidegger's understanding of the being of Dasein is "an essentially 'excentric' being, since it is nothing outside of the *relation* to the other than itself."[25] Accordingly, being cannot be understood in terms of "constant presence," as Heidegger claims that the Greeks understood it in calling it *idea, ousia,* or *energeia.* However, Heidegger also notes that discourse (philosophical or otherwise) has the tendency to make present *(Gegenwärtigen).* Therefore, we can raise questions concerning the relationship between *Being and Time* as a discourse and the problems of metaphysics. This is not to imply that Heidegger conceptualizes being in terms of constant presence or of Dasein in terms of a subject. Even when one avoids the immediate implication of presence and subjectivity, the question still remains as to whether a philosophical discourse "about" the ecstatic unity of temporality has to be thought in terms of description, and as a question of cognition. Is Heidegger's own discourse in *Being and Time* subject to the same difficulty of treating its subject matter as an object *(Gegenstand)?* It is true that Dasein is not an object, and being is not understood as subjectivity. However, is it not the case that a "non-cognitive" relation to negativity becomes a cognitive problem in and through its description? Is it not the case that Heidegger himself transforms this negativity into a *Gegenstand* of thought? The potential problem of *Being and Time,* in other words, concerns whether it manifests a desire to articulate the confrontation with negativity within the terms of scientific phenomenology. I will elaborate this difficulty specifically in terms of two places in *Being and Time:* In the context of Heidegger's discussion of truth on the basis of unconcealment *(aletheia),* and in his discussion of historicity.

TRUTH AND HISTORY

In section forty-four of *Being and Time,* Heidegger raises the question of truth. If Dasein's being has to be understood other than as presence-at-hand, the traditional concept of truth has to be displaced. Heidegger enumerates three theses concerning the traditional concept of truth: 1) The "locus" of truth is the proposition (judgment); 2) The essence of truth lies in the "agreement" of the judgment with its object; 3) Aristotle, the father of logic, attributed truth to judgment as its primordial locus, and thereby also started the definition of truth as "agreement" (SZ, 214). Heidegger does not accept the third thesis. Nevertheless, the traditional conception of truth remains that of the correspondence between a proposition and its object. Heidegger now raises the following question: if the true is the agreement between knowledge and its object, how can we explain this agreement as a relation? Not every relation is an agreement, and indeed it is possible that there is a relation between a judgment and its object even when the judgment is false. Consequently, agreement presupposes a relation to beings on the basis of which propositions can be true or false. How are we to explain this relation ontologically? An assertion about a being in the world first discovers that toward which it is. This initial "discovering" is that which allows the proposition to be true or false. Hence, to say that a statement is true means that it discovers the beings in themselves. It asserts, it shows, it lets beings "be seen" *(apophansis)* in their discoveredness. We will return to Heidegger's understanding of unconcealment in the next chapter. At this point it is important to underline what Heidegger concludes from his discussion of truth as discovering. "Discovering is a way of being-in-the world" (SZ, 220). Dasein does not discover beings by making assertions about them, but rather by "taking-care of things." Therefore, Dasein's being, rather than assertion, is the original locus of truth. Heidegger writes that "Dasein is in the truth" in terms of disclosedness, thrownness, and project. In terms of falling, however, where Dasein understands itself for the most part in terms of the "they," it is also in the untruth in accordance with its constitution of being (SZ, 222). In its being-alongside entities and taking care of them, Dasein discovers. "Truth (discoveredness) must always first be wrested from beings. Beings are torn from concealment. The actual, factical discoveredness is, so to speak, always a kind of *robbery*" (SZ, 222). But Heidegger adds that:

> to the disclosedness of Dasein discourse essentially belongs. Dasein expresses itself: *itself*—as a being toward beings that have been discovered in statements. Statements communicate beings in the how of their discoveredness. Dasein, perceiving the communication, brings itself to a discovering being toward the beings discussed. The statements are made about something, and in what they are about they contain the discoveredness of beings. This discoveredness is preserved in what is expressed. What is expressed becomes, so to speak, an innerworldly thing at hand that can be taken up and spoken further. (SZ, 224)

Yet in and through such expression, statements are made public, and what is discovered becomes an issue for the "they." Thereby the relation between the statement and beings becomes a present-at-hand relation, even though it preserves its original discoveredness. However, "understood in its most primordial sense, truth belongs to the fundamental constitution of Dasein" (SZ, 226). It is precisely at this point that the status of *Being and Time* as a discourse becomes a problem. If truth is indeed to be understood on the basis of the constitution of Dasein, and if this unity is to be understood as care and finally as the unity of ecstatic temporality, how are we to understand the statements of *Being and Time?* Does not *Being and Time* as a discourse turn against itself? Does not *Being and Time* imply its own inevitable impossibility? These questions are not meant to be a criticism. The important point to emphasize here is that Heidegger does not fall into a predicament of inevitable distortion in expressing something outside his discourse. The problem here is not the inability to express something exterior to discourse. Indeed, if discourse is a way of being of Dasein, the question concerns the very nature of discursivity, the very form of the movement of thinking.[26] Therefore, to reject "consciousness" as the basis of truth and existence do not obviate the problem of expressing this rejection in discourse and to a certain extent of undermining the possibility of this rejection. This problem is especially pressing as Dasein's being is articulated as *a priori*. As Heidegger writes:

> The ideas of a "pure ego" and "a consciousness in general" are so far from including the *a priori* character of "real" subjectivity that they pass over the ontological character of facticity of Dasein and its constitution of being, or do not see it at all. Rejection of a "consciousness in general" does not mean the negation of the *a priori*, any more than the positing of an idealized subject guarantees a factually based *a priori* character of Dasein. (SZ, 229)

A similar problem can be observed in Heidegger's discussion of historicity in chapter five of the second division of *Being and Time,* entitled "Temporality and Historicity." In this chapter Heidegger explicitly takes up the question of Dasein's existence as a movement *(Bewegung).* In terms of the question of the self, the movement concerns the "connection of life" which is between birth and death. Consistent with the main thrust of *Being and Time,* Heidegger distinguishes Dasein's existence as a movement from "the motion of something present at hand" (SZ, 375). Dasein's existence has to be distinguished from a motion between two ends, birth and death. In other words, birth and death cannot be understood as "not-anymore," and "not yet." Hence, Dasein's existence is to be understood as a "stretching along" *(Erstreckung)* in which the "between" of birth and death already lies in the being of Dasein. Therefore, Dasein is not in time in the sense that life experiences can be considered to be in time, and its historicity cannot be constructed out of a connectedness of these experiences. As Heidegger writes: *"The analysis of the historicity of Dasein attempted to show that this being is not 'temporal,' because it 'is in history,' but because, on the contrary, it exists and can exist historically only because it is temporal in the ground of its being"* (SZ, 376). Heidegger's strategy in this chapter follows a line similar to his analysis of truth. After an explication of the vulgar understanding of history as a succession of events which were once present and no longer are, Heidegger states that the ground of this conception of history, which he calls historiography, has to be thought in terms of

Dasein's historicity. "Historical objects" are only such because they are revealed by Dasein's existence. Yet Dasein, whose destiny is bound up with present-at-hand beings, tends to understand its historicity in terms of the historical character of these beings. However, Heidegger argues that the historicity of Dasein is to be understood in terms of its temporality: "*Only authentic temporality that is at the same time finite makes something like fate, that is authentic historicity, possible*" (SZ, 385). "*Authentic being-toward-death, that is, finite temporality, is the concealed ground of the historicity of Da-sein*" (SZ, 386). Inauthentic historicity, "lost in the making present of the today," understands the "past" in terms of the "present." By contrast, the temporality of authentic historicity, as the moment that anticipates and retrieves, undoes the making present of the today (SZ, 391). Consequently, "the possibility and the structure of historiographical truth are to be set forth in terms of the authentic disclosedness ('truth') of historical existence" (SZ, 397).

Yet this understanding of history on the basis of Dasein's temporality raises the question of the historical status of *Being and Time*. What is the status of a discourse with respect to history that claims to "make present" that which makes historicity possible? Does not the language of "making possible" (or the "condition of possibility") precisely undermine Dasein's historicity by claiming to articulate its "ground"? It is true that for Heidegger this ground is ultimately an abyss, or non-ground. Yet is it even possible to "express," "make present" this abyss without making it into "something"?

These two problems concerning truth and historicity determine the direction of Heidegger's work after *Being and Time*. Accordingly, my claim is that Heidegger himself is aware of these problems, or at least his work allows us to articulate what is at stake in these problems. After *Being and Time* Heidegger repeatedly states that this work has to be understood other than within the problematic of subjectivity. This claim is correct. Yet *Being and Time* is certainly not the only place where Heidegger deals with the question of subjectivity. Indeed, after *Being and Time* the question of subjectivity becomes even more urgent.[27] Heidegger effectively displaces the conception of human existence as understood in terms of a subject over and against a field of objects. Accordingly, Heidegger does indeed displace a corresponding (to subjectivity) understanding of being as constant presence. Yet the problem of subjectivity exceeds the understanding of the grounding of philosophy on the human subject, and an understanding of being as constant presence. For Hegel the question of subjectivity is not the question of the human subject, and for Hegel, being is not "constant presence." The dialectical movement of spirit, understood in terms of radical negativity, allows one to reconstruct Hegel's understanding of being other than as "constant presence." Indeed, one can argue that there is never a simple presence in the dialectical movement of thinking. Therefore, Hegel already overcomes a certain understanding of subjectivity in terms of the constant presence of a subject. In order to see the thrust of Heidegger's later philosophy, we have to trace what Heidegger calls a confrontation (*Auseinandersetzung*) with Hegel. In the next chapter I will argue that Heidegger's rethinking of unconcealment and historicity in terms of philosophy's confrontation with negativity can be articulated in terms of his understanding of madness. In this confrontation between Hegel and Heidegger, the issue is what kind of thinking, language, and rationality are possible after Hegel.

FOUR

Heidegger

Madness, Negativity, Truth, and History

The madman.—Have you not heard of that madman who lit a lantern in the bright morning hours, ran to the market place, and cried incessantly: "I seek God! I seek God!"—As many of those who did not believe in God were standing around just then, he provoked much laughter. Has he got lost? asked one. Did he lose his way like a child? asked another. Or is he hiding? Is he afraid of us? Has he gone on a voyage? emigrated?—Thus they yelled and laughed.

The madman jumped into their midst and pierced them with his eyes. "Whither is God?" he cried; "I will tell you. *We have killed him*—you and I. All of us are his murderers. But how did we do this? How could we drink up the sea? Who gave us the sponge to wipe away the entire horizon? What were we doing when we unchained this earth from its sun? Whither is it moving? Whither are we moving? Away from all suns? Are we not plunging continually? Backward, sideward, forward, in all directions? Is there still any up or down? Are we not straying as through an infinite nothing? Do we not feel the breath of empty space? Has it not become colder? Is it not night continually closing in on us? Do we not need to light lanterns in the morning? Do we hear nothing as yet of the noise of gravediggers who are burying God? Do we smell nothing as yet of the divine decomposition? Gods, too, decompose. God is dead. God remains dead. And we have killed him."
—Nietzsche

THE QUESTION OF MADNESS is intimately connected with the question of truth. The way in which Plato and Hegel "overcome" madness is based in turn on their conviction that madness is necessary. Madness is necessary as an access to the suprasensuous world, or to the next stage of dialectical thinking.

Thus, they understand madness on the basis of the question of truth and error, albeit in different ways. By contrast, for Heidegger, the question of truth itself has to be thought differently. Heidegger does not simply articulate another discourse about truth, but the difference lies in the way discourse itself is shown to be so fundamentally caught up in its "error" that it cannot overcome its "madness." Heidegger does, therefore, seem to reserve a privileged role for madness, and the question will remain as to whether Heidegger's articulation of madness ultimately betrays a desire for presence in the sense of presentation. We will take up the same question in the next chapter in the context of the debate between Foucault and Derrida. The aim of the present chapter is to respond to the questions articulated at the end of the previous chapter concerning the status of Being and Time as a discourse. Furthermore, is it possible to make a case for Heidegger's conception of negativity after Being and Time as constituting a response to both Plato and Hegel?

Heidegger's understanding of being is in accordance with the role that Plato attributes to the forms in making perception possible. In chapter one we saw how Plato's notion of forms can be interpreted as making beings accessible to human perception. In the Zollikon Seminars Heidegger articulates this accordance: "Before we can perceive the table as this or that table, we must have already perceived beforehand that there is such a thing as presence."[1] At the moment of the perception of a table, this apprehension of presence, although necessary, is not explicit. We "see" the table on the basis of a referential totality that Heidegger analyzes in Being and Time; this referential totality relates to the questions of the unity of presence, to the unity of the existential structures of Dasein, and to the ecstatic unity of temporality. Heidegger's understanding of madness manifests a similar relationship to presence, to presencing, and to truth as unconcealment. This is to say, for Heidegger madness provides a specific access to that which makes presence possible.

THE ZOLLIKON SEMINARS

In the Zollikon Seminars Heidegger repeatedly argues that human existence has to be distinguished from a present-at-hand object. After a lengthy discussion of the assumptions of the modern sciences, Heidegger argues that psychology and psychopathology are also based on the presuppositions of the modern physical sciences. I will not recount Heidegger's entire discussion of the presuppositions of the modern sciences. The basic point in this discussion is that through the sciences, the real becomes that which is measurable or objectively present for a subject. Accordingly, the human being is understood as the subject of his or her cognitions, desires, and impulses. Thereby, the human subject too can become the object of scientific research. Any scientific approach to the human being already objectifies human existence. Heidegger's argument cannot be discounted simply by claiming that psychiatry and psychology are not concerned with this "philosophical problem" of the determination of human existence. Such a separation between scientific and philosophical problems cannot be sustained because the fact that one is not concerned with the philosophical determination of the human being does not mean that one is not already operating within one. In other words, the desire of scientific, medical discourse to disentangle itself from philosophical difficulties by ignoring them is itself a philosophical presupposition. When one makes a claim about how a human being should behave, think, or speak in order to be "healthy," one is already within the domain of philosophical scrutiny. For Heidegger the scientific understanding of human existence presupposes (in the sense of both *suppositio* and *acceptio*) that being is presence-at-hand. This presupposition in turn is based on an understanding of time as a sequence (*Abfolge*) of "now" points. Yet when such an approach confronts the sick human being, "one fails [breaks down, *scheitert*]."

For Heidegger, the fundamental presuppositions of the modern sciences can be traced back to conception of time as a series of "now" points. By contrast, Heidegger maintains that time, in the first instance, is not to be understood in terms of clock time, but in terms of the way in which it is given to human existence. Time is given first in terms of its significance (*Deutsamkeit*). One "has" time *for* something. The significance in terms of which beings are revealed is based upon the givenness of time within the world. The second characteristic of time, its datedness (*Datiertheit*), is also based on its givenness in terms of being-in-the-world. Time can be dated only on the basis of Dasein's being-in-the-world. Once time is understood in terms of being-in-the-world, the "now" points are communicable in terms of their publicness (*Öffentlichkeit*), which constitutes the third characteristic of time. Finally, on the basis of Dasein's involvement in the world, time has an expanse (*Weite*). Heidegger argues that these characteristics of time, understood in terms of being-in-the-world, have "priority" over clock time (the sequence of nows), and consequently being-in-time has to be understood differently from clock time in the case of human existence. Heidegger asks:

> Which is the 'true' time? Assuming for a moment that time were given to us as mere 'one after the other' [*Nacheinander*], in which all the above-named characters of datedness, significance, expanse, and publicness were leveled out into an empty now-sequence, then we would have to be mad, from the perspective of time represented as such, or worse yet, we would no longer even have the possibility of being mad. For in order to be mad [*verrückt*] we must in the first instance be able to be moved away [*weggerückt*] from one now, and be moved into another now in the first place. With regard to time we must have the possibility of being moved away from the

time that is otherwise given to us, and must be banished into an empty sequence of time. This manifests itself as a uniform oneness [or sameness, *Einerlei*] without a wherefore [*Wofür*]. (Z, 63–64)

There are two claims here. First, living in a now-sequence without any of the characteristics of significance, expanse, datability, and publicness would lead us to madness. Consequently, Heidegger intimates that the scientific understanding of time as a sequence of nows is inadequate for assessing the relationship between human existence and time. Yet is this move a mere reversal of the scientific understanding of time? Is Heidegger claiming that scientific understanding is mad, and that the existential understanding of time is rational? It is true that without the existential structure of temporality we would not even be capable of madness. Therefore, an understanding of temporality is not only the basis of an understanding of madness, but temporality forms the very distinction between madness and rationality: "The disturbed relation to time of the psychologically sick human being can be understood from the originary, naturally apprehended, constantly significant and datable human relation to time, not from the perspective of calculated time, which stems from the representation of time as sequence of empty "nows" without 'character'" (Z, 55).

The German term Heidegger uses for "madness" in this context is *verrückt*, which consists of the prefix *ver* and the verb *rücken*, meaning to "move" or "shift." The word has the connotation of a movement. Heidegger elsewhere uses cognates of *rücken* at several important junctures in characterizing the resolute disclosedness that runs ahead in the *Augenblick*.[2] In *Being and Time*, Heidegger writes:

> In resoluteness, the present is not only brought back from the dispersion in what is taken care of nearest at hand, but is held in the future, and having-been. We call the *present* that is held in authentic temporality, and is thus *authentic*, the *moment [Augenblick]*. This term must be understood in the active sense as an ecstasy. It means the resolute rapture *[Entrückung]* of Dasein, which is yet *held* in resoluteness in what is encountered as possibilities and circumstances to be taken care of in the situation. (SZ, 338)

Being held is not a static or passive state, but rather a sudden movement of time in the *Augenblick,* a kind of rapture *(Entrückung)* that is ecstatic. Both authentic resoluteness and madness *(verrücktsein)* manifest a similar phenomenon concerning our relationship to time. Yet authentic temporality is not madness to the extent that the latter is understood within the framework of mental illness.

Heidegger uses a similar language of movement back and forth in "The Origin of the Work of Art." Here he describes the confrontation with the work of art in its solitude:

The more solitarily the work, fixed in the figure, stands on its own and the more cleanly it seems to cut all ties to human beings, the more simply does the thrust come into the open, that such a work *is*, and the more essentially is the extraordinary thrust to the surface and the long-familiar thrust down. But this multiple thrusting is nothing violent, for the more purely the work is itself transported into [*entrückt*] the openness of being . . . the more simply does it transport us [*einrücken*] into this openness and thus at the same time transport us out of the realm of the ordinary [*herausrücken*]. To follow this displacement [*Verrückung*] means: to transform our accustomed ties to the world and to earth and henceforth to restrain all usual doing and prizing, knowing and looking, in order to stay with the truth of what is happening in the work.[3]

The moment of confrontation with the work of art is Heidegger's reformulation of the disclosedness that runs ahead (*vorlaufende Entschlossenheit*).[4] A certain displacement or dislocation is characteristic of Dasein's confrontation with the negativity of its own existence, and this displacement is the moment of authentic temporality. This displacement of temporality opens up the possibility of any relation to the world. Yet is it madness? If not, how is it to be distinguished from madness? In the *Zollikon Seminars*, Heidegger gives a hint. In his conversation with Medard Boss about the nature of the drive [*Drang*], Heidegger says:

> That which drives [*das Drängende*] is Dasein. That which drives is being-in-the-world itself. Someone manic who is erratically carried away from one thing to the other wants to devour everything. Dasein exists only in this snatching [*an sich reißen*]. It is not letting oneself be drawn [*Sich-ziehen-lassen*], but rather a seizing [*an sich raffen*]. The manic also overruns being-ahead-of-oneself [*Sich-vorweg-sein*] so that he does not reflect upon that which he can be authentically. Therefore, his being-ahead of himself is an inauthentic one. (Z, 219)

"The one who is erratically carried away from one thing to the other" is ahead of himself inauthentically. Here Heidegger suggests that there are different ways of understanding being ahead of oneself; if being ahead rushes ahead and does not reflect upon that which can be authentically, it is a kind of madness (mental illness) that is to be distinguished from the being-ahead of Dasein. It seems that Heidegger, here, understands "manic" as being mentally ill, as having a deficient relationship to time. This understanding of madness is different from Heidegger's conception of madness later in his career. Later in his career, Heidegger will speak of a more originary madness, which is prior to both authenticity and inauthenticity. Heidegger will discuss such a conception of madness after an articulation of a more radical negativity. Madness, in this sense, would be historical, not in the sense in which madness is determined historically, but in the sense that madness would be the condition of historicity in general. This would require a different configuration of the relationship between history and Dasein. As we indicated in the previous chapter, Heidegger is aware of the problem of predicating the possibility of historicity on Dasein: "In *Being and Time* historicity is only related to Dasein, but not to the destiny of being *(Seinsgeschick)*. One cannot explain the destiny of being from the historicity of Dasein. On the contrary human historicity belongs to the destiny of being" (Z, 230). What exactly does this inversion imply, and what does it mean for madness? We will return to the discussion of the destiny of being in "The Anaximander Fragment," below. However, this discussion necessitates a detour that will explain Heidegger's rethinking of madness and his confrontation with Hegel.

BASIC QUESTIONS OF PHILOSOPHY

Perhaps Heidegger's most sustained reflection on the question of truth after *Being and Time* and before the publication of his essay "On the Essence of Truth"[5] is to be found in his 1937–1938 lecture course entitled *Basic Questions of Philosophy*.[6] This lecture course coincides with his much more famous text *Beiträge zur Philosophie*. I do claim that this lecture course marks a significant shift in Heidegger's position. This text, however, signifies an important deepening in Heidegger's thinking concerning the question of truth and historicity.

Heidegger starts his lecture on truth by raising the question concerning the basic presupposition of truth defined as the correctness of an assertion. This question, Heidegger claims, "involves a confrontation with the whole of Western Philosophy and can never be broached without this historical confrontation" (GdP, 12). This conviction modifies the project of *Being and Time* where the question of truth was broached on the basis of the existential constitution of Dasein. However, what is at stake in investigating the essence of truth is not an abandonment of Dasein's existence, but rather a rethinking of Dasein's existence out of historicity and eventually out of the eschatology of being. The movement of this lecture course follows a similar path to that of Heidegger's essay "On the Essence of Truth," even though in this lecture course Heidegger articulates a more detailed analysis of the traditional conception of truth. Truth as the correctness of an assertion implies that the assertion conforms to *(sich richtet nach)* its object. Hence truth is correctness *(Richtigkeit)*. Correctness is also understood as adequation, assimilation, and correspondence. For Aristotle, truth is in *logos* as assimilation *(homoiosis)* where the representation is assimilated into what is grasped. What is represented corresponds to what it represents. Heidegger maintains that both realism and idealism accept this correspondence even though they differ on whether an assertion corresponds to its object or to a representation. Even

Kant, who transforms the direction of correspondence, accepts its basic pre-supposition.[7] Yet if an assertion is to correspond to its object, the object itself must somehow be open in advance. This is an important step within Hei-degger's argument. With the necessity of this prior openness the question of truth is carried to a different level. The being, which the assertion is about, has to somehow be open. In contrast to *Being and Time* Heidegger does not claim that the assertion discovers, which in turn was based on the disclosed-ness of Dasein. Indeed there is a four-fold openness presupposed by the cor-rectness of an assertion. The human being who makes the assertion has to somehow be open in order to encounter the thing: "He must be open for what encounters him, so that it might encounter him. . . . The person must also be open to his fellows, so that, co-representing what is communicated to him in their assertions, he can, together with the others and out of a being-with them, conform to the same thing and be in agreement with them about the correctness of the representing" (GdP, 18). Hence the four-fold openness is 1) of the thing; 2) of the region between the thing and the human being; 3) of the human being with regard to the thing; and 4) of the human being to fellow human beings (GdP, 19).

Heidegger insists that the "essence" of the human being has to be under-stood with regard to this openness. At the very beginning of this lecture course Heidegger connects the conception of truth to the essence of the human being. For Heidegger the traditional conception of the human being as a "rational animal" *(zoon logon echon)* has been gained from this openness. The human being is "rational" where reason means the immediate perception of beings. There is, indeed, a difference between reason and perception. Yet here Heidegger understands reason *(Vernunft)* in accordance with its root *"vernehmen"* ("apprehension," or literally "taking in"). Human perception, he claims, is never an "animal" perception, and "reason" is not an addition to this perception. As we have seen in the first chapter, for Plato, the percep-tion of individual beings has been made possible by a prior access to forms. This is the same dimension of perception that Heidegger has in mind.

The question of truth does not ask whether a specific assertion is true or not, or whether something particular is really what it is. Rather, it asks the essence of truth, that which makes everything true. Heidegger raises the ques-tion of the essence of truth in terms of its form, not because truth as uncon-cealment is to be understood in these terms, but because he wants to demon-strate the basic presupposition of the Platonic-Aristotelian conception of truth. The truth of something, according to Plato, is to be found in its "what-ness" understood as its form. We have seen how Plato transforms the question of "what something is" to the question of its form, or essence. We have also seen how Plato ultimately understands the question of the absence of beings (that are subject to time, and consequently *me on*, nonbeings) in terms of the presence of forms. "Everything we see in particulars is always determined by what we have in view in advance" (GdP, 67, 60). Heidegger's statement that "the essence of truth is the truth of essence" has to be understood in connection to this Greek understanding of essence. There are four characteristics of the essentiality of the essence in Plato and Aristotle: 1) The essence is what something is in general (to katholou), what applies over the entire extent of the particular instances; 2) The essence is that from which anything, in what it is as such, has its origin, whence it stems (to genos); 3) The essence can therefore be designated as what something already was, before it became what it is as an individual. It is precisely this characteristic of essence that connects the order of reason (and perception) with the order of being. What we have to have access to in advance in order to perceive a being is also that which constitutes the essence (being, ousia) of that being. As we have seen in the discussion of Being and Time, Heidegger understands this characteristic of essence as to ti en einai in terms of the a priori perfect character of Dasein's involvement.[8] What Dasein has access to is not a constantly present form, but rather the totality of involvements, the unity of presence which is understood on the basis of the ecstatic unity of temporality; 4) In all these determinations, the essence is what lies over or before the individual, or what lies under it as its ground (to hupokeimenon) (GdP, 58).

Through these characteristics of essence, one can also understand how the essence of the human being is understood as parallel to this conception of essence. The human being is the being that is present to this openness of beings, which the Greeks initially understood as unconcealment. Yet the Greeks transformed this movement of the unconcealment of being into constant presence by trying to secure the constant presence of the human being to this unconcealment. Heidegger writes: "The Greeks understand by being the constant presence of something. What is constant in any particular being is what-it-is, and what is present is precisely this 'what' as the being's prevailing look, eidos" (GdP, 67). By contrast, for Heidegger, this look in advance is in the first instance a "productive look," that which brings beings out of concealment into unconcealment. This bringing-forth undermines the possibility of the constant presence of an idea. What happens in the understanding of being as constant presence is the covering over of absence and negativity (the lethe of a-letheia). Therefore, Heidegger says, "the concealment of beings as a whole, un-truth proper, is older than every openedness of this or that being. It is older even than letting-be itself, which in disclosing already holds concealed and comports itself toward concealing."[9] The second sentence in this quotation reveals Heidegger's desire to think concealment differently than he did in Being and Time. Dasein's "letting-be" comports itself toward concealing. Yet something more is at stake here. Heidegger realizes that the possible understanding of this relationship between concealment and unconcealment as "condition of possibility" has to be resisted. That is to say, concealment cannot be thought as the condition of possibility of unconcealment, just as unconcealment cannot be thought of as the condition of possibility of truth in its traditional conception. Truth as *aletheia* is not to be understood as making truth as correctness possible, or grounding it in the sense that there is the possibility of thinking a linear progression from the former to the latter. Heidegger resists such an understanding because it would be assimilated into the structure of thinking within a Hegelian system. Heidegger recognizes that the language of the grounding of beings has to be transformed as it leads to "nothingness" as the ground. He explains this necessity at the end of his essay "Plato's Doctrine of Truth":

> To pursue this relationship [of unhiddenness to looking, apprehending, thinking, asserting] means to give up the essence of unhiddenness. No attempt to ground the essence of unhiddenness in 'reason,' 'spirit,' 'thinking,' '*logos*,' or in any kind of 'subjectivity,' can never rescue the essence of unhiddenness. Because thereby, that which is to be grounded, the essence of unhiddenness itself, is not sufficiently sought out [*erfragt*], but only an essential consequence of the uncomprehended essence of unhiddenness is always explained [*erklärt*].[10]

If we accept this problematic relationship to concealment, then we have to renew our questions concerning *Being and Time*. What is the status of *Being and Time*? Is it not a series of assertions? Is it not "thinking" in the broadest sense of the term? Is it not a text of "explanation"? Heidegger becomes more and more aware of the "failure" of *Being and Time*, not because what it asserts is incorrect, but because it undermines the possibility of its own "asserting." This is not to say that what Heidegger tries to think has to be abandoned, but rather that thinking itself has to be transformed. This transformation requires a dislocation (*Verrückung*) of the human being from its traditional understanding of him or herself. In "On the Essence of Truth" Heidegger calls concealment "the mystery." Hence "the disclosure of beings as such is simultaneously and intrinsically the concealing of beings as a whole. In the simultaneity of disclosure and concealing, errancy holds sway."[11] The translator of these lines, John Sallis, observing the simultaneity of concealment and unconcealment, writes:

> . . . what is essentially other than truth belongs to the essence of truth, even though within that essence its otherness is preserved, not just dialectically but as oppositional. . . . An other so essentially other than truth that it would be absolved from truth, as absolutely as madness can be. Let us, then, ponder whether what the question of truth is all about is in the end akin to madness.[12]

Unfortunately, Sallis does not discuss Heidegger's discussion of madness at the end of *Basic Questions of Philosophy*, where Heidegger does ponder the affinity of truth to madness.

Evidently Sallis has Hegel in mind when he writes that "the preservation" is "not just dialectical, but oppositional." Yet is it possible to be oppositional without the dialectic? What exactly does "absolved from truth" mean,
and is it different from Hegel's notion of the absolute? And finally, does not
something essentially other than truth, indeed madness, belong to the
essence of truth, understood as the dialectic movement, according to Hegel?
These questions lead us back to the confrontation between Hegel and Heidegger concerning the status of madness as negativity.

HEGEL AND HEIDEGGER

I now return to the question of whether Heidegger's interpretation of negativity is different from that of Hegel.[13] Heidegger returns to Hegel at several
junctures in his career. However, I will not exclusively discuss Heidegger's
writings about Hegel. The problem with this approach would be that a Heideggerian "criticism" of Hegel presents the possibility of interpreting Hegel
differently. By the same token, a Hegelian intervention transforms the thrust
of Heidegger's thought. However, their positions do not allow a dialectical
transformation. It is also correct that Heidegger criticizes Hegel's notion of
subjectivity. It is correct that Heidegger complicates, albeit indirectly, Hegel's
conception of madness. Yet we need to think the nature of these criticisms.
Does Heidegger come up with a separate position? And if so, does not Hegel's
dialectic, whose chief virtue is nothing other than the assimilation of other
positions, have an answer to Heidegger? In order to understand Heidegger's
criticism of subjectivity we have to understand what exactly subjectivity is for
Hegel, and what Heidegger means by subjectivity beyond this Hegelian
notion. We need to ask whether there is any possibility of thinking differently
than in terms of subjectivity. We have already seen how this problem mani-
fested itself in *Being and Time*.

There are two main issues I will discuss in this section: the question of
truth, and the question of historicity. Hegel is perhaps the first thinker who
challenged the correspondence theory of truth. Like Heidegger, Hegel realizes that every correspondence account of truth presupposes something prior
that is true. Hegel's reaction to this difficulty is a desire to achieve a presup-
positionless beginning in order to explain truth in logic. He rejects the claim
of natural consciousness that truth is self-evident and accessible. Thereby,
he also undermines the law of non-contradiction as the criterion for truth.[14]
Truth is a kind of certainty for Hegel, but certainty is never immediate.[15]
Truth emerges as a result of the dialectical movement of consciousness.
However, the result of this movement (truth) is not separate from the movement itself. Nevertheless, the truth of a certain moment in this dialectical
movement does indeed emerge in the next moment, upon the completion of
the previous shape of consciousness. Therefore, the truth of consciousness is

self-consciousness, and the truth of the deranged soul is the rational soul. When Hegel states that the absolute alone is the truth, he does not mean that truth is only reached at the end of the dialectical movement to absolute spirit. The absolute spirit *is* the dialectical movement. Therefore, there is a sense in which the absolute is always "with us from the start." Truth, consequently, is not separate from untruth, error, illusion, and madness to the extent that they are the necessary moments of this movement. Moreover, Hegel would connect this conception of truth to the historicity of thinking, of the dialectical movement.[16]

For Heidegger two questions remain in this connection between history and truth. Is thinking radically historical for Hegel? That is, is the historicity of thinking not subsumed under the dialectical structure of thinking culminating in absolute spirit? Secondly, does not Hegel's displacement of correspondence ultimately represent its infinite affirmation? That is to say, does not the suspension of correspondence in the dialectical movement ultimately secure the correspondence of being and thinking? These questions are different from the question of whether there is an end of dialectical thinking for Hegel, or from the question of whether absolute knowledge *emerges* in history, and what happens after its emergence. I want to avoid these questions, because they seem to overlook the fact that Hegel's aim is not to describe a history of ideas, but to spell out the logic of thinking. There is a sense in which Heidegger "concedes" that with Hegel we reach a completion, regardless of whether absolute knowledge "emerges" or not. Even though Heidegger admits a completion in Hegel's thinking, he does not want to think the completion in the way that Hegel does, that is, he does not want to think completion as the consummation of the movement of spirit that is now in the past. These two points, historicity and truth, therefore, are also themes that preoccupy Heidegger's thinking after *Being and Time* and help to frame his confrontation with Hegel.

Heidegger's reading of Hegel is spread out over his entire career. Contrary to what the critics say, Hegel's *Logic* more than his *Phenomenology* is constantly at the background of Heidegger's reading of Hegel.[17] Heidegger's early reading of Hegel concentrates on the question of time in Hegel's *Encyclopaedia*.[18] In *Being and Time*, Heidegger states that Hegel's understanding of time as "now" and "not yet" and its formal similarity to spirit shows that it is a "vulgar" understanding and has to be based on the authentic temporality of Dasein. This is the aspect of *Being and Time* that becomes increasingly problematic. However, Heidegger's conviction that the movement of spirit as a fundamental "inability" to remain with the present is based on a specific understanding of time that does not change. The reason why Heidegger does not come back to this reading is not because he finds it incorrect, but because he wants to move away from explaining authentic temporality as a condition of possibility for the vulgar understanding of time.[19] Yet even in *Being and*

Time, Heidegger designates the domain of confrontation with Hegel in broader terms of negativity and of the movement of spirit. What is at stake in this movement with respect to time is the question of whether, for Hegel, the movement "proceeds" on the basis of the completion of a previous "shape" of consciousness. This question is important because ultimately the problem will be whether this movement is a movement of cognition or of a different understanding of being. Heidegger would insist that there "is" a finitude on the basis of which the movement of spirit has to be thought. However, the articulation of this finitude should not take it to be a "condition of possibility." After *Being and Time*, Heidegger articulates finitude other than on the basis of the authentic temporality of Dasein. This is not to say that Dasein's finitude is not the issue anymore. However, if the negativity of Dasein is articulated as that which makes the worldhood of the world possible, even though that which makes possible is, strictly speaking, nothingness, then there is a possibility of taking this negativity up into the dialectic movement of the historical thinking. In *Being and Time*, Heidegger articulates this finitude in a way that makes articulation problematic (i.e., the non-communicable nature of death). However, Heidegger recognizes that this designation itself has to be thought out of the historicity of being in such a way that the discussion itself has to be finite. It does not articulate anything outside itself that can ultimately be reduced to an object, as the *Gegenstand* of thought (not simply an object over and against a subject). Nor does it articulate an experience of Dasein with itself that could be raised to the level of cognition. Concealment at the very heart of being undermines the very possibility of its own articulation, and this is the finitude of being *and* thinking, which is also their *difference* as *difference*.[20]

There are relatively constant themes in Heidegger's reading of Hegel after *Being and Time*. Hegel is also at the background of several other texts by Heidegger, and his thinking itself is in general a response to Hegel, even though Heidegger's thinking is not reducible to such a response. Therefore "The Anaximander Fragment" and "Language in the Poem," also have to be thought in terms of a Hegelian problematic. The most important theme that preoccupies Heidegger in his later readings of Hegel is the concept of experience *(Erfahrung)*.[21] Even though Heidegger deals with this concept extensively in "Hegel's Concept of Experience" (1943), his interpretation in *Hegel's Phenomenology of Spirit* (1931)[22] already concentrates on the notion of experience.

Heidegger identifies Hegel's desire for a system as a desire to reach absolute knowledge. However, Heidegger recognizes that absolute knowledge does not mean an unchanging knowledge of something that is constantly present. Absolute knowledge is not finite in the sense that it is not the knowledge *of* an object. Finite knowledge is relative in the sense that it is bound to an object. "Such a relative knowledge would be caught up in and imprisoned by what it knows. Hegel calls such knowing consciousness" (HPS, 15). The dialectical movement is the process of absolution from this relativity. "In the process of its unfolding alongside things, consciousness absolves itself in a certain way from them as soon as it becomes aware of itself *as* consciousness" (HPS, 15). Therefore, the dialectical process is a process of freedom. At this point Heidegger refers back to the first title Hegel used for distinguishing the first part of the system of science: "Science of the Experience of Consciousness." Heidegger distinguishes Hegel's concept of experience from an empiricist conception of the experience *of* something, and from Husserlian phenomenological intuition. For Hegel, *Er-fahrung* is to be understood as that which consciousness has to undergo with itself (HPS, 21). Experience of consciousness, in the first instance, is an experience *of* consciousness as a subjective genitive: "Only because consciousness in the quite specific sense of absolute knowledge is the subject of experience is consciousness the object of experience and can undergo an experience with itself" (HPS, 21). Heidegger's point is not that consciousness is subjective as opposed to being objective, but rather that spirit's subjectivity consists of the fact that it "creates" its own object *(Gegenstand)*, that which stands over and against itself in contradiction and thereby comes back to itself in the process of ab-solution. Therefore, phenomenology does not mean a description of something like consciousness from a different point of view. The presentation of consciousness is also that which is presented, that is, its own unfolding. Consciousness realizes that the "in-itself" of its object is an in-itself *for* consciousness, and therefore is capable of making this very identity into its own object. Thus, the experience has both a positive and a negative aspect: "Through the experience which consciousness undergoes with itself, consciousness becomes other to itself. But this becoming-different-to-itself is exactly a coming-to-self" (HSP, 22). Therefore, experience is a movement and, as Hegel puts it in the *Phenomenology of Spirit*, "inasmuch as the new true object issues from it, this dialectical movement which consciousness exercises on itself and which affects both its knowledge and its object, is precisely what is called experience" (Phen., 78, 55). Absolute knowledge is nothing above and beyond this dialectical movement. Spirit is this "absolute restlessness." Hegel calls this restlessness "absolute negativity." Therefore, the *Phenomenology of Spirit* is not a description of different stages of spirit, but spirit's own self-presentation. Thereby, Hegel effectively undermines the dichotomy between a philosophical discourse and what this discourse is about. One's implication in one's own text is dissolved, or rather absolved. "In and through its character as movement, the exposition becomes *itself what is to be exposed*. The exposition and what is to be exposed coincide, not by chance but necessarily" (HPS, 27).

In the movement from consciousness to self-consciousness the *"of"* of relative knowledge disappears. The dialectical movement not only generates its "object" at every stage, but the method of dealing with this object is also generated through dialectic. Hegel understands the method not as a tool to be applied to gain knowledge, but in its original sense as *met-hodos*, as being "on the way." Therefore, the movement of spirit as *Erfahrung* does not presuppose the constant presence of a substance *(hupokeimenon)* underlying the experiences. Hence, for Hegel, being is not a constant presence of beings. Indeed, one can argue that the movement of the dialectic itself is "made possible" by a constant negativity (and absence), which Hegel understands as the negation of negation; that is to say, contradiction is that which moves spirit. Thereby, Hegel displaces a conception of human subjectivity as the substance of experiences by arguing that consciousness is self-consciousness.[23] Accordingly, for Hegel, being is to be understood as a movement, which is not simply dependent on a "natural" understanding of time, but on the historicity of thinking. Finally, Hegel has a conception of beginning in terms of "indeterminate immediacy," where the negativity of thought is radicalized as the unity of being and nothing, which means that his notion of being is not as a simple presence.

Heidegger takes up Hegel's concept of experience in his essay "Hegel's Concept of Experience." This text basically consists of a close reading of the Introduction of the *Phenomenology of Spirit*.[24] The main thrust of Heidegger's argument appears in his reading of paragraph eighty-six of Hegel's Introduction, which, as we quoted above, names experience as the dialectical movement. Heidegger writes that by the word "experience" Hegel names the being of beings (HBE, 163–64, 113). This is not the only time that Heidegger tries to interpret a Hegelian concept by substituting his own for it, but it is the most important one for explaining the relation between Hegel and Heidegger. Consciousness qua consciousness *is* its own movement. It expresses its truth in its own exposition, through *(dia)* uttering *(legein)*, in a *dialogue* with itself, that is, dialectically. Heidegger writes that "Hegel does not conceive experience dialectically; he thinks dialectic in terms of the nature of experience. Experience is the beingness of beings whose determination, *qua subiectum*, is determined in terms of subjectness" (HBE, 169–70, 119). Dialectic proceeds by making its previous shape, and the unity of this shape, its own object. Therefore, Hegel does not see negativity as an abstract negativity, but as a determinate negation, one that has a content *(Inhalt)* (Phen., 51, 74). This also explains why negativity has to be understood on the basis of determinate negation for Hegel. For Hegel, negativity does not yield an utter despair or complete annihilation because it always concerns a determinate content. Indeed, that which is negative transforms itself into a content of consciousness by being *determined*. Therefore, negativity does not exclusively yield a negative for Hegel, but also a determinate positive content. It is the unity of the negative and positive that allows for the ab-solution of thinking. We observe this in sense-certainty, where pure immediate description inevitably becomes other than itself, and finds its truth in coming back to itself. Heidegger recognizes that "there is generally nothing like pure immediate description in philosophy" (HPG, 74, 53).[25] It is precisely this conception of negativity as determinate negation that Heidegger tries to formulate differently.

Perhaps Heidegger's most enigmatic and provocative interpretation of Hegel is his 1938–39 text *Die Negativität: Eine Auseinandersetzung mit Hegel aus dem Ansatz in der Negativität.*[26] Heidegger designates negativity as the fundamental determination (*Grundbestimmung*) of his confrontation with Hegel. After emphasizing the importance of the notion of negativity in Hegel's determination of substance as subject, that is, as the dialectical movement, Heidegger tries to articulate the origin of Hegel's understanding of negativity. "Negativity is the energy of unconditional thinking" (H, 14). However, negativity is ultimately dissolved in the positivity of the absolute, because for Hegel negativity is determined as the difference of consciousness (*als Unterschied des Bewußtseins*). Obviously, consciousness is only the first stage of the dialectical process, and therefore it cannot account for the entire movement of thinking. However, for Heidegger, consciousness here indicates a determination of the entire dialectical process. It moves cognitively, that is, it moves by making the negativity of a previous shape its own object (*Gegenstand*), since that which stands over and against is a content for thinking, and therefore *of* thinking. Yet Heidegger asks whether negativity thereby is swallowed by positivity, by being dissolved in the subject-object relation. Once again, "subject" here does not simply mean a particular thinking being as opposed to an object in the world, but rather designates thinking and its content.[27] Therefore, Heidegger's aim is not to criticize Hegel for falling back into something that the dialectic claims to have overcome. Heidegger asks whether overcoming subjectivity is enough to account for negativity thought in terms of nothingness. Heidegger claims that Hegel does not think negativity out of nothingness; because nothingness is the same as being, there is no *difference* there and therefore no negativity (H, 14). Yet Heidegger also concedes that negativity cannot be thought out of Dasein's finitude either. Rather, Dasein's finitude has to be thought out of this "originary" difference that is neither present nor originary in the sense of being connected to thinking in a linear way, as a condition for its possibility. Hegel, according to Heidegger, renders negativity an object of thought, or more precisely, a difference within the movement of thinking. Yet we should ask what it would mean to "think" negativity otherwise, without making it the "object" of thinking, without making it present. Heidegger's attribution of representational thinking to Hegel has to be thought in terms of this broader concept of re-presentation. Hegel does indeed overcome representational thinking to the extent that representation refers to a mental content of a subject. Hegel's conceptual thinking is representational in a different way. It re-*presents* negativity in terms of the difference of cognition. For Hegel, nothingness is indeterminate immediacy.

However, negativity is determinate negation, and absolute negation is the negation of negation. Between being and nothing there is no difference. Thus, negativity has to be thought in terms of the difference of consciousness. Yet there still remains a difference for Heidegger that is unthought, that is covered over, namely the difference between being and beings, the ontological difference. Heidegger agrees with Hegel that pure being and pure nothing "do belong together, not because . . . both agree in their indeterminateness and immediacy, but rather because being itself is essentially finite and reveals itself only in the transcendence of Dasein which is held out into the nothing."[28] This sentence remains true, except that the finitude of being does not become "present" in Dasein's transcendence, and transcendence does not provide the condition for the existence of Dasein. What remains the same from "What is Metaphysics?" until the end of Heidegger's career is a resistance to understanding negativity in terms of *being conscious (Bewußt-sein)* of it. Heidegger tries to think negativity in terms of being disposed to it, that is, as a non-cognitive confrontation with negativity.

For Hegel "negativity as being-torn *(Zerrissenheit)* and separation is 'death,' the absolute master, and life of the absolute spirit means nothing other than to bear and carry out death" (H, 24). Heidegger adds in parenthesis, "but it can never become serious with this death; no *katastrophe* is possible, no fall, no fall down possible, everything is caught up and evened out, (or cancelled out)" (H, 24). Negativity is understood in terms of spirit's being alongside itself *(bei-sich)* and in terms of the contradiction involved in this being-alongside itself. Ultimately, by being assimilated into the content of thinking negativity becomes something other than "us," something "containable" in contradiction, something we can be indifferent to. This is precisely what Heidegger tries to resist. Yet is this resistance desirable, or even possible? Did not Hegel articulate everything that is possible to articulate in terms of negativity? I am raising these questions not because I will answer them, but because they remain questions. Is it inevitable that every thinking of negativity, even if it were formulated in terms of absence or concealment would transform it into a difference of consciousness? It is precisely with this question that we come back to the questions of madness and engagement in philosophy. Is there, in other words, anything that forces us to think, to engage, not, perhaps, with the task of philosophy, but with that of thinking after, as Nietzsche declares, God is dead?

Our question is whether Hegel's conception of the negativity of being, that is, of the unity of being and nothing, is similar to the moment of concealment and unconcealment in that it opens up the possibility of not only truth but also historicity? If the relation between concealment and unconcealment is different from the unity of being and nothing in a Hegelian sense, what is the *historical* status of a discourse that addresses this difference? Does this discourse fall outside of this history? Here we have to emphasize Heidegger's distinction between the historicity of being and the eschatology of being.[29] The eschatology of being situates Heidegger's discourse both within and outside of history. It is not beyond and above history, in that it describes its condition of possibility. Indeed, the eschatology of being signifies that the historical understanding of being always unfolds out of the recognition of this historicity. That is, the movement of history (eschatology) is not a series of interpretations of being that could be captured dialectically, but rather a history of the very capturing of historicity itself.[30] Different ways of understanding this condition of possibility together constitute the eschatology of being. An understanding of being is not understanding being as it happens historically, but an understanding of the condition of the possibility of historicity. Ultimately, for Heidegger, the question is whether the negativity of being, the ontological *difference*, can be *thought* cognitively in terms of the negativity of spirit. This question appears to be somehow meaningless. What does it mean to ask whether *negativity* can be thought other than cognitively? There is a sense in which every thinking of negativity has to be *thinking*, and, for Hegel, ultimately a content of thought. Yet for Heidegger the nature of negativity is such that it necessitates not only a different way of thinking, but also a different conception of thinking itself. This can only be thought in the sense of "our" confrontation with negativity, in terms of the question as to whether this confrontation itself is cognitive or can be made into cognition. If any kind of discourse about negativity somehow makes it "present" in and through language, don't we need another language, another discourse, and ultimately another beginning in order to continue to think? For Heidegger, such a beginning is indeed necessary, and this necessity arises from what he calls "the distress of not knowing the way out or the way in" (GdP, 151, 131). This need, according to Heidegger, is "a lack, absence, away," yet "not every negation is negation in a depreciatory sense. Silence, for example, means the 'absence,' the 'away' the 'not' of noise and disturbance."

For Heidegger, confronting negativity requires a fundamental attunement *(Grundstimmung)*. It is not an intellectual "problem." Negativity touches us in our very being, it is not to be reduced to the indifference of a "contradiction." The Greeks initially thought of this non-cognitive relation in terms of wonder *(thaumazein)*, which is the true "beginning" of philosophy. Yet this particular beginning is lost, in the sense that we cannot simply go back to and retrieve such a beginning:

> Hence we gained the recognition of a loss. But it is not at all decided that we have here a genuine loss. . . . Is the past not irreparably gone? And even if we wanted to adhere to this past in memory, would that not lead to the opposite of what is necessary? We do not want to turn back history, and of course we cannot; instead we must think and act out of our present (or future) necessity. (GdP, 109–96)

The *thaumazein* that first opened up the negativity of being is irretrievable. Heidegger does not aim to turn back history. Negativity *now* is to be thought through the dislocation of humanity, through a radical conception of madness, one that is other than the distinction between the rational and the irrational, what Heidegger calls the "unthought in the matter of philosophy": "Perhaps there is a thinking outside the distinction of rational and irrational, more sober-minded still than scientific technology, more sober-minded and hence removed, without effect, yet having its own necessity."[31] The simultaneity of concealment and unconcealment cannot be thought as "oppositional." Therefore, Dasein's existence is not opposed to the subjectivity of the subject, nor is there the possibility of thinking their relationship in a linear transition. There is no continuous movement from Dasein to the subject, which would make the unity of thinking and being possible. Indeed, there is *nothing* that makes being and thinking possible. The relation to this negativity of being is madness, a madness that can never be overcome in and through the movement of the dialectic. Heidegger articulates his radical understanding of madness at the end of *Basic Questions of Philosophy*:

> We must insist over and over that what is at stake in the question of truth as raised here is not simply an alteration of the previous concept of truth, nor a supplementation of the usual representation, but a transformation of being-human [*eine Verwandlung des Menschsein*] itself. . . . The determination of the essence of truth is accompanied by a necessary transformation of human being. Both are the same. This transformation signifies the dislocation of being human [*Verrückung des Menschseins*] out of its previous home—or, better, from its homelessness—into the ground of its essence, in order for man to become the founder and the preserver of the truth of being, to be the "there," as the ground employed by the essence of being itself. (GdP, 215)

For Heidegger, to raise the question of truth does not mean to supply a new conception of truth, but rather to transform what it means to be human. According to Heidegger, such a transformation stands in a different relationship to previous conceptions of truth and conceptions of what it means to be a human being. The being of the human is not to be understood in continuity with previous conceptions, but through a fundamental break. The human being is not a rational animal. Therefore, rationality cannot be presupposed in defining the being of human being. Heidegger continues:

> The dislocation of being-human—to be this ground—turns the human being away from himself the furthest and into a relation to being itself [*rückt den Menschen am weitesten von sich weg in den Bezug des Seyn selbst*]. But only out of this furthest distance can man truly find himself back, i.e., be who he is. We have been speaking of "human being," expressing ourselves as concisely as possible. But the human being that concerns us is historical human being, which means

the one who creates history, is sustained by history, and is beset by history. This historical human being is not a separate "individual," dragging his past behind himself. Nor does it mean several individuals belonging together in the form of society. Individuation and society are themselves only possible and necessary modes of historical humanity and do not at all exhaust it. Historical human being: that shall mean for us the unexhausted unique fullness of essential human possibilities and necessities, specifically—which is decisive here—one's arising from human being's relation to the truth of being itself. (GdP, 215–16)

Historical human being, whom Heidegger will associate with a certain madness, does not participate in history understood as the occurrence of events. Historical human being is neither an individual nor a group of individuals. In fact, historical human being is not to be understood as a human being who has certain properties. Heidegger tries to understand the very notion of human being from out of this dislocation. This dislocation requires a different conception of history, according to Heidegger:

Questioning on the basis of such a pre-view, we would represent precisely the possibility of the beginning of an entirely different history, in which the destiny of the single individual as well as of society would be determined differently, so differently that the previous representations could no longer suffice. (GdP, 215)

I think it is this idea of difference that distinguishes Heidegger's understanding of history from those of his predecessors. For Heidegger, there is no continuity, movement, or transition from one moment in history to the next. Rather, the radical difference in the idea of the dislocation of being-human (*Verrückung des Menschseins*) disrupts the continuous movement of historical rationality and leads to a kind of madness. Hence, this dislocation (*Verrückung*) manifests itself as madness (*Verrücktheit*) in certain individuals:

Thus the dislocation of being-human back into his ground has to be carried out in the first place by those few, solitary, uncanny ones, who in various ways as poets, thinkers, as builders and artists, as doers and actors, ground and shelter the truth of being in beings through the transformation of beings. Through the rigor of the decisions, which lie ahead, they become, each in his way and unknown to the many, a silent sacrifice.

If we appraise the reflection on this dislocation [*Verrückung*] of man from the standpoint of sound common sense and its predominance, we reject it as deranged [*verrückt*], to play cleverly with a word, and will not even take the pains to reject such reflection but will simply ridicule it. (GdP, 215)

Heidegger thus radicalizes his understanding of madness. Madness as a historical phenomenon manifesting itself in poets, thinkers, and artists has nothing to do with mental illness. In fact, the madness of these individuals cannot be understood with regard to the ordinary conception of truth. I believe Heidegger's conception of madness, in its relation to truth, is fundamentally different from that of Hegel. As we discussed in chapter two, for Hegel, madness is, in a sense, opposed, and thereby defined, by the concept of truth. For Heidegger, madness cannot be defined by or reduced to the question of truth if madness manifests a completely different conception of truth than that which has been historically dominant hitherto. Heidegger raises the question as to whether our rationality and conception of truth can capture madness as it manifests itself in historical individuals:

> But this will not mislead the ones who know, to the extent that there are any. For a case, which has not yet been mastered, is still in the air, the latest in the history of German thought, the case of Nietzsche. Fortunately, we have the inconvertible fact that this thinker lapsed into madness [Wahnsinn]. By means of this circumstance it is possible to ward off his most decisive meditation—the thought of the eternal recurrence of the same—in its totally strange character and its inexorableness of its perspectiveness and questioning, by interpreting it as a precursor of madness [Wahnsinn] and an offspring of despair. But what about the other one, still greater, whose poetry was further in advance, namely Hölderlin?
>
> Have we at all sufficiently considered that something wondrous has come to pass ever since the history of the West in its deepest meditations, has surmised its unrolling to its end? The wondrous [Wunderbares] is that those who suffered such meditation, and created it, and hence bore the knowledge of the entirely other, were prematurely torn away from the sanity of their Dasein—and this is in wholly different ways in their own respective domains: Schiller, Hölderlin, Kierkegaard, van Gogh, Nietzsche. Are all these "broken down," as an extrinsic calculation could perhaps ascertain, or was a new song sung to them, one that never tolerates an "and so forth," but demands the sacrifice of the "shortest path" (Hölderlin)?
>
> These names are like enigmatic signs, inscribed in the most concealed ground of our history. We hardly give a thought to the sheer power of this series of signs, which is not to say that we would be strong enough to understand it. These signs point in advance to a change of history, which lies deeper, and reaches further than all "revolutions" within the realm of activities of men, of peoples, and their contrivances. Here something comes to pass, for which we have no measure and no space—at least not yet—and we therefore force it into disfiguration and disguise, if we speak about it by means of language as constituted hitherto (GdP, 216).

For Heidegger, there is a radical break between the madness of these individuals and a rational understanding of history dominated by a certain understanding of truth. When Heidegger refers to the dislocation (Verrückung) of the human being, he makes clear that he is speaking of a historical transformation, which cannot be made sense of in terms of a linear conception of history as the occurrence of events. Therefore, this radical conception of madness intimates a break from history that cannot be assimilated in continuity with this history. I contend that this break effectively displaces the very movement of the dialectic, and thereby Hegel's radical conception of subjectivity, because the previous "event" of history manifesting itself as madness cannot be made a content of thought. The reason for this displacement is that this break, according to Heidegger, cannot be brought to rational consciousness. Hence, the modern madness that takes over thinkers and artists cannot be overcome in and through the movement of spirit, because they testify to that which makes the movement of spirit *impossible*. The passage above reiterates Heidegger's conviction that the human relationship to negativity is not cognitive. Thus, the relation between unconcealment and history is neither one of a "condition of possibility" nor a linear unfolding where consciousness "experiences" its own absolution. Indeed, rather than being ab-solved from radical finitude, human existence becomes entangled in finitude in a manner of engagement. This engagement is not assimilated into a problem of explanation or expression, and is ultimately not one of cognition in the sense of "making present." This engagement is madness, which is *not* the *Zerrissenheit* of spirit. Most importantly, the negativity of madness is *not* confronted as a contradiction *of* consciousness, which would recuperate a possibility of continuity with history. The negativity of thinking cannot be taken up into the movement of thought, because this negativity is not "experienced," but is revealed in a fundamental *attunement*. Heidegger no longer formulates this attunement as an anxiety arising from the confrontation of Dasein's mortality, but as a madness arising from the very finitude of being in its historicity. Consequently, Heidegger takes up this question of madness again in terms of the eschatology of being. Within this conception of madness, the truth of madness cannot be revealed in the next shape of the dialectical movement, for madness displaces this very movement. Therefore, for Heidegger, the negativity of madness is *historical* in a radical fashion, not because we understand madness differently in different periods in history, but because madness that is yet to seize us opens up a radically different movement of history. Let us turn, then, to this madness in another context, but once again in terms of the questions of history and truth. Heidegger takes up the theme of madness more explicitly in "The Anaximander Fragment."

"THE ANAXIMANDER FRAGMENT"

> . . . *unter den Männern erhob sich*
> *Kalchas der Thestoride, der weiseste Vogeldeuter,*
> *Der erkannte, was ist, was sein wird oder zuvor war,*
> *Der gen Ilion auch der Danaer Schiffe geleitet*
> *Kraft seiner Wahrsagerkunst, der Gabe Phoiobos Apollons.*

. . . among the men stood up
Kalchas, the son of Thestoride, the wisest of the bird-interpreters,
who knew all that is, is to be, or once was,
who guided into the land of Ilion the ships of the Achaens
by virtue of his truth-sayer art, the gift of Phoibos Apollo.[32]

Heidegger quotes these lines from Homer's *Iliad* in order to illustrate the difference between the Greek words *eon* and *eonta* on the one hand, and from
on and *onta* on the other. The main point Heidegger makes is that in its
"original" form being was not understood in terms of presence (*Gegenwart*)
but in terms of a unity of past, present, and future. Thus Kalchas, the one
who has seen, sees all that is, that is to be, and that once was. "To see" in
this sense, however, is "to have seen." The vision of Kalchas is to be understood as his essential way of being. Therefore, Kalchas is not first a human
being who then additionally has the ability to see. His essence is constituted
by a particular way of seeing. What does he see, or rather, from what perspective does he see? Achilles asks Kalchas to interpret the wrath of Apollo,
who sent the plague, which has raged, in the Greek camp. The plague, as
Achilles says, brings death. Kalchas has to interpret the rage of the god from
the perspective of death. Yet Apollo, who sends the plague, also gives
Kalchas his visionary ability as a gift.[33] By virtue of this gift Kalchas sees all
that is, that is to be, and that once was. He does not see three different
things, but sees from the unitary perspective of death. Apollo sends death in
the form of a plague, and as a visionary ability. As Heidegger elsewhere
writes, "[i]n death the highest concealment of being [*des Seins*] gathers
itself."[34] Kalchas sees from the perspective of the highest concealment: "The
seer stands in sight of what is present, in its unconcealment, which has at
the same time cast light on the concealment of what is absent as being
absent" (SpA, 320, 35). Kalchas is touched by the highest concealment, by
an absence. Therefore, says Heidegger "the seer is the *mainomenos*, the madman [*der Rasende*]" (SpA, 320, 35). The power of vision leads the seer to
madness. The madman is out of himself, away (*weg*); away "from the sheer
oppression of what lies before us, which is only presently present, away to
what is absent . . ." (SpA, 320, 35).

Heidegger does not comment on this madness any further. He concludes
this paragraph by saying that the "madness of being-away of the seer does not
consist of the fact that the madman raves, rolls his eyes, and tosses his limbs;
The madness of vision can be accompanied by the inconspicuous tranquility
of bodily composure" (SpA, 321, 35–36). If we reflect upon this enigmatic
reference to madness, we realize that a mad "doubling" takes place in Heidegger's text: Heidegger seems to intimate that to recognize what is to be seen
in Anaximander's fragment requires a certain madness of vision on our part.
Quite literally, the power to see the eschatological character of being is

accompanied by madness. In order to be able render this intimation fully, let us follow the path of the text up to this point.

Even though Heidegger emphasizes the necessity of trans-lating our-selves to Anaximander's saying before translating the fragment itself, he starts his essay by quoting a translation of it. "Whence things have their ori-gin, there they must also pass away according to necessity; for they must pay penalty and be judged for their injustice, according to the ordinance of time" (SpA, 296, 13). This translation, however, is not an arbitrary one. It is Niet-zsche's. It is the translation of the oldest fragment of Western thinking by someone Heidegger calls the last thinker of Western thinking. Yet it is remarkably similar to the "standard translation." Heidegger claims that throughout the philosophical tradition, Anaximander has been interpreted as either presocratic (by Diels), preplatonic (by Nietzsche), or prearis-totelian (by Hegel). Heidegger's juxtaposition of Anaximander with Niet-zsche and Hegel is not accidental, but speaks to his attempt to "delimit" a tradition, which is "racing towards its end" (SpA, 300, 16). Yet can the ear-liest saying of this tradition still say something to us, "who stand in the very twilight of the most monstrous transformation of the entire earth and of the time of the historical space in which earth itself hangs suspended" (SpA, 300, 17)? Does the "the most monstrous transformation," the modern, tech-nological age, intimate the end of a certain kind of thinking? Are we merely at the end of a history, or at the dawn of an altogether different age? Hei-degger distinguishes his questions from a desire to predict the future. He claims that such an attempt is, in fact, the desire of historiography, which attempts to predict what is to come from the images of the past determined by the present and, thus, systematically destroys the future (SpA, 301, 17). However, the antiquity pervading the Anaximander fragment would be inaccessible to historiography if that which is early outdistanced everything late; if the very earliest far surpassed the very latest (SpA, 301, 18). If so, what once occurred in the dawn of our destiny would then come, as what once occurred, at the end *(eschaton)*, that is, at the departure of the long-hidden destiny of being. Heidegger does not raise the question of to "whom" the end can appear. If he had, he would have said: To the seer who sees the future by having seen in advance; To the one who sees the future tense *(Futurum)* out of the perfect *(Perfectum)*. Hence, Heidegger appeals to the notion of a seer, not only because of the seer's vision of what is presently and not-presently present, but also because the seer has the power to see the eschatological character of being, the earliest and the latest of a history which comes to an end. Yet these are not two different visions. In other words, the eschatological character of being, or the history of being, "deter-mines" the way in which our bodies are affected by that which is presently and non-presently present. This intimation gives a different twist to Hei-degger's claim that we have to translate ourselves to what the fragment

speaks of before translating the text. This translation is a transposing of ourselves into the uncanny realm of madness. In other words, Heidegger's text
invites us to the perspective of death, to a tranquil realm of madness.

Immediately after quoting Homer, Heidegger indicates that Homer refers
to Kalchas as the one who had seen (in the "before-past," or past present,
Vorvergangenheit), the one who had *already* seen. Only because one has already
seen can one truly see: "to see is to have seen." Heidegger's allusion to a prior
familiarity refers back to his discussion of involvement in section eighteen of
Being and Time. As we saw in the previous chapter, Heidegger claims that
"having already let something to be involved, which frees something for that
involvement, is a perfect tense *a priori* that characterizes the way of being of
Dasein itself" (SZ, 85). In the same way, in order to be able to see something
as something one already needs to be "outside" of it (not physically, but in the
sense of being "away" from it). At this point, one can recognize the similarity
of Kalchas being "away" and the care structure of *Dasein.* Both Kalchas and
Dasein are in a sense "away." Kalchas is away *(weg)* from presence into
absence, whereas Dasein is always "away," ahead of itself *(Sichvorweg).*[35] In the
first instance what one sees is something other, something that is not present
to the seer. As we have seen before, to see what is present as present requires
a look "away" from the present, into the presence of what is present, the way
in which what is present comes into presence. Without this looking away, one
cannot see what is present, or delimit what is present as a unity, as distinct
from another "constituted present." Yet how can one account for this presence? Or *is* there such a presence, can "it" be accounted for as a delimited, constituted unity? Would not an attempt to delimit such a presence reduce it to
what is present? On the other hand, how can one insist on the difference
between what is present and the way in which it comes to presence, without
reducing this presencing to a constituted presence? Such a reduction would be
what Heidegger calls "the oblivion of being":

> From early on it seems as though presencing and what is present were each
> something for itself. Presencing itself unnoticeably becomes something pre-
> sent. Represented in the manner of something present, it is elevated above
> whatever else is present and so becomes the highest being present. As soon
> as presencing is named it is represented as some present being. Ultimately,
> presencing as such is not distinguished from what is present: it is taken
> merely as the most universal or the highest of present beings, thereby
> becoming one among such beings. The essential unfolding of presencing
> and with that the difference of presencing from what is present remains for-
> gotten. The oblivion of being is the oblivion of the difference of being from
> beings. (SpA, 335–36, 50)

As we have emphasized, however, one cannot simply assert the difference
between what is present and presencing, remind oneself of the ontological dif-

ference, and solve the problem. The difficulty is that "the very relation between presencing and what is present remains unthought." The oblivion of being, of the difference between being and beings is not a simple forgetfulness that happened in the history of metaphysics; rather it "belongs to the self-veiling essential unfolding [Wesen] of being" (SpA, 335, 50). The oblivion of being in the history of metaphysics is oblivion of absence at the very heart of being, the irreducibility of presencing to a constituted presence. This oblivion is not something purely "negative," but is a founding "gesture" of metaphysics, which approaches its consummation in the age of modern technology.

The thought of a delimited, constituted presence accompanies the modern technological way of seeing a field of objects standing over and against a subject. Indeed, Heidegger's appeal to Kalchas is an attempt to displace this way of accounting for the unity of presence. The perspective from which one sees may be characterized as the perspective of a subject looking at a field of objectivity. Only by virtue of accounting for the presence of what is present in terms of subjectivity can one see what is present as a field of objectivity. To explain the unity of presence in terms of its presence to a subject presupposes that the way in which what is present comes to presence can be delimited in terms of a particular constituted presence. This presupposition is accompanied by a certain interpretation of the presently present and the non-presently present. Heidegger warns that what Homer suggests as "what is to be," and "what once was," that is, the non-presently present, cannot be understood as a particular case of a broad universal concept of presence: "Whatever is presently present is not a slice of something shoved in between what is non-presently present; it is present insofar as it lets itself belong to the non-present" (SpA, 329, 44). The relationship between what is presently present and non-presently present is fundamentally different from that of two present-at-hand entities standing over and against a subject at different points on a present-at-hand scale of time. Subjectivity regards what is to be, and what once was, in terms of what is present at a particular moment. Subjectivist thinking accounts for the externality required in seeing in terms of a constituted presence. One sees what is present, according to this scheme, by virtue of something that was once present, or that will be present. The unity, which allows one to see, is accounted for in terms of a modification of the present, in terms of something that underlies all three moments, namely the subject. The presence of the subject throughout what once was, what is, and what is to be, explains the appearance of everything outside of this subject. According to this scheme, Kalchas would be a subject looking at a field of objects. As we have seen, for Hegel, the dialectical movement proceeds through the completion of the reduction of presencing into presence. In this reduction, however, there still remains the question concerning the nature of "an eye" that sees Kalchas and the field of objects standing over and against him. From what perspective does this eye see?

What *is present* is threefold: what is, what is to be, and what once was. The externality required to see this threefold cannot be reduced to one of its modes. What becomes present is not simply what is presently present, but also what is non-presently present. What, then, is the perspective from which one sees both the presently present and the non-presently present? Heidegger's aim is no longer to "explain" this perspective, precisely because it does not lend itself to explanation, and it "is" not in the sense of something there to be explained. The attempt to explain the perspective of presence presupposes that the way presence comes to presence can be explained in terms of a constituted presence which *is*, and which can be explained. Presencing cannot be *reduced* to a constituted presence. Hence, the expanse of presencing is occupied by an absence. A discourse concerning this expanse is stillness, a "negative" discourse, not in the sense of negating something which is present-at-hand, but in the sense of displacing the conception of a discourse, which speaks *about* something.

This character of the movement of presencing has to be distinguished from a different sense in which the eschatological character of being is characterized. Early in his essay Heidegger writes: "we think the eschatology of being in a way corresponding to the way the phenomenology of spirit is to be thought, that is, from within the history of being. The phenomenology of spirit itself constitutes a phase in the eschatology of being, when being gathers itself in the ultimacy of its essence, hitherto determined through metaphysics, as the absolute subjectity [Subjektität] of the unconditioned will" (SpA, 302, 18). Yet for Hegel the subjectivity of the subject is not exactly constituted through the presence of a subject, namely as a *hupokeimenon*. As we have noted earlier, for Hegel, subjectivity is the way in which phenomenology moves, that is, the subject is never "present" throughout the movement, but emerges in and through the movement. What Heidegger tries to contest is the possibility of understanding the movement of being as subjectivity. For Heidegger, it is not possible for a phase within the movement to be sublated in and through this movement. Madness as a necessary phase, for example, cannot be contained and sublated within the movement, because madness thereby becomes a present-at-hand stage within this movement by being confronted cognitively and stripped of its character of being a way of relating to the world. Madness becomes a cognitive problem precisely by being reduced to a question of error, the truth of which (of madness as well as of error) is revealed in moving to the next step in the movement of spirit. It is precisely the way in which madness is "objectified" that Heidegger contests. This objectification does not proceed by treating the madman as an object, but by treating madness as "something earlier" that is overcome. Heidegger resists this tendency because it pretends to solve the problem of being implicated in one's own text.

Kalchas, the seer, sees the presently present and non-presently present because he occupies the realm of unconcealment which presencing brings along with itself. "Unconcealment itself is presencing. Both are the same, though they are not identical" (SpA, 341, 55). That is to say that uncon-cealment of being is presencing, yet this presencing is a simultaneous con-cealment. Unconcealment and presencing speak to the same phenomenon, but cannot be identical as they are not to be thought as things that can be identical. The expanse Kalchas occupies is not a stretch of a unifying subject because, as Heidegger writes, ". . . for Greek thinking . . . the seer as the one who has seen, is himself one who comes to presence, who belongs in an exceptional sense to the totality of what is present" (SpA, 323, 38, the trans-lation is modified). Kalchas belongs to the totality of what is present,that is, in a sense he sees "himself" within that totality. Yet what does this belonging mean? Can one see "oneself" within the totality? Belonging to the totality of what is present makes an "external point of view" to this totality impossible. This belonging displaces any conception of a subject in front of a field of objects, and any "formal" discourse about the totality of beings. The vision of the totality of what is present implies that the human being is never simply present-at-hand within that totality inasmuch as the totality itself is never present as such. The presencing of what is present does not belong to the human being but, on the contrary, the human being belongs in an extraordi-nary way to presencing. This implies that the essence of the human being does not *belong* to itself. There *is* no human being to whom presencing would belong independently of presencing itself. Kalchas, the one who sees the presently present and non-presently present, *is* nothing other than the gaze of absence, the gaze of death. The external perspective from which one is sup-posed to see oneself within the totality of what is present is never the exter-nality of a subject, but that of a madman, who is away into absence, an absence that ultimately is not different from presencing itself. The perspec-tive from which one sees oneself as within the totality of what is present also displaces the idea that one can simply be present within that totality, not only because one needs to be precisely "not oneself" for such a vision, but also because the totality of what is present is not present as such. As Heidegger says, the most extreme possibility of subjectivity, that is, the way in which one considers oneself as a subject, and accounts for the unity of presence in terms of this notion of subject, also leads to its displacement, to the over-coming of subjectivity. This overcoming is not simply a triumph of yet another discourse, but rather is something quite extraordinary, something at the edge of madness.

Kalchas is able to see the presently present as well as the non-presently present through God given power to see. Heidegger states that the seer is the madman, and immediately raises the question of what the essence of madness is: "A madman is outside himself. He is away" (SpA, 321, 35). The seer is away from the presently present (*gegenwärtig Anwesende*), to what is non-presently present (*ungegenwärtig Anwesende*), to what is absent: "The seer is outside of himself in the solitary region of presencing of everything that in some way becomes present. Therefore he can find his way back from the 'away' of this region, and arrive at what has just presented itself, the raging epidemic" (SpA, 321, 35). The seer is away from the presently present, and since he belongs to this presence in an extraordinary way, he is also outside himself. When, as Heidegger says, the seer finds his way back from the "away," he can never come back to him*self*. The perspective from which he sees, the region he occupies, makes it impossible for him to be present to himself as a subject. Indeed, he sees precisely because he is *outside* of himself, he is *not* him*self*, understood as a subject, or as a delimited and constituted presence.

Kalchas sees the threefold nature of *eonta,* what comes to presence, by virtue of having seen presencing, or being. As Heidegger says earlier in the essay, "as it reveals itself in beings, being withdraws" (SpA, 310, 26). A prior look at being that withdraws allows Kalchas to see that which comes to presence. But how can one see that which withdraws, or more radically, that which is never in the first place there to withdraw? Heidegger calls this withdrawal of being the *epoche* of being in its history, a history that "approaches" its end as "the absolute subjectity [*Subjektität*] of the unconditioned will to will" (SpA, 302, 18). What does it mean to look away from presence to presencing itself? It means to be "the placeholder of the nothing" (SpA, 321, 36).[36] Occupying the place of the nothing is not different from preserving the truth of being, namely, presencing. As Heidegger elsewhere writes: "The nothing is never nothing; it is just as little a something, in the sense of an object; *it is being itself,* whose truth will be appropriated over to man when he has overcome himself as subject, and that means when he no longer sets beings before himself as objects."[37] The irreducible absence at the heart of presencing is not "something" different than presencing itself. This is to say that unconcealment is itself concealment. As Heidegger would say, they are the same although not identical. On the other hand, "man's inability to see himself corresponds to the self-concealing of the clearing of being" (SpA, 311, 26). Similarly, the negativity of death surrounding human existence is not different from human existence itself. Hence, the nothing translates itself into death, because, as Heidegger says, "the most readily experienced correspondence to the epochal character of being is the ecstatic character of *Dasein.* The epochal essence of being appropriates to the ecstatic nature of *Dasein*" (SpA, 311, 27).[38] To be alongside of being is to be alongside of the nothing, alongside of death, to be constantly exposed to death as Kalchas is surrounded by the wrath of Apollo in the form of plague. Death is not something that waits at the end of the existence of a present-at-hand entity or a subject. It is never present, just as nothingness is never present. Death is a "place" the seer has to occupy in order to see. The truth of being is given over to Kalchas, because he can see, and when he sees, he never quite experiences himself as a subject. Death surrounding him in the form of the raging epidemic, to which he belongs in an extraordinary way, is not something that he can represent to himself as a subject is supposed to do. *Seeing* the nothing, which Heidegger says has nothing to do with the completion of an optical process, seeing presence from the perspective of death, with the intervention of death which can never be present, renders it impossible for Kalchas to see himself simply as present. Likewise the vision of "something" that can never be present is the reason that Heidegger calls Kalchas the madman. To see the totality of what is present in its presencing makes the seer the one who stands in knowledge. To have seen, says Heidegger, is the essence of knowledge. Knowledge is indebted to presencing. Therefore "knowledge is the remembrance of being. That is why *Mnemosyne* is mother of the muses" (SpA, 322, 36). But as we have "seen," the perspective from which Kalchas sees the nonpresently present is not simply a modification of constituted presence. In fact the question remains how it is possible to remember something that can never be present.[39] The realm of absence Kalchas is delivered over to is a realm which is more radical, more ancient than the past that memory is conventionally supposed to remember. What he remembers is not something that happened in the past but, in fact, something that has never been present, and never will be present as such. Remembering such an absence, something that has never been present, is what makes Kalchas the madman. Yet the madness of Kalchas is different than that of Hölderlin or that of Nietzsche. The difference lies in the epochal character of being, in historicity. For Heidegger the possibility of expressing madness as a radical vision requires a different kind of language. In "Language in the Poem" Heidegger addresses the problem of language concerning madness.

"LANGUAGE IN THE POEM"

The question of finding a proper language for madness proves to be immature. Heidegger recognizes that philosophical language, as it is historically conceived, is insufficient to express the negativity of its own movement of presencing. To disentangle thinking from its productive[40] and problematic dimension requires a different language, a different expression of language. However, Heidegger also recognizes that his own discourse is also subject to the same difficulties he finds in philosophical language. There *is* no other language that we can invent or discover that may articulate the problem of articulation. Yet for Heidegger poetic language appears to be different in nature than the series of assertions that form philosophical language. Their difference lies in their movement, or rhythm, rather than their content. In his "Language in the Poem: A Discussion of George Trakl's Poem,"[41] Heidegger tries to articulate the movement of Trakl's poetry. I will follow the text's movement up to the point where the themes of madness and death emerge in Trakl's poems.[42]

Heidegger refers to his own essay as a discussion. The German word for "discussion" is *Erörterung,* which includes the word *Ort,* "place," or "site." Thus by "discussion" Heidegger means a placement, or placing. This essay has been the focus of several essays by Derrida.[43] These essays have been mostly focused on the themes of *Geschlecht* (a word which is almost untranslatable, but can be rendered as "sex," "genre," "family," "stock," "race," "lineage," "generation"), and spirit *(Geist).* Reading Heidegger's essay exclusively in light of these themes overlooks another significant dimension of the text, and misses its main thrust by reducing it to one singular conviction. For Heidegger, Trakl's poetry does not represent a different language that addresses that which is originary in a better way. The language of poetry does not stand in a linear relationship to philosophical language in that the former expresses that which is the condition of possibility of the latter. Poetic language has a different movement than that of philosophical language, which, by contrast, progresses rationally. Poetry does not follow a linear rationality. As Heidegger puts it in the context of his discussion of Trakl's poem *"In ein altes Stammbuch,"* "the one who poetizes first becomes a poet, to the extent that he follows the madman, who dies away into the earliness, and calls the brother who follows him through the melody of his steps from detachment" (S, 71). Heidegger will discuss all these themes in terms of Trakl's poems, which do not move as a series of arguments, but nevertheless express a certain univocal site.

Heidegger brings several poems of Trakl together in order to designate the site of his poem. Heidegger interprets some of Trakl's words in terms of his own vocabulary of being. Heidegger utilizes this strategy with respect to various thinkers. However, in the case of Trakl this substitution is quite different. Instead of replacing Trakl's poems with an interpretive framework, Heidegger allows Trakl's words to invade his own meditation of being. The discussion of a poem, its placing, is dictated by the content of Trakl's poems. There is no static "site" of interpretation that Heidegger is trying to designate. The whole essay is a placing-movement. The site of poetry is a movement, and the direction, that is, the meaning of this movement, is presented by Trakl's own poetry. Heidegger's various interpretations of poetry have been mostly understood as attempts to find the right vocabulary to speak of that about which Heidegger has a prior inkling. The essay "Language in Poem," however, moves according to the content of Trakl's poetry. It is as if Heidegger tries to take the reader into the movement of placing as a "stranger on the way."

Heidegger begins with an analysis of the following line from Trakl's poem entitled "Springtime of the Soul [*Frühling der Seele*]": "The soul is a stranger on the earth [*Es ist die Seele ein Fremdes auf Erden*]." Heidegger immediately disqualifies a possible Platonist interpretation of this line, which he calls a "common representation." The common representation interprets the earth as earthly in the sense of transitory. The soul, on the other hand, belongs to the suprasensuous world. If the soul appears on earth at all, it is because it is foreign to the earth, cast away to the earth. The soul is immortal; it is imprisoned in the body, in the realm of the sensuous. Thus, the soul seeks to abandon the realm of the sensuous, which is not truly a being (*Nicht-wahrhaft-Seiende*), a world that decomposes (*das Verwesende*). It is important to note that Heidegger designates the earth as that which decomposes, according to the Platonist interpretation, because he is going to retain, yet also reverse this decomposition.[44] Yet Heidegger claims that Trakl is saying almost exactly the opposite of this common representation. Heidegger appeals to the old high-German root of the word *fremd* (strange), *fram*, which means, "forward to somewhere else," or "on the way to."[45] On this interpretation, the soul does not escape the earth but seeks the earth in the first place. Heidegger adds that seeking the earth is not an additional characteristic of the soul, but a determination of the soul's very being (*Wesen*). The remainder of this section discusses the place that the soul is called to, and Heidegger's reading will follow the soul that is underway to a site. This movement ties Heidegger's reading of Trakl as a placement (*Erörterung*) to the content of Trakl's poetry, namely to the site or place to which the soul is called. The poet responds to this call. Heidegger finds the first hint of this call in another poem, "Sebastian in Dream":

> O how still a course down the blue river,
> Sensing the forgotten, there in green branches
> The thrush called the stranger into down-going.

The stranger is called into down-going or descension (*Untergang*). Yet down-going is neither a catastrophe, nor a disappearance in falling. Heidegger quotes from "Transfigured Autumn":

> It goes down in peace and silence.

The down-going is in peace and silence. "Into what peace does it go? The peace of the dead? But of which dead? And into what silence?" (S, 42) Heidegger finds the answer from the same poem, "Springtime of the soul":

> The soul is a stranger on earth
> Spiritually dusks
> The blueness over the thickening forest.

The peace and silence are those of the dusk (*Dämmerung*). Yet the German word for "dusk" signifies not only the down-going of the day, but also its rising. The blueness dawns spiritually (*geistlich*) as well. *Dämmerung* is the drawing to a close of the sun's course. It also designates the end of the year, namely the springtime. The year is also drawing to a close (Neige). Therefore, in "Summer's End," Trakl writes:

> The green summer has become so quiet (leise)
> And through the silvery night there rings
> The step of the stranger.
> The blue game were to remember its path,
> The melody of its spiritual years.

"So quiet" is a figure that recurs in Trakl's poems, designating, according to Heidegger, slipping away into the fall. At this point, Heidegger indicates the difference between the stranger (Fremdling), with which he associates the soul, and a series of figures in Trakl's poems identified with mortals, "the blue game (ein blaues Wild)," "the shy game (das scheue Wild)," and "the gentle animal (das sanfte Tier)" (S, 44). Mortals follow the stranger who is called to the down-going of death. Heidegger designates the down-going of the stranger as the silence of the dead. The death of the stranger does not refer to decomposition, but rather to an abandonment of the decomposed structure of the human being (S, 46). The gentle animal follows the stranger into the darkness of the night. Yet the darkness of the night does not necessarily designate a gloom (Finsternis). Trakl uses the expression "gentle corn flower sheaf of the night" to designate the depth of the holy. The holy withdraws into the darkness of the night. The animal that follows the stranger comes face to face with the blueness, with the holiness of the blueness. The animal is petrified face to face with the holy. It is this confrontation that determines the animality of the gentle animal. The gentle animal, according to Heidegger, is the human being whose animality is not yet determined. Heidegger, therefore, once again evokes the question of the essence of human being. This animal follows the stranger to death.

The theme of death together with that of decomposition continues Heidegger's displacement of the reading of Trakl's poems in terms of a Platonist interpretation. Death is not a leaving behind of the decomposed nature of the sensuous, nor is it itself a decomposition. It is the abandonment of the decomposed structure of the human being, that is, of the structure of the body and the soul understood as a combination of the sensuous and the suprasensuous. Therefore, what is designated as that which is decomposed is precisely the metaphysical interpretation of the human being. "Down-going" means leaving behind the interpretation of the human being as belonging to something *above* the sensuous world. Heidegger approaches this separation in a double move. First, he reads Trakl's phrase "the blue game" (animal) as the human being whose animality has not been determined, that is, as that which is on the way to a site. Second, in contrast to the tradition of Western European metaphysics since Plato, Heidegger reads this separation other than as a striking apart *(Schlag)* into sensuous and suprasensuous worlds. The latter move is important to notice in order to read Heidegger's understanding of "decomposing *(verwesen)*" and *"Geschlecht."* Heidegger states that the wanderer who follows the stranger is separated from his or her loved ones (or from the others), that is, from all those who are determined by the blow of the decomposed structure of the human being *(der Schlag der verwesten Gestalt des Menschen)*. Heidegger calls the *being* of the human that is stamped by a blow, and cast away into this blow, the *Geschlecht.* Thus, *Geschlecht* designates an entire generation that is determined by the metaphysical conception of the human being that is also stamped into the duality of the sexes. At this point, it is quite evident that Heidegger does not simply overlook an entire stock of questions arising from sexual difference, but reads it in terms of another duality. This is not to say that the duality as such is a curse, but rather that the dissension in such duality is the curse *[Nicht das Zwiefache als solches, sondern dies Zwietracht ist der Fluch]* (S, 50). Hence, rather than designating sexual difference as a curse, Heidegger claims that the metaphysical dualism that carries this duality into an opposition between the feminine earth of the sensuous and the masculine sky of the suprasensuous is what leads to the decomposition of the human being. Heidegger's strategy is to undermine precisely that which claims to do away with the decomposition of human nature by attributing its source to the earth, to the sensuous. As a result, Heidegger's aim is to appeal not to another kind of pure source of unity, but to another kind of scission or separation. It is true, however, that Heidegger appeals to a gathering as the site of all the themes introduced in his interpretation of Trakl's poems. Heidegger states that Trakl names this site "detachment" (or departedness, *Abgeschiedenheit*). The word "detachment," *Abgeschiedenheit,* also means apartness or decease in the sense of being dead, deceased.

Heidegger interprets this site in terms of what Trakl calls the "earliest earliness." The one who dies dies away into the earliest earliness. Heidegger interprets this earliness other than in terms of a linear understanding of time. The beginning, as the earliest earliness, has already overtaken the end. Heidegger writes, "The earliness preserves the originary essence of time which is always yet covered over." Yet "the true time is the arrival of what has been. This is not that which has been past, but the gathering of that which comes to presence, which precedes all arrival in that it brings itself back as such a gathering to that which is always earlier" (S, 57). Is this, then, an appeal to an originary gathering? If so, does it become the condition of possibility of what comes to presence? Derrida seems to think so. In his interpretation of these lines Derrida writes "once again, after covering a huge amount of ground, it is on the basis of a more originary thinking of time that we will open ourselves to a more appropriate thinking of spirit."[46] Therefore, Derrida sees Heidegger's designation of a more promising earliness as a desire "to think that on the basis of which all metaphysics is possible."[47] However, Heidegger does indeed cover a lot of ground, which in fact displaces a reading of his interpretation in terms of conditions of possibility. Even though Derrida himself acknowledges an inevitable promise of language, he seems to attribute to Heidegger an unquestioned attachment to gathering, which ultimately betrays a desire for presence. It is true that Derrida designates this tendency as one of Heidegger's hands.[48] Yet it is a hand nevertheless. Derrida's concern seems to be the result of his own interpretation of gathering in opposition to dispersion and difference. Hence, Derrida interprets Heidegger's designation of spirit as flames as a commitment to a gathering as opposed to dispersion. Therefore, Derrida wants to suggest that there is a certain complicity between Heidegger and Hegel. Despite his attempts, Heidegger is not always able, according to Derrida, to escape a Hegelian tendency towards unity and presence. Yet Heidegger designates spirit not only as that which is in flames, but also that which "raises, displaces," "brings out of grasp." "Spirit is outside itself" (S, 60). Yet, contrary to what Derrida thinks, being outside is not based on ecstatic time, but rather on a certain displacement of language. Spirit is understood in terms of a kind of madness, which displaces the linear, rational movement of conditions of possibility. As Heidegger puts it, there is "the clear knowing of the mad, who sees the other" (S, 80). Heidegger does not, as Derrida contends, modestly and discreetly think that on the basis of which every metaphysical or Christian interpretation of being is possible. Heidegger's discourse stands in a fundamentally different relationship to these discourses. The difference is that, for Heidegger, gathering is never a unifiable presence, it is an ambiguous ambiguity, and the word of the poet remains unspoken.

The site of detachment is where the themes of madness and death come together. Heidegger displaces the metaphysical interpretations of these themes. According to Plato, death and madness are two interrelated ways in which the soul has access to the world of forms. In the *Phaedo*, death, as the separation of the soul from the body, leads to the knowledge of being(s) as they are. In the *Phaedrus*, madness, in the form of love, as a kind of manifestation of death in life, provides access to the forms. With his notion of detachment, Heidegger *displaces* these interpretations of madness and death as ways of access to the suprasensuous world. Heidegger argues this point through his reading of Trakl's poems. The one who is detached is also the one who is dead. Heidegger asks into which death did the stranger die? (. . . *in welchen Tod ist der Fremdling gestorben?*) (S, 53). Without giving an immediate answer Heidegger continues by quoting several lines from Trakl's poems:

> The one who is mad has died.
> One buries the stranger.
> The white magician plays with his snakes in his grave.

Heidegger writes that the dead one *lives* in his grave. The dead one is the mad one. Madness *(Wahnsinn)* does not mean a sensing *(Sinnen)* that imagines *(wähnt)* the senseless *(das Unsinnige)*. Heidegger's strategy at this point is also a double move to displace the Platonist interpretation of madness. As we might recall, Plato distinguishes two kinds of madness: the first is the philosophical madness of love that remembers the being of sensible things as they are, the second is madness as a disease, which clings to the sensuous world of desires. Heidegger displaces this opposition by claiming that madness belongs to the sensuous world, and yet at the same time remains away from it. This strategy, therefore, interprets madness as "neither, nor" in terms of the Platonist structure. Heidegger once again appeals to the old high German root of *Wahnsinn*. The word *"wana"* means "without." Hence, the mad one senses, and senses like no one else. The word "to sense" *(Sinnan)* originally means, "to travel," "to strive toward." The mad one is on the way to somewhere else. Thus, Heidegger retains an aspect of Plato's understanding of madness as detached from immediate presence. Yet, unlike Plato, Heidegger does not circumvent the absence (being-away) at the heart of human existence in terms of the presence of forms.

Heidegger does not interpret madness and death in terms of their possible access to presence. Indeed, his reading of death is even different from his analysis of being-towards-death in *Being and Time,* which could still be construed in terms of a condition of possibility. Heidegger's emphasis on the madness of the poet manifests his attempt to rethink the movement of philosophical language. His designation of *Geschlecht* has to be read from the perspective of this decomposition of the history of metaphysics. The themes of madness and death give a different accent to the text. The text is an attempt to understand the place of poetry, not as a space to be occupied, but in terms of the path that one can follow into madness and death. For Heidegger, the place is not something static, but a movement. This movement is the movement of the soul. Throughout his essay, Heidegger performs this movement by following Trakl's poems without articulating an explicit program or outcome. Therefore, the style of Heidegger's reading *(Erörterung)* and its trajectory converge with the content of Trakl's poetry. This place of convergence, this gathering, is the singularity of Trakl's poem, as well as the place of death and madness. Yet this gathering *(Versammlung)* is not a gathering as opposed to dispersion. It is not a unification of an absolute spirit. Detachment is precisely the displacement of absolution. The relationship to the withdrawal of holiness which seems to promise an "unborn earliness" is indeed the promise of madness, yet it always remains unsaid in Trakl's poem. It is not the promise of presence.

The question of finding the "proper" language to articulate negativity proves to be immature, because language is not a "tool" with which we can try to approach a "thought" that is accessible. Even though I argued throughout this chapter that Heidegger attempts to keep a Christian interpretation of Trakl's poetry at bay and to displace any type of romanticism regarding the "originary" experience of being and unconcealment, we might ask whether there is still a questioning of a *Versammlung* of "something earlier" in Heidegger's thinking. Does Heidegger's interpretation of madness still promise a presence, something that is present to thought? Does Heidegger, unlike Derrida, want to keep us until the dawn of a new thinking?[49] Does Heidegger not promise an engagement, as madness, as soon as he enters the question of language?[50] Perhaps, but what if this "repetition" of metaphysical difference was not simply yet another metaphysical gesture, what if

> the thinking of this *Frühe* to come, while advancing towards the possibility of what you think you recognize, is going towards what is quite other than what you think you recognize. It is indeed not a new content. But access to thought, the thinking access to the *possibility* of metaphysics or pneumato-spiritualist religions opens onto something quite other than what possibility makes possible.[51]

Is this enough for Derrida? In other words, does Heidegger's discourse become entangled by the difficulties of the metaphysics of presence? Does Heidegger's deconstruction ultimately betray another desire for unity, for presence? Derrida sometimes seems to suggest that this is the case, but not always. Derrida's reading of Heidegger's interpretation suggests that there is always a double gesture in Heidegger's text. Heidegger, according to Derrida, always writes with two hands. It is this ambiguity that fascinates Derrida. On the one hand, Heidegger seems to be continuing with a metaphysical promise of a presence. The dawn of a new beginning seems to suggest the promise of a yet another originary presence. On the other hand, thinking of the earlier opens onto something quite other than what possibility makes possible. Heidegger's response to this opposition, which is recognized by Derrida, will be that the thinking of difference is not simply beyond the metaphysics of presence, but other than the opposition between metaphysics and another kind of thinking.

FIVE

Foucault

The History of Madness

THE CONFRONTATION BETWEEN Hegel and Heidegger concerns the possibility of whether madness and death can be articulated as instances of negativity without being reduced to the movement of rational thinking. Hegel incorporates madness into the dialectical thinking by displacing the principle of noncontradiction as a criterion of truth. However, such a displacement exhibits the power of reason over madness, rather than the finitude of thinking. After Hegel, the relationship of madness to history and truth continues to provoke thinking. Does the overcoming of madness open up the possibility of (rational) history? And if so, is madness the condition of possibility of history? Does such a conviction preserve a privileged position for madness? Is madness, far from being "outside" the history of metaphysics, its fundamental element? And if so, does any discussion of madness not simply repeat the gesture of the metaphysics of presence in its presentation of madness? These questions that emerge through the confrontation between Hegel and Heidegger also animate a debate between Foucault and Derrida.

By the term "debate," I refer to a series of exchanges between Foucault and Derrida concerning Foucault's *Histoire de la folie*.[1] Two years after the publication of this text on March 4, 1963, Derrida, who had been Foucault's student in his course on psychology at the École Normale in the early 1950s, delivered his talk "Cogito and the History of Madness." This "critique" of *Histoire de la folie*, delivered in Foucault's presence, consists of two lines of questioning. First, Derrida questions Foucault's reading of Descartes' first Meditation in the second chapter of *Histoire de la folie*. Derrida argues that Descartes, rather than excluding madness, incorporated madness into the project of radical doubt through the figure of the evil genius. Derrida's second line of "critique" concerns Foucault's project as a whole. Derrida interprets Foucault's project as attempting to lend a voice to madness, or to articulate the silence of madness. Derrida argues that any work that claimed to be speaking "in the name" of madness would inevitably end up betraying madness by virtue of being a "work." These two lines of questioning should not be treated separately. The implication of this connection is not that Foucault's entire project would have to be dismissed if his reading of Descartes were incorrect. These lines of questioning are inextricably bound together. First, because Descartes is a figure who represents "modern philosophy." Hence, one's reading of Descartes could be a sign of how one understands modern philosophy. Second, the exclusion Foucault associates with Descartes occupies a significant position within the history of madness. Finally, in and through this debate we observe how an apparently innocent interpretation of a text can carry a host of assumptions about truth and historicity. In interpreting the debate between Foucault and Derrida, I will try to keep these two lines of Derrida's questioning together. Foucault responded to Derrida's critique nine years later in an appendix to the second edition of *Histoire de la folie*. The text, entitled "My Body, This Paper, This Fire," was mainly a response to Derrida's reading of Descartes, or more precisely to Derrida's critique of Foucault's reading of Descartes. In this text Foucault does not explicitly address Derrida's general criticisms of *Histoire de la folie*. However, since Derrida's two lines of critique were inextricably bound together we can infer significant implications from Foucault's response concerning Derrida's general critique. In what follows, therefore, I will first interpret the debate between Foucault and Derrida in light of this assumption. At one point in this debate Derrida accuses Foucault of operating with a conception of madness that has "never been submitted to a thematic scrutiny" (CHM, 41). This statement may perhaps be true of *Histoire de la folie*. However, it is ultimately an unfair statement, because Foucault thought and wrote on madness extensively early in his career. In the second part of this chapter I will concentrate on some of Foucault's early writings on literature in order to show his understanding of madness. However, Derrida's accusation is not the only reason that I emphasize Foucault's early writings on literature. I also respond to a growing tendency to praise Foucault's later writings on politics and ethics at the expense of his earlier reflections on literature, textuality, and language. I contend that Foucault's later critical writings cannot be understood without comprehending the thrust of his reflections on literature and language.

For the purposes of my work, I will discuss this debate in terms of the question of the articulation of madness. Foucault seems to share a Heideggerian conviction that madness has to be understood as a re-consideration of philosophical thinking. Heidegger's desire to articulate a non-cognitive relation to negativity in general and madness in particular is reiterated by Foucault in his discussion of a history of the "exclusion" of madness. Like

Heidegger, Foucault understands the problem of negativity to be closely related to the emergence of the discourse of subjectivity in modernity. Derrida, however, even though he does not agree with Hegel's conclusion, agrees with Hegel that the question of negativity can only be formulated from the perspective of reason. Derrida does not accept the inevitable mastery of reason over negativity as a positive aspect of reason. Yet Derrida concedes to Hegel that any notion of negativity is exhausted within the language of metaphysics. Even though I will not emphasize this coupling between Heidegger and Foucault, on the one hand, and Hegel and Derrida on the other, it may provide the starting point of our reading of the debate between Foucault and Derrida.

The debate between Foucault and Derrida concerns madness. This may seem to be an obvious statement, but it is not. The debate has been the focus of various commentaries. Even though these commentaries mention that the debate concerns madness, they do not explicitly discuss the question of madness itself. The debate is said to be about the French intellectual scene, about Hegel, about the question of mastery, and about ethics. Yet it is also about madness, in fact, it is primarily about madness. Why is this debate completely abstracted from its context? By raising these questions, I do not want to imply that all of these suggestions are wrong. In fact some of these suggestions are true and interesting. My aim is simply to designate the fate of madness as a topic within philosophical discourse. The implication is that all concerns about madness are not really, or not exclusively about madness in the final analysis. Madness stands for something else, something more profound, more "philosophical." This is the fate of madness as a philosophical topic. My aim in this chapter is to discuss what Foucault and Derrida understand by the term "madness." I will suggest that their understanding of madness betrays a common ground between them. This understanding is in line with the argument I have been developing throughout this study. Both Foucault and Derrida think the question of madness in terms of the question of death and negativity.

This is not to deny that there are important differences between the ways in which Foucault and Derrida think concerning questions of subjectivity and historicity. For Foucault, the conception of madness since the classical period has been based on the emergence of subjectivity as the locus of philosophical thinking. This, for Foucault, marks a significant configuration in history, a divergence from the Middle Ages. The modern attitude toward madness is based on an understanding of the madman as the subject behind his disease. Madness becomes localized, is said to *belong* to a person. Thereby, madness is no longer regarded as a tendency within discourse and becomes a "quality" of a person. Even when madmen are not always considered to be responsible for their actions, it is assumed that there still is—or ought to be—a subject, however troubled it may be, behind the appearance. Since Foucault's investigation concerns the experience of madness in the classical age, it presupposes the possibility of delimiting the experience of madness with respect to different epochs. Thus, for Foucault, madness as an experience does not remain the same throughout history. This is not simply to say that the definition of madness, the social norms and assumptions of what madness is, have changed over history. Foucault's claim concerns the experience of madness. Yet what do we mean by the word "experience"? Does this necessarily imply a naive appeal to a phenomenon that a subject undergoes? Or is it possible to think of madness as a more fundamental phenomenon that shapes the question of the subject?

Madness as a phenomenon underwent a transformation in modernity. Nietzsche's madness is not the same as that of Kalchas. Foucault's claim concerns how discourse *(logos)* shapes and animates the human body. Obviously, we recognize that our understanding of madness changes, as we understand more about its physical causes, its psychological determinants, and so on. Yet neurobiological considerations often presuppose that there is a relatively stable physical or chemical basis of different variations of mental illness. Even though these neurobiological explanations themselves change, it is also assumed that these explanations are relatively independent of the "actual" causes of mental diseases. The causal explanation separates our understanding of "madness" from its "causes," causes which ultimately constitute "the reality" of madness.[2] Most of such assumptions are based on the conviction that madness can be explained in terms of a causal model. This notion is put into question in the debate between Foucault and Derrida. Perhaps madness is a sign which gives us the illusion that we are speaking about the same experience. Evidently, the various experiences of "madness" discussed in this study are not unrelated. Yet these are related to each other through ruptures, breaks, and discontinuities. Foucault investigates these ruptures in *Histoire de la folie*.

The disagreement between Foucault and Derrida concerns this question of rupture in history. What is the "place" of madness as an instance of negativity with respect to philosophy? In a crucial footnote to "Cogito and the History of Madness," Derrida explains the relationship of philosophical language to negativity. Derrida recognizes that madness "stands for" negativity. However, for Derrida, one cannot write the history of this negativity as madness, because history itself is always the history of reason and of meaning. Yet if "philosophical language, as soon as it speaks, reappropriates negativity or forgets it, which is the same thing even when it allegedly affirms or recognizes negativity" (CHM, 308), then Foucault cannot restrict the exclusion of negativity to the classical period. For Derrida, this exclusion and appropriation of negativity is an economic structure rather than a historical one. At times Derrida seems to propose a silent affirmation of the negativity which is the driving force of history. As Derrida recognizes, Foucault's aim is not simply to write a history of negativity. Foucault seems to recognize the impossibility of writing a history of madness. Yet Foucault attempts to write a history of exclusion, and he thinks that the experience of this negativity undergoes a transformation. For Foucault, the negativity of madness is not experienced and excluded in the same way at all historical junctures. For Derrida, one has to "affirm negativity *in silence* to gain access to a nonclassical type of dissociation between thought and language" (CHM, 308). This affirmation, Derrida claims, may perhaps lead to a dissociation of thought and philosophy as discourse "if we are conscious of the fact that this schism cannot be enunciated, thereby erasing itself, except within philosophy" (CHM, 308). Derrida's refusal of the distinction between the classical and the Socratic *logos* parallels his conviction that negativity can only be affirmed *within* philosophy. Thus, Derrida understands madness as an instance of negativity, not as an experience, but as a "tendency" or operation of reason itself. Derrida agrees with Foucault that madness is to be understood within the self-dissension of reason. Yet this is not a historical "fact" (as Derrida repeatedly claims that it is for Foucault) for Derrida, but an essential and eternal feature of reason. Does Derrida himself inadvertently propose an invariable and historical notion of madness, even though this is what he accuses Foucault of doing? What is the nature of this tendency in reason "in general"? Derrida contends that this "in general is not to be confused with an ahistorical eternity [which is a possible interpretation of his understanding of madness], nor with an empirically determined moment of the history of facts" (CHM, 54) (as Foucault believes, according to Derrida). Is Derrida's notion of "historicity" itself, then, ahistorical? Even if Derrida is right with respect to the Socratic *logos*, namely, that it is not different from classical reason with regard to its exclusion of madness, does this mean that the experience of madness within the Socratic *logos* is the same as the experience of madness in modernity?

The debate between Foucault and Derrida reflects the fate of madness: it appears to be more and more about reason rather than madness. Yet we need to avoid reducing the question of madness to a simple oppositional structure between madness and reason. We will not approach the question of historicity in this debate in terms of the question of whether madness is excluded in the classical period with Descartes. Even if, as Derrida claims, madness *by definition* has to be radicalized (and incorporated) by reason (I think, therefore I am, even if I am mad), this does not exclude the possibility of a transformation of the meaning of madness from the Middle Ages to the classical period. The point to consider between Foucault and Derrida, then, is not whether there was an exclusion in Descartes which did not exist before him, but whether there is a shift in the experience of madness itself from the Middle Ages to the classical period.

BEFORE THE EXCLUSION OF MADNESS

The debate between Foucault and Derrida concerns the second chapter of Foucault's work, *Le grand renfermement*, where Foucault presents his reading of the First Meditation. Foucault's interpretation of this specific passage from Descartes has to be understood against the background of his first chapter, "Stultifera Navis." There are two important dimensions of the first chapter of *Histoire de la folie*: the discussion of madness in terms of the theme of death, and the nature of the transformation of madness prior to the classical period. In order to understand how Descartes modifies madness, we have to see how madness is symbolized in the Renaissance. This pre-Cartesian transformation is not the same as the exclusion Descartes is responsible for. It represents a different shift in the experience of madness. This prior transformation enables Descartes to transform the experience of madness by excluding it from the domain of reason.

Foucault starts the first chapter of *Histoire de la folie* with a discussion of leprosy: "At the end of the Middle Ages, leprosy disappeared from the Western world" (HF, 13). What, if any, is the relationship between leprosy and madness? Foucault claims later that madness replaced leprosy as an illness that exists in the margins of society. Leprosy is connected to madness in that both are instances of death. Leprosy is an illness. It leads to death. How is madness related to death? Foucault writes:

> Fear in the face of the absolute limit of death turns inward in a continuous irony; man disarms it in advance, making it an object of derision by giving it an everyday, tamed form, by constantly renewing it in the spectacle of life, by scattering it throughout the vices, the difficulties, and the absurdities of all men. Death's annihilation is no longer anything because it was already everything, because life itself was only futility, vain words, a squabble of cap and bells. The head that will become a skull is already empty. *Madness is the déjà-là of death.* . . . From the vain mask to the corpse, the same smile persists. But when the madman laughs, he already laughs with the laugh of death; the lunatic, anticipating the macabre, has disarmed it. . . . The substitution of the theme of madness for that of death does not mark a break, but rather a torsion within the same anxiety. What is in question is still the nothingness of existence; but this nothingness is no longer considered an external, final term, both threat and conclusion; it is experienced from within as the continuous and constant form of existence. . . . (HF, 26–27)[3]

Madness is the *déjà-là* of death. This is not simply a historical relationship for Foucault, at least not in the way in which we understand history as a succession of events. There is also an affinity between madness and death in the sense that they articulate one and the same experience. What is experienced in madness and death is the "nothingness of existence." However, in madness nothingness is no longer experienced as an external intervention, but from within. There occurs a "transformation" of the experience of exteriority to one of interiority. This transformation is the fundamental contribution of the Renaissance to the history of madness. The nothingness of existence (that is, a certain negativity) does not belong to an outside anymore, but is interiorized. Yet Foucault's claim is not simply that death belongs to exteriority, and madness to interiority. Both death and madness can be experienced as exteriority. Yet the substitution of the theme of madness for death is historically parallel to the experience of nothingness from within the subject. Throughout his career Foucault refers to an experience of exteriority.[4] The experience of madness that Foucault refers to as "the silence of madness," or the "archaeology of madness," is not an unchanging "pristine experience" from the past, but that which is to come beyond the interiorization of madness in the Renaissance, and beyond its exclusion from the domain of subjectivity in the classical age.[5] Therefore, when Foucault says that Descartes excludes madness, he already speaks on the basis of his discussion of the interiorization of madness. Through the Renaissance transformations, madness becomes a property of human being, and hence plays a decisive role in the constitution of subjectivity as a discourse.

Foucault articulates this interiorization through a discussion of the representation of madness in the plastic arts and literature. It is important to note, however, that it would be a reductive reading to restrict this entire chapter to the question of the "representation" of madness. Foucault's interpretation concerns the relationship between subjectivity and madness. Even though madness is associated with death in the plastic arts and in literature, a gap opens between word and image: "The unity begins to dissolve; a single and identical meaning is not immediately common to them" (HF, 28). This dissolution between figure and speech, according to Foucault, "is a barely perceptible scission, which will be the greatest cleavage (partage) in the Occidental experience of madness" (HF, 28). Foucault claims that the dawn of madness on the horizon of the Renaissance is first perceptible in the decay of gothic symbolism. The close knit network of spiritual meanings begins to unravel. The meaning of things becomes clear only in the forms of madness: "Freed from wisdom and from the teaching that organized it, the image begins to gravitate about its own madness" (HF, 29). This liberation, which derives from a proliferation of meaning, from a self-multiplication of significance, can no longer be deciphered except in the esoterism of knowledge: "Things themselves become so burdened with attributes, signs, allusions that they finally lose their own form. Meaning is no longer read in an immediate perception, the figure no longer speaks for itself; between the knowledge which animates it and the form into which it is transposed, a gap widens. It is free for the dream" (HF, 29). The gap between the word and image of madness leads to two different experiences of madness. The pictorial image of madness leads to an obliteration of its form, whereas literary, philosophical, and moral themes attribute a different form to madness. Madness assumes a different relationship to knowledge, "madness does not control the secrets of knowledge, but it becomes a punishment of a disorderly and useless science. . . .

Learning becomes madness through the very excess of false learning" (HF, 34–35). The substitution of madness for the theme of death speaks to this phenomenon. The nothingness of existence is experienced from within. Thus, the liberation of madness in the Renaissance is a reconfiguration of the relationship between madness and death. Before the Renaissance the experience of nothingness was mainly an experience of death. With the Renaissance, with the liberation of madness, the experience of nothingness is interiorized. This is a liberation of madness to the extent that it dissociates madness from an experience of exteriority. Now the theme of madness reigns not with an explicit association to the exteriority of death, but to the interiority of the human subject. The experience of interiority *is* the experience of human existence as subjectivity. The experience of madness in the Renaissance is a double phenomenon, according to Foucault: on the one hand, the experience of madness contributes to the constitution of subjectivity: on the other hand, given the constitution of subjectivity, madness itself is experienced differently by the human subject. Foucault articulates this phenomenon in the following words:

> madness is not linked to the world and its subterranean forms, but rather to man, to his weaknesses, dreams, and illusions. . . . Madness no longer lies in wait for mankind at the four corners of the earth, it insinuates itself within man, or rather it is a subtle rapport that man maintains with himself . . . only "follies" exist—human forms of madness. . . . There is no madness but that which is in every man, since it is man who constitutes madness in the attachment he bears for himself and by the illusions he entertains. . . . In this delusive attachment to himself, man generates his madness like a mirage. . . . Madness deals not so much with truth and the world, as with man and whatever truth about himself he is able to perceive. (HF, 35–36)

This anthropomorphization of madness is an interiorization: "Madness is no longer the familiar foreignness of the world; it is merely a commonplace spectacle for the foreign spectator; no longer a figure of the *cosmos*, but a characteristic of the *aevum*" (HF, 28). Madness is reduced to an interior experience, and subsequently it will be reduced to the relationship of the subject to itself. Hence, the subject of madness, as well as the object of discourses on madness, is the human subject itself. Descartes' "exclusion" of madness from thought is only possible after this interiorization of madness. "The classical experience of madness is born. . . . Madness has ceased to be—at the limits of the world, of man and death—an eschatological figure." (HF, 53)

When Foucault speaks about Descartes and the classical experience of madness, he does not simply articulate a categorical dichotomy between an authentic and inauthentic experience of madness. It is not as if Descartes single-handedly excluded madness. Foucault's notion of the classical experience of madness speaks to a historical phenomenon stretching well beyond

Descartes. Therefore, it is not fair to claim, as Derrida does, that Foucault's entire project can be pinpointed in his reading of Descartes' *Meditations*. Descartes could exclude madness because it was already interiorized, had already lost its connection to the world. Descartes could understand madness in terms of the question of truth and falsehood only because the word and the image were already dissociated, and because truth had become a correspondence between the thought in the mind of the subject and the things themselves. Madness had already become a mistake, an evil, or a flaw. Descartes realized that madness had to be excluded from philosophical reason because madness was not an excess of philosophical wisdom in the way it had been for Plato.[6] This is not to say that Plato had a more authentic understanding of madness than Descartes. It is to say, rather, that Plato did not think of madness exclusively as a property of the human being, of the human subject, because he did not think human existence in terms of a self-present subject. It is important to be aware of the preCartesian interiorization of madness in order to understand Foucault's treatment of Descartes' *Meditations*, as well as his fascination with Hölderlin, Nietzsche, Nerval, and Artaud. Foucault's relation to these madmen is not simply a nostalgic longing for an authentic experience in the past, but an anticipation concerning the implosion of subjectivity, and a new (post-subjectivist) relationship to exteriority.

In the entirety of the 637 pages of *Histoire de la folie*, Foucault devotes only three pages to a passage from Descartes's First Meditation.[7] These three pages occur at the beginning of the second chapter called "The Great Incarceration." Foucault opens this chapter with the following reference to the Renaissance: "The Madness [*folie*] whose voices were freed by the Renaissance, but whose violence had already been mastered by it, was, during the Classical Age, going to be reduced to silence by a strange act of force [*étrange coup de force*]" (HF, 56). This sentence is already a reference to what happened in the Renaissance. Descartes already operates with an interiorized experience of madness. He excludes this experience from the domain of the thinking subject, not because man cannot be mad, but because thought essentially and fundamentally cannot be mad.

In the First Meditation Descartes seems to introduce his method of doubt by way of a "dialogue" between a commonsense voice and a voice of radical doubt.[8] These voices are characterized in terms of sanity and madness. It never becomes quite clear whether a radical doubt concerning certain beliefs has an affinity with madness. The path to the Cogito will maintain a difficult relationship to the possibility of doubt and to madness. The question remains, however, to what extent this path involves an exclusion *or* radicalization (and, thereby, incorporation and appropriation) of madness.

In order to secure a certain and indubitable foundation for knowledge it is necessary to get rid of all false opinions. However, it is not necessary to show that all opinions are false. Indeed, Descartes admits that this is something that he could perhaps never manage. Therefore, if there is a reason to doubt an idea, this is enough for it to be dismissed. Yet this enterprise, too, is not possible; one cannot possibly go through all of one's opinions and check whether they are dubitable or not. Consequently, some sort of foundationalism has to be assumed beforehand so that the method of doubt can proceed. Descartes assumes this foundationalism by holding that it is enough that one attacks the foundations of one's opinions through doubt rather than going through all beliefs. This foundation is sense perception, because most beliefs are acquired either from or through the senses. Once the reliability of the senses is put into question, all beliefs stemming from them are subject to doubt. At this stage the common sense voice intervenes: Is it possible to doubt the senses altogether even if they may deceive us occasionally? Primarily,

> how could it be denied that these hands or this whole body are mine? Unless perhaps I were to liken myself to madmen, whose brains are so damaged by the persistent vapors of melancholia that they firmly maintain they are kings when they are paupers, or say they are dressed in purple when they are naked, or that their heads are made of earthenware, or that they are pumpkins, or made of glass. But since such people are insane [des fous], I would be thought equally mad [extrauagant] if I took anything from them as a model for myself.[9]

The last sentence of this paragraph, which begins "But since such people . . . ," and the beginning of the next paragraph constitute the main focus of the textual debate between Foucault and Derrida. The next paragraph starts as follows: "A brilliant piece of reasoning! as if I were not a man who sleeps at night, and regularly has all the same experiences while asleep as madmen do when awake—indeed sometimes even more improbable ones."[10] Descartes continues this paragraph with a description of the "errors" occurring in dreams and points out the difficulty of distinguishing dreams from being awake. What, then, is the character of this transition? Does Descartes radicalize the question of madness in the next paragraph on dreaming, or does he exclude the possibility of madness and carry over the discussion to a domain that is continuous with the meditating subject? Foucault thinks that the latter is the case.

In order to understand Foucault's claim, we have to make a distinction between what madmen perceive (what they believe to have perceived, in other words, the content of their perception and belief) and the "fact" that they think and perceive, that is, the act of believing. In Histoire de la folie, it may appear to be unclear whether Foucault attributes Descartes' exclusion of madness to the content of beliefs or to the madman's act of believing. Does Descartes say that what madmen think is so outrageous that I (or we) cannot possibly believe it, or does he say that the problem with madmen is not that they believe this or that, but that they believe it in such a way that they would not even be able to doubt their beliefs as a rational person would? Madmen are so present to that to which they are exposed that they cannot even step back and doubt the content of what they perceive. In his response to Derrida, Foucault makes it clear that he means the latter "type" of exclusion: ". . . in madness *I believe* that an illusory purple covers my nudity and my poverty . . . the madman believes falsely that his body is made of glass, but does not consider himself as believing it falsely."[11] The problem with madness is not that it makes us believe strange things, but that it does not allow for the possibility of doubting them. Hence, madness is the perversion, the other of thought, not in the sense of outrageous contents of thought, but of the absence of thought in general. If madness were not excluded, Descartes could not have continued with the *Meditations*. Not to exclude madness would result in the *aporia* of thought, the absence of thought, such that one could not even move toward the Cogito. This interpretation seems to be supported by the fact that the possibility of "cogito ergo sum" is based upon the actuality of thought. I have to doubt, and thereby I have to think. If madness makes me not doubt, it also makes me not think, and thus unable to intuit "I think, therefore I am." However, how can one say that madmen do not think? Is this what Descartes says? This reading seems to be weakened by what Descartes says in the synopsis of the following six meditations: "The great benefit of these arguments is not, in my view, that they prove what they establish— namely that there really is a world, and that human beings have bodies and so on—*since no sane person has ever seriously doubted these things.*"[12] This statement may suggest that Descartes seems to associate doubt with insanity. Therefore, the claim that the madman does not doubt may be regarded to be false. Indeed, there seems to be a sense in which it is mad to doubt these things. So what does the rational human being do? Does he or she pretend to doubt, or is he or she really madder than madness (as Derrida seems to suggest)? Yet Descartes' statement does not necessarily diminish the force of Foucault's reading of an exclusion. It would only seem insane for a rational person to doubt all these perceptual beliefs, but a madman would not be able to sustain this doubt in such a way that he would reach an absolute certainty.

In *Histoire de la folie*, Foucault claims that there is a fundamental disequilibrium between Descartes' treatment of madness on the one hand, and dreams and error on the other. Descartes does not treat madness in the way he deals with dreams and errors. While refusing to compare himself to madmen who believe uncritically whatever is presented to their perception, Descartes still presents the example of dreams in which he finds a legitimate ground for doubt. Yet even if we admit that our eyes deceive us, or if we assume that we are asleep, "the truth will not slip entirely into the night." Yet the same is not true for madness. Foucault makes it clear that the truth here does not concern the content of the thought of madman: "if [the] dangers [of madness] do not compromise the process, nor the essence of its truth, it is not because some thing, even in the thought of a madman, cannot be false; it is because I, the one who is thinking, cannot be mad" (HF, 56). Foucault continues:

> It is not the permanence of a truth that guarantees thought against madness, as it did when it allowed thought to lose its attachment to an error or to emerge from a dream; it is the impossibility of being mad, which is essential not to the object of thought but to the subject who thinks. . . . One cannot . . . suppose even in thought that one is mad, for madness is precisely the condition of the impossibility of thought. (HF, 57)

For Foucault, Descartes excludes madness not from the object of thought, but from the subject who thinks. Hence, the disequilibrium between madness, on the one hand, and errors and dreams, on the other, concerns the possibility of *the continuity of meditation.*

Foucault claims that with Descartes madness is excluded from the domain of reason: "Madness can no longer concern Descartes. It would be an insanity to suppose that one is insane: as an experience of thought, madness implies itself, and is henceforth excluded from the project" (HF, 58). With Descartes, reason attains a full self-possession in a way that was not possible in the sixteenth century:

> *The path of Cartesian doubt* seems to testify to the fact that in the 17th century the danger is conjured away and madness is placed outside the proper domain where the subject retains its right to truth. This domain for Classical thought is reason itself. Henceforth madness is exiled. If man can always be mad, thought, as the exercise of the sovereignty of a subject whose duty is to perceive the true, cannot be insane. (HF, 58)

There are two series of questions concerning Foucault's reading of Descartes. First, does Foucault give a definition of madness by claiming that madness is the impossibility of thought? Does he mean that madman cannot think? Is the Cogito impossible to reach if one is mad? Clearly, Foucault does not present a definition of madness to the extent that definition always presupposes the possibility of thought. He does not claim that the madman does not think. Indeed, it is quite possible that madmen are thinkers. One cannot object to Foucault by claiming that madmen usually know that they are mad, that self-consciousness is a prerequisite of madness, because this experience of madness is quite recent, and presupposes a certain conception of mental illness. Foucault's claim *concerns the continuity of thought,* the possibility of a subject meditating, remaining the substrate of meditation, not only having control over the discourse, but also being present to itself. Thought is a process, and Descartes thinks that it is possible for the subject to be present throughout this process; in fact the subject *is* this self-presence. It is true that Foucault will challenge the possibility of this self-presence, but this does not preclude the fact that Descartes does believe in the possibility of self-presence. Even if a madman can say "I think, I am" he cannot be self-present throughout the process of meditation, because he is excessively present to the presence of appearances of things around him to the extent that he does not even doubt that he is not a king, that his head is not made of glass.

The second set of questions concerns the relationship of Descartes' exclusion to the preCartesian interiorization (and liberation) of madness. Foucault makes it clear that Descartes' exclusion of madness is possible only on the basis of a madness that threatens thought from within. One can exclude madness only if it is a phenomenon belonging to man, rather than the exteriority of thought. The discourse of subjectivity can exclude madness if it is said to be a possibility for a subject. The subject that can be mad is inevitably an empirical self that can be excluded from the domain of pure thought. Therefore, Foucault's argument regarding Descartes cannot simply be reduced to an "either/or": either Foucault is right and Descartes excludes madness, or Foucault is wrong, Descartes does not exclude madness. Perhaps the crucial point about Foucault's reading of Descartes does not lie in the question of exclusion, but in the transformation of the experience of madness.

THE CONFRONTATION BETWEEN DERRIDA AND FOUCAULT: "COGITO AND THE HISTORY OF MADNESS"

Derrida's reading of Foucault's *Histoire de la folie* is multilayered. He starts his interpretation with an epigraph from Kierkegaard: "The Instant of Decision is Madness." The epigraph shows why Derrida thinks that he will be right from the start: Descartes could not have excluded madness by a decision, precisely because the instant of decision is madness. Yet Foucault would not have disagreed with Kierkegaard. Many commentators have noted that Derrida's allusions to a master-disciple relationship at the beginning of his essay reflect the relationship between him and Foucault, and this seems to be true. Yet the next question concerns the nature of this relationship. The allusion to a master also invokes another master, a master who is going to delimit the heart of the debate. That master is Hegel, whom Derrida invokes at a crucial juncture of his essay. Derrida suspects that the crucial absence of Hegel in *Histoire de la folie* betrays the ultimate problematic of the text. Foucault almost naively seems to forget that "the revolution against reason can be made only within it, in accordance with a Hegelian law" (CHM, 36).[13] Derrida states that he was very sensitive to this law in Foucault's book "despite the absence of any precise reference to Hegel" (CHM, 36). Obviously there could not be explicit references to Hegel, because then Foucault would have realized that

> since the revolution against reason, from the moment it is articulated, can operate only within reason, it always has the limited scope of what is called,

precisely in the language of a department of internal affairs, a disturbance. . . . A history, that is, an archaeology against reason doubtless cannot be written, for, despite all appearances to the contrary, the concept of
history has always been a rational one (CHM, 36).

It is not exactly clear whether Derrida accuses Foucault of forgetting this
Hegelian law, or of remembering it too well (perhaps they will be the same
thing). Foucault himself acknowledges the impossibility of writing a history
of madness itself. As Derrida quotes Foucault in "Cogito and the History of
Madness": "The perception that seeks to grasp them [in question are the mis-
eries and murmurings of madness] in their wild state necessarily belongs to a
world that has already captured them. The liberty of madness can be understood only from high in the fortress that holds madness prisoner" (CHM, 37).
This passage which Derrida quotes from Foucault comes after Foucault
declares that writing a history of madness is an impossible task: "But no doubt
that is a doubly impossible task."[14] Foucault continues:

> To do the history of madness will therefore mean: to make a structural study of
> the historical ensemble—notions, institutions, juridical and police mea-
> sures, scientific concepts—which hold captive a madness whose wild state
> can never in itself be restored; but, short of this inaccessible primitive purity,
> structural study must ascend back to the decision which at once joins and
> separates reason and madness; it must strive to discover perpetual exchange,
> the obscure common root, the originary affrontment which gives meaning
> to the unity as much as to the opposition of sense and the senseless.[15]

However, the most important qualification comes later, when Foucault states
that the decision is to be investigated as "heterogeneous to the time of history,
but ungraspable outside of it" (my emphasis). The relationship between the
decision to exclude madness and history is the key to thinking the difference
between Foucault and Derrida. If the decision of madness is that which opens
the possibility of (rational) history, it cannot be situated historically. We will
come back to this question. At this stage, it is clear that Foucault is aware of
the problem of writing a history of madness, and Derrida's critique is not
restricted to this question. Why does Foucault attempt to write the history of
madness? Is this attempt based on "our desire to measure our strength against
the greatest possible proximity to madness" (CHM, 55)?

After his appeal to Hegel and mastery, Derrida divides his remarks into
two areas. As we already discussed, the first one concerns Foucault's reading
of Descartes' Meditations. Derrida raises several questions regarding the justi-
fication of this reading. The second set of questions concerns Foucault's project as a whole, the possibility and feasibility of writing a history of madness.
However, as Derrida himself admits, these two areas are not unrelated: "the
sense of Foucault's entire project can be pinpointed in these few allusive and

somewhat enigmatic pages" (CHM, 32), namely, the pages where his reading of Descartes is presented. Consequently, even though Foucault does not address Derrida's general concern in his response, his answers concerning his reading of Descartes make interesting allusions to the general concerns of the debate in his response to Derrida.

Derrida starts his remarks with a "commentary" on Foucault's project by describing the aim of *Histoire de la folie*. "In writing a history of madness, Foucault has attempted—and this is the greatest merit, but also the very infeasibility of his book—to write a history of madness itself. Itself. Of madness itself. That is, by letting madness speak for itself" (CHM, 33). Therefore, madness is the subject of Foucault's book in every sense of the word. Both the theme and the narrator or author are madness, madness speaking about itself. Foucault did not plan to write on madness. His project, in his words, is "a history not of psychiatry but of madness itself, in its most vibrant state, before being captured by knowledge" (CHM, 34). Therefore, Foucault wants to avoid the objectivist naiveté that would write a history of untamed madness from within the language of classical reason. Derrida claims that Foucault's constant attempt to avoid this objectivist trap is "admirable," yet also "the *maddest* aspect of his project" (CHM, 34). What does Derrida mean by "the maddest aspect" of Foucault's project? What is the force of the word "maddest" in the superlative *(le plus fou)*, as Derrida states after reassuring us that he is not being playful? Does "maddest" refer to something that he could never have done, but tried to do in vain? How does Foucault execute this "maddest" aspect of his project? Yet Derrida's critique is not simply that Foucault is naively trying to write a history of madness *itself*.

Sometimes Foucault seems to reject the language of reason, claiming that he tried to write an archaeology of silence, whereby madness is tied to "words without language" or "without the voice of a subject." The history of madness, therefore, is the archaeology of a silence. Yet Derrida is very skeptical as to whether a history of silence is possible. Does not archaeology share the same fate as other languages? Is it not an organized language, an order, a project repeating the act perpetrated against madness? Derrida thinks that it is insufficient and unfair to reduce the exclusion and silencing of madness to psychiatry, because if there is a responsibility for imprisoning and exiling madness, it does not exclusively belong to the language of psychiatry, but concerns all languages. Thus, it is not enough to avoid the language of psychiatry; rather one has to refuse all Western European language in general:

> All our European language, the language of everything that has participated, from near or far, in the adventure of Western reason. . . . Nothing within this language and no one among those who speak it, can escape the historical guilt—if there is one, and if it is historical in a classical sense—

which Foucault apparently wishes to put on trial. But such a trial may be impossible, for by the simple fact of their articulation the proceedings and the verdict unceasingly reiterate the crime. (CHM, 35)

Derrida, therefore, is suspicious about whether Foucault himself can avoid speaking within order, using the tools of the very order that he must put into question. The implications of Derrida's claim are quite far reaching. The fate of madness is that it will be inevitably betrayed. Madness is bound to remain the madness of reason, that is, already incorporated into reason, into language. Does this mean that there is only madness in and through such language (or *logos*), and if so does this mean that madness can be reduced to such language? The crucial point of the debate between Foucault and Derrida seems to lie in this question. Foucault realizes the importance of this question when he states in "My Body, This Paper, This Fire": "The stakes of the debate are clearly indicated: could there be anything anterior or exterior to philosophical discourse?"[16] Foucault intimates that there is a strong Hegelian conviction in Derrida's objection to Foucault's project. In fact, this is the context in which Derrida invokes Hegel's insight against Foucault. Total disengagement from the totality of the historical language responsible for the exile of madness is possible for Derrida, and in not just one but two ways: "Either do not mention a certain silence, or follow the madman down the road of his exile" (CHM, 36). In a sense, both of these alternatives seem to amount to the same thing. Do not mention a certain silence, be silent about the silence of the silent, and remain silent as the truly mad one does. Consequently, follow the mad down the road of their silence. What does following the mad down the road of their exile mean? Does Derrida suggest that there is only one way of escaping from the totality of historical language, by going mad? Does he accuse Foucault of not following the madman when he states that

> [t]he misfortune of the mad, the interminable misfortune of their silence, is that their best spokesmen are those who betray them best; which is to say that when one attempts to convey their silence itself, one has already passed over to the side of the enemy, the side of order, even if one fights against order from within, putting its origin into question? (CHM, 36)

Does Foucault betray the madman? What is there to be betrayed, according to Derrida, if "madness" is a concept *of* reason. How can Derrida suggest that there is a road to be followed, if there is no madness *itself*? Derrida takes this inevitable betrayal quite seriously. Foucault's fidelity (as the best spokesman) would inevitably be a betrayal. There would be no betrayal without this desire to be a spokesperson, but only indifference. Hence, there cannot be two ways of escaping the totality of the language that exiled madness. One has to mention silence and one cannot follow the mad because the mad are exiled to nowhere. They are at the margins of language. Perhaps the mad are "within" language, as Derrida insists, but this "within" has the potential of opening this language to its margins. Derrida claims that Foucault's archaeology, as an attempt at revolution, can only be made within reason. By invoking Hegel, Derrida intimates that Foucault's project ultimately remains within reason. A revolution against reason is always an internal affair. One cannot speak against reason except by being in it. A history of madness is impossible, because history has always been rational. Derrida's argument seems to be that Foucault's project of articulating the voice of madness as the other of reason is an act of reason that perfects itself by appropriating the other. Thus, Foucault does seem to appreciate a Hegelian law, namely, that the other is always the other *of* reason, or *of* the same.

The issue here requires us not to take sides within this dichotomy, because any side taken transforms into its opposite. By invoking his relationship to Foucault in terms of the master-disciple relationship at the beginning of his essay, Derrida does not speak of an empirical relationship to Foucault. The question of Derrida's relationship to Foucault and of his reading of and objections to Foucault's project is immediately transformed when Derrida invokes Hegel. If, as Derrida claims, Foucault remains within the very language of reason that he criticizes, if Foucault inevitably, despite his "mad" efforts, remains within the oppression of reason, what is Derrida's perception of his own discourse "against" Foucault? Can Derrida, then, represent the "outside" better than Foucault does? Derrida knows everything he states "against" Foucault can be said against himself, and that he may end up being the one who betrays madness by being "closer" to it than Foucault. Derrida's opening remarks on Hegel also speak to his own predicament as a disciple. What does it mean to say that Derrida is a disciple? Is he an infant, who by definition cannot speak, and thus, in the words of Foucault, the "madman"? Is Derrida expressing a desire that he himself criticizes, namely, the desire to be strong through a proximity to madness? Derrida is aware of this possibility, not subsequent to his essay, but always already, from the beginning, even before beginning to deliver his lecture.[17] Thus, my aim here is not at all to criticize Derrida. In fact, I believe this recoil is at the heart of Derrida's reading of Foucault. And I believe this recoil constitutes the heart of Derrida's and Foucault's understanding of madness. This recoil makes a "theory" or even a "position" on madness impossible from the start. Both Foucault and Derrida are aware of this impossibility.

Derrida recognizes that Foucault is aware of the problem of a language "about" madness. There are two issues to be distinguished here: First, Foucault seems to appeal to a more profound notion of reason, as Derrida will mention in his discussion of the Greek *logos*. Second, Derrida acknowledges that Foucault may be speaking of something within reason that escapes the content of reason. In Foucault's admission of the difficulty of speaking about madness, that is, that it inevitably gets articulated in terms of the language of

reason, Derrida discerns another project, a more ambitious one than archaeology. The resolution of the difficulty of speaking of madness only in terms of
the language of reason and of thereby betraying madness at the times when
one is closest to it, according to Derrida, is *"practiced* rather than *formulated"*
(CHM, 37). Why does Derrida say that this is another project? Derrida does
reduce Foucault's book to a single project.[18] There are several projects in Foucault's book. In Foucault's book "the silence of madness is not *said*, cannot be
said in the *logos* of this book, but is indirectly, metaphorically,[19] made present
by its *pathos*—taking this word in its best sense" (CHM, 37). This is a new
and radical praise, whose intentions cannot be admitted because the praise
(*éloge*) of silence always takes place within *logos* (CHM, 37). The distinction
Derrida appeals to here does not concern the form and content of Foucault's
language. The *pathos* of Foucault's book does not lie in its form, but in the
performance of a certain silence. What is this *pathos*? Is it simply a declara-
tion of the difficulty, stating the difficulty of stating without surmounting it?
Foucault's *pathos* leaves a number of philosophical and methodological problems unanswered, according to Derrida. Derrida asks "who enunciates the
possibility of nonrecourse, who wrote and who is to understand the history of
madness" (CHM, 38)? Thereby, Derrida suggests that Foucault's project itself
participates in a historical transformation of madness and reduction of it to
nonreason. Derrida admits that Foucault is sensitive to the historical situatedness of his own project. Yet one can ask whether this situatedness can ever
be fully apparent to the author. Foucault would be the first to admit that his
own discourse obeys rules that he cannot appropriate. However, there is still
a difference between a discourse that is sensitive to its own limitations, and
one that ignores these limitations and regards itself as a purely descriptive discourse. Perhaps this is the unsaid silent pathos of Foucault's discourse that
Derrida does not acknowledge enough. What would be the status of a discourse that neatly addresses its philosophical and methodological difficulties?
Is this what Derrida demands from Foucault? And if he does demand such a
transparency from Foucault with respect to Foucault's own discourse, does not
Derrida himself require precisely what he criticizes Foucault for, a complete
self-possession of the discourse?

  Derrida claims to have recognized a different project behind archaeology.
He insists that this project is *different*, because it does not appeal to an original muteness, but tries to reach the point at which the dialogue between reason and madness breaks off. Foucault calls this act of separation between reason and madness a decision through a single act, a dissension, and a
self-dividing action. There is therefore a unity between reason and madness,
according to Foucault, a common *logos* of all dissension, an archaic notion of
reason that is "prior" to the classical age. Derrida interprets this split as an
internal dissension, an interior that delimits its own exterior, just as reason
always delimits madness. Derrida claims that the historical grounds of this

decision remain in the shadow for the following reasons: First of all, in *Histoire de la folie*, Foucault appeals to a Greek *logos* which, Foucault claims, had no contrary; indeed, it had a nonoppositional relation to a kind of madness, namely, *hybris*. Yet Foucault, at the same time, claims that Socratic discourse was reassuring. Derrida finds these claims to be incompatible, as the capacity to be reassuring presupposes the expulsion, exclusion, and, at the same time, the assimilation and mastery of its opposite. Hence, Derrida finds this appeal to the Greeks' relationship to madness unacceptable, since what allegedly happens in the classical age is already at work in the Greek *logos*. Derrida, therefore, concludes: "The attempt to write the history of the decision, division, difference runs the risk of construing the division as an event or a structure subsequent to the unity of an original presence, thereby confirming metaphysics in its fundamental operation" (CHM, 40). Does this statement imply that Foucault appeals to an original presence? What would it mean to avoid confirming metaphysics, according to Derrida? Is avoiding metaphysics a matter of decision? Can one intentionally avoid metaphysics? How is one supposed to avoid this "confirmation"? By claiming that there is no decision? Is not Derrida's entire essay subject to the same risk? Does he not, at the times when he is polemical, reduce Foucault's entire project to a definable intention? Does he not circumvent Foucault's project in the very same fashion that Foucault allegedly circumvents madness? Once again, I believe that Derrida is indeed aware of the possibility of recoil. He knows that his discourse is haunted by the very same possibility of confirming metaphysics that he attributes to Foucault's discourse.

Perhaps the most troubling questions Derrida poses to Foucault concern Foucault's appeal to the Greek notion of *hybris*. Derrida asks: "in the name of what invariable meaning of 'madness' does Foucault associate, whatever the meaning of this association, madness and *hybris*? . . . [I]f madness has an invariable meaning, what is the relation of this meaning to the *a posteriori* events which govern Foucault's analysis?" (CHM, 41). These questions are troubling not only for Foucault's project, but also for Derrida's reading of it. Derrida does not simply raise these questions, but goes further in pointing out the troubling aspects of Foucault's use of the concept of madness. The concept of madness, according to Derrida, is never submitted to a thematic scrutiny by Foucault. Foucault simply rejects the psychiatric material that has always mastered madness, but thereby appeals to a popular and equivocal notion of madness taken from an unverifiable source. Derrida claims that everything transpires as if Foucault knew what "madness" meant. These questions seem to be quite destructive for Foucault's project. Yet what do they really demand? What does it mean to accuse Foucault (if this is indeed an accusation) of not having a rigorous concept of madness? Is madness reducible to a concept? Does Foucault ever appeal to an invariable meaning of madness? What would it mean to practice thematic scrutiny, to verify one's source? Does Derrida demand from Foucault precisely that which he had claimed to be impossible? Finally, in the name of what mastery, what authority, does Derrida criticize Foucault for either having or not having a unequivocal notion of madness? Derrida claims that the concept of madness as intended by Foucault "overlaps [with] everything that can be put under the rubric of negativity" (CHM, 41). Evidently, this is a problem for Derrida, as negativity is *the* philosophical notion under a Hegelian law. Derrida contends, "one can imagine the kind of problems posed by such a usage of the notion of madness" (CHM, 41). Yet can one also imagine the kind of problems posed by *not* using the notion of madness in this way? Are the latter perhaps the problems of deconstruction?

Let us leave these questions as questions and move to Derrida's reading of Foucault's argument that the exclusion of madness is necessary for historicity. If, as Foucault seems to suggest, the decision *of* reason through which it constitutes itself by excluding and objectifying madness is the condition of historicity itself, then this exclusion could not have been born with classical reason. For Derrida, classical reason is not an example as a model, but simply an example as a sample. Hence, Descartes' discourse has no exemplarity in the sense of executing an exclusion that had not existed before. Derrida believes that Descartes' exclusion is part of a structure of a sign of appropriation. It reiterates an act of appropriation of madness. Like every sign, it has the structure of iterability; it reiterates an act in its difference. Yet what is this act? According to Derrida, it is not an "act of force," as Foucault claims, if an act of force is understood as a specific act of a singular subject. For Derrida, Descartes' act does not have a singularity and specificity as opposed to iterability; rather, Descartes' act reiterates a more general structure.[20] That is to say, Derrida reads Descartes' text in such a way that it does not show a sign of exclusion, but rather an incorporation and appropriation of madness.

These questions take us to the disagreement concerning textuality between Foucault and Derrida. The relationship between Derrida's general arguments concerning Foucault's project, and his specific reading of Descartes' *Meditations* is difficult to assess, because it involves questions concerning the textuality of the text. Is Descartes' text caught in a historical and sociopolitical drama, or does it have an independence which cannot be reduced to anything beyond the text? Foucault does not simply assert that the text is to be understood in terms of "something" beyond it. On the other hand, Derrida does not think that every text controls itself in such a way that there is no need to go beyond it. Both of these "positions" are far too simplistic to give insight into what is to be thought in terms of the textuality of the text. In fact, the heart of the debate between Foucault and Derrida seems to lie in this question of a text (a work) and what is exterior to it. Both Foucault and Derrida would admit that there is a dimension in the "happening" of a text that cannot be captured by the content of the text. A text can be attentive to the negativity that makes it possible (as well as impossible as a complete self-possessed articulation of a thought, of a content). Derrida's philosophical career *is* in fact an example of attentiveness to the being of the text. However, to assert that all that counts for Derrida is the text is premature and tells us nothing. Derrida does indeed believe that we cannot understand the relation of a text to exteriority as a relationship between two independent and present-at-hand entities. Hence, a text is not simply a thing that articulates something outside itself, be this a thought, an object, or its own negativity. Foucault, on the other hand, tries to understand this relationship of a text to an exteriority in terms of a madness that nevertheless cannot be captured within the text. Both Foucault and Derrida acknowledge the strange being of the text; for both of them this question of textuality concerns the question of madness, and for both the question of madness concerns the question of margins, margins of reason, of the text, and of philosophical discourse.

Obviously Foucault and Derrida do not state the same thing. Instead of delineating the differences and similarities between these two thinkers, we need to think what is at the margin of "their" discourses. If madness does indeed stand for a negativity, we should ask the question as to whether this negativity can only be thought as a "capital of reason." Is it possible to affirm and think this negativity without allowing it to be reappropriated by positivity, by reason? In other words, is it possible to think that which is not independent of the philosophical *logos*, yet also not reducible to it? What would the desire to think that which can never be appropriated by reason involve? Is the desire to think this negativity a self-destructive desire, in a double sense? First, the possibility of being thought is also negativity's possibility of being appropriated by reason and language. Secondly, why would one try to undermine reason? Would this attempt not ultimately be a self-destructive attempt? Would it not be a "pure" resistance without recourse? Perhaps madness signifies this self-destructive desire. But this resistance cannot be by design. Resistance happens when design is given up, when one resists one's own discourse, when one refuses to appropriate one's discourse there where the work ends. Here we can observe the radical nature of the notion of "the absence of the work" in these questions. We will return to such questions in a moment. Our immediate question concerns Derrida's reading of Descartes and whether it presupposes a certain mastery by Descartes of his own discourse.

What is the relationship of Descartes' text to what happens in the classical age? Derrida states that Descartes does not exclude the possibility of madness, but carries this possibility of madness over to dreams and errors. For Derrida, madness as a possibility of error is not a strong case that does justice to the radical nature of doubt. Descartes, according to Derrida, speaks with a second voice, the voice of a nonphilosopher, when he compares his doubts with the errors of madmen. It is difficult to understand the nature of this comparison. Why does Descartes compare his situation with that of madmen? They are not at all similar to him. Madmen believe various kinds of outrageous and "false" perceptions, whereas the "I" refuses to believe even the most straightforward and immediate perceptions. The problem with madmen, according to Derrida's reading, is not that they are wrong, but that they are not "wrong often enough" (CHM, 51). Therefore, according to Derrida, Descartes leaves the paragraph on madness not with exclusion, but with a temporary postponement, only to take it up in a radical way in the case of dreams, and especially in the case of the evil genius. In fact, it is not appropriate to discuss the possibility of madness at the naive, natural and premetaphysical stage. This stage is the stage of natural doubt before Descartes introduces the possibility of the evil genius. With the evil genius, the possibility of madness comes from the outside, is inflicted upon the subject; it is total derangement that brings subversion to pure thought. In fact, the power of Descartes' discourse, according to Derrida, comes from its proximity to madness. Reason is closer to madness than the madman himself. Madmen are not mad enough, because they are not wrong enough, but reason is madder than the madman, because it can envision total derangement. Derrida's reading of Descartes tries to show that Descartes' reference to madness is an example, not a model. Descartes does not exclude madness, but rather appropriates madness in such a way that reason is seen to be more powerful than madness, even in being mad. Descartes' strategy, according to Derrida, is yet another example of the iterable structure of the metaphysics of presence. This structure does not simply work by excluding the other, but appropriates its other by being "more other" than its other. Therefore, madness is fundamentally a concept of reason, the product of reason. Hence, reason defines the intelligibility of its own violence and destruction. Thus, we come back to the Hegelian law: the subversion of reason is only possible within reason. It is not simply that Foucault's project of madness is problematic, but that the powers of reason are far reaching. Negativity is both a product of reason and metaphysics and their main capital. The strategy of metaphysics is the "production" as well as the appropriation of its other. When one tries to be maddest, one is most rational. Hence, Derrida thinks that Foucault not only forgets Hegel (Hegelian law), but is himself too Hegelian (precisely because he forgets Hegel). Therefore, Derrida associates Foucault's project with that of Descartes:

> . . . any philosopher or speaking subject (and the philosopher is but the speaking subject par excellence) who must evoke madness from the *interior* of thought . . . can do so only in the realm of the *possible* and in the language of fiction or the fiction of language. Thereby through his own language, he reassures himself against any actual madness—which may sometimes appear quite talkative, another problem—and can keep his distance, the distance

for continuing to speak and to live. But this is not weakness or a search for security proper to a given historical language (for example, the search for certainty in the Cartesian style), but is rather inherent in the essence and very project of all language in general; and even in the language of those who are apparently maddest; and even and above all in the language of those who, by their praise of madness, by their complicity with it, measure their own strength against the greatest possible proximity to madness. Language being the break with madness, it adheres more thoroughly to its essence and vocation, makes a cleaner break with madness, if it pits itself against madness more freely and gets closer to it; to the point of being separated from it only by the "transparent sheet" of which Joyce speaks. . . . In this sense I would be tempted to consider Foucault's book a powerful gesture of protection and internment. A Cartesian gesture for the twentieth century. A reappropriation of negativity. To all appearances, it is reason that he interns, but, like Descartes, he chooses the reason of yesterday as his target and not the possibility of meaning in general. (CHM, 54–55)

The difficulty in interpreting Foucault's and Derrida's readings of Descartes is the question of the situatedness of Descartes. Derrida seems to regard Descartes as a particular occurrence of a sign, repeating (in its difference) the gesture of all language (reason) in general. Descartes is the father of modern subjectivity. Is it possible, then, to regard every philosopher as a "speaking subject," not simply "le sujet parlant," but "le sujet parlant par excellence"? Is Descartes' project the same as that of Plato even in this regard? How is it possible that Foucault and Derrida can have such a disagreement on Descartes, the French philosopher par excellence? With regard to the above passage, one may ask what Derrida means when he says "actual madness." Actual? Actual as opposed to feigned? In which case, the power of those who praise madness would come not from an actual madness, but from an appearance of madness? Does this imply that there is a deep (real) structure of madness? Are we to assume that Descartes has full possession of his own discourse? We have to acknowledge that the discourse may escape Descartes' own intentions. Does Derrida not derive his own power by attributing to Descartes an enormous control over his (Descartes') own discourse? Does Descartes come closer to madness than Foucault does? In the name of what "unchanging conception of madness" does Derrida ascertain the proximity of Descartes' and Foucault's discourses? Does Foucault indeed appropriate negativity as madness in the same general way that every Western European language inevitably does? What is the force of Derrida's attribution of an "in general" appropriation of madness to every discourse? Derrida insists that "in general" is the dimension of historicity: "within the dimension of historicity in general, which is to be confused neither with some ahistorical eternity, nor with an empirically determined moment of the history of facts . . ." (CHM, 54). Descartes' discourse is to be read in terms of this "general appropriation of negativity." If this is the case, does this mean that it is impossible to write on madness? Or is it simply Foucault's writing that has to be dismissed? If Foucault did not find a way to write about madness, even though it is still possible to write madness, then the meaning of writing, rather than madness (or alongside madness) has to be rethought. Madness is the other "produced" by reason itself. Hence, there is an ultimate inevitability of reason. Reason may be violent, but it is impossible to overcome it. What is the implication of this Hegelian law for Foucault's project? Is Foucault ultimately deriving his authority, his masterhood, from his own proximity to madness? Is this an appropriation of the power of the victim? Finally, if for Derrida, to make madness speak is impossible, what is the problem? The problem is that Derrida himself writes "about" madness. Perhaps this is a problem that emerges at a particular point in history. Perhaps Descartes is the one who makes it possible for Derrida to regard this difficulty "in general." Perhaps before Descartes, without Descartes, this "in general" would not have been possible. What Descartes does is perhaps not to participate in this "in general," but to institute it. Descartes institutes the sovereignty of the speaking subject over his discourse. Ultimately, it is this sovereignty that allows Derrida to enunciate this "in general." However, is it not questionable for Derrida to say that this "in general" is not to be confused with "an empirically determined moment of the history of facts"? Thereby, Derrida suggests that to claim that Descartes institutes the sovereignty of the speaking subject by excluding madness is to state that this moment of exclusion is "an empirically determined moment in the history of facts." Obviously, this is not what Foucault suggests. Foucault's claim about Descartes cannot be reduced to a detection of a historical fact. Descartes is not in the past; his discourse is not finished. And this is the difficulty of reading Foucault and Derrida on Descartes. Descartes' discourse, as well as the debate between Foucault and Derrida, is not something in the past. They are not controlled, prepared, and finished by their authors.

Derrida claims that the Cogito is valid, not at the expense of madness; rather, its validity is attained and ascertained within madness itself (CHM, 55). I think, therefore I am, even if I am mad. Descartes does not exclude and circumvent madness, but appropriates it. The Cartesian Cogito is a mad audacity which "consists in the return to an original point which no longer belongs to either a *determined* reason or a *determined* unreason, no longer belongs to them as opposition or alternative. . . . Whether I am mad or not, *Cogito, sum*. Madness is, therefore, in every sense of the word, only one *case* of thought (*within* thought)" (CHM, 56). Even if this is the case, is it still possible that Descartes' project takes place within a historical configuration of thought that allows us to accept everything Derrida asserts? Derrida is aware of this problem when he says that we no longer perceive Descartes' mad audacity, unlike Descartes' contemporaries, because "we are too well assured of ourselves and too well accustomed to the framework of the Cogito, rather than a critical experience of it" (CHM, 56). Is it possible that we are accustomed to the framework of the Cogito in such a way that we read this experience not as a historical transformation that continues shaping us but as a "tendency" within language and reason "in general"? These questions are not simply meant to question Derrida's reading of Descartes, but also our reading of Derrida "in general."

Derrida's most penetrating thoughts come when he seems to be least polemical. The last part of his essay is an attempt to articulate the enigmatic structure of the "in general," and the zero point where Descartes' mad audacity ventures and establishes the Cogito in the midst of madness. For Derrida, the moment of the Cogito is outside both madness and reason. To be sure, the Cogito is a work, that is, as soon as it is assured of what it says it becomes the absence of madness. Yet Descartes' Cogito is not outside madness, but the moment of its enunciation, its temporal origin; or rather, temporal originality is hospitable to both madness and reason. The instant of the Cogito, according to Derrida, is the origin of historicity and meaning. The relationship between reason and negativity (in the form of madness or death—Derrida recognizes that they are intimately connected for Foucault, even though Derrida does not investigate this connection) is an economy, "a structure of deferral whose irreducible originality must be respected" (CHM, 62). Derrida recognizes that ultimately the Cogito *is* protected from madness, but this happens through God, the ultimate ground of presence. Derrida is referring to the moment when Descartes enunciates the Cogito, where thinking and saying are the same. Yet this moment, even after it is enunciated, is surrounded by the constant of nonexistence. Descartes introduces the question of time precisely at this point. "I think, I exist, but for how long? As long as I think, I think, I exist" (*Meditations,* 18). God sustains my existence even when I do not think. Yet why does Descartes not entertain the possibility of the "I" (displaced in every moment) being incapable of thinking at all (a complete absence of thought). Such an absence would not be a modification of presence: It is not that I think that I do not think, but it is an absence which is much more radical than that, a madness which is, as Derrida says, outside both reason and madness, an absence which does not even allow me to think that I do not think. Foucault's response to Derrida seems to concentrate precisely on this point.

Foucault, despite the sharp tone of his response, recognizes the difficulties Derrida raises with respect to his reading of Descartes. Foucault reiterates that the dissymmetry between the paragraph on madness, and that on dreams, does not consist in the fact that dreams have a residue of truth in the sense of content. The truth that does not disappear is the being of thinking, that is, the element which allows Descartes to continue with his meditation.

Here we discern a dichotomy between Foucault and Derrida similar to the one we observed between Hegel and Heidegger. Foucault, like Heidegger, understands madness as a break that concerns the continuity of thinking. Hegel and Derrida seem to interpret madness in terms of the content of beliefs (whether they are true or not). Even though Descartes' meditation is not identical to Hegel's dialectic, both manifest an "exclusion" of madness that allows their discourses to go forward. To be fair to Derrida, he does not accept a Hegelian assimilation of madness into reason. However, his critique of Foucault seems to rely on a certain affirmation of reason's operation of assimilation.

The problem with madness, according to Foucault, is not simply that it makes us believe outrageous things, but that it does not allow us to doubt these beliefs (i.e., it is the absence of doubt, the absence of thought). Foucault reconstructs the relationship between Descartes' paragraph on madness and that on dreams in terms of the question of actuality, namely the way in which the author is present to things around him. The presence of the madman to the actuality around him is radically different from the presence of the dreaming subject. Descartes, according to Foucault, can ascertain continuity between the subject of the *Meditations* and the subject of dreams, but not between the rational subject and the madman, because the rational subject *is* the doubting subject. It may appear to be mad to doubt, but in fact it is mad *not* to doubt. Derrida's claim that reason is madder than madness seems to be correct, yet this is also precisely how madness is excluded from the domain of reason. Madness is reduced to not doubting and not meditating. Madness is the absence of the actuality of thought. "But madness does not allow itself to be reduced in this way."[21] This is precisely why Derrida's invocation of the evil genius as total derangement does not work, according to Foucault, "since in madness *I believe* that an illusory purple covers my nudity and my poverty, whilst the hypothesis of the evil genius permits me *not to believe* [thus to doubt] that my body and hands exist."[22]

The debate between Foucault and Derrida cannot be decided by claiming that one or the other reads Descartes correctly. Descartes could have been doing what both Foucault and Derrida say he was doing. To the extent that we recognize the singularity of Descartes' text and resist engaging in a confrontation between a Foucauldian and Derridian way of reading, the question of what Descartes was "really" doing remains always yet to be determined. There is no Foucauldian or Derridian "way" of reading that will provide us with a theory of reading. It is true that Foucault and Derrida emphasize different aspects of Descartes' text. Hence, we can ask questions concerning what Descartes does with his text or what he was allowed to do. However, ultimately, both Foucault and Derrida agree that a text is animated by that which cannot be controlled or articulated by the author and the reader. Thus, both Foucault and Derrida are aware of the problematic relationship they have with their own texts. For us, there is no way of reading them without taking this question into account. In fact this question amounts to the question of madness, because madness is thought in terms of its relationship to writing and to art in contemporary philosophy. The textuality of the debate is figured by (and figures) the content of the debate. This folding of a text over onto itself characterizes a kind of madness.[23] Foucault describes this relationship between the content of a discourse and madness in his inaugural lecture delivered at the Collège de France, translated as "The Order of Discourse."

BEFORE THE DEBATE: FOUCAULT ON MADNESS

In "The Order of Discourse," through a reflection on his relationship to discourse, Foucault introduces his future line of work. He writes: ". . . in every society the production of discourse is at once controlled, selected, organized and redistributed according to a certain number of procedures whose role is to avert its powers and its dangers, to cope with chance events, to evade its ponderous, awesome materiality."[24] These lines introduce what is at stake in Foucault's subsequent discussion of the rules of exclusion. Foucault's aim is not simply to lay out the conditions under which the discourse is excluded and to thereby emancipate us from this oppression, but to underline the way in which we do not and cannot adequately or exhaustively experience the materiality of discourse. The purpose of the discussion of these exclusions is not to set us free from political domination, but to expose us to the invasion of discourse. That is to say: the relationship between the body and discourse has to be mediated by a series of rules, otherwise the body is exposed to danger. This danger is precisely the invasion of discourse on the body in a specific way, resulting in madness. Foucault names the opposition between reason and folly as a specific exclusion, one that is not a prohibition, but a division and a rejection. In the Middle Ages the words of the mad were not considered to be a part of the common discourse; their words were considered to be null and void. Yet their words were also believed to have strange powers, to reveal some hidden truth, predict the future, reveal what the wise were not able to perceive. In a strange way, madness was considered to be more true than the discourse of a rational person. And yet the belief that the mad person has the power to reveal a hidden truth did not mean that the content of mad speech was listened to or interpreted. Foucault notes that many of us would think that this attitude of not listening to the words of the mad is not the case anymore. We do listen to madness. Perhaps we listen too much. Madness is considered to be closer to us than we thought it was; we take notice of the words of the mad "in those tiny moments when we forget what we are talking about."[25] Foucault recognizes that there is an attentiveness to the words of the mad, yet lending an ear to madness still takes place in the context of a hiatus between listener and speaker. Foucault maintains that the fate of madness moves parallel to another system of exclusion, the division between truth and falsehood. Thereby, Foucault shares Heidegger's insight concerning the relationship between truth and madness. The division between the true and the false is a historically constituted division. Therefore, the connection between the will to truth and madness is a complex one. Foucault argues that the division between madness and rationality tended toward the will to truth, in the sense that the latter has been attempting to assimilate the former and to provide a firm foundation for the exclusion of madness. With regard to the exclusion concerning the will to truth, Foucault claims that a certain will to truth started with Plato:

> . . . with the 6th century Greek poets, true discourse—in the meaningful sense—inspiring respect and terror, to which all were obliged to submit, because it held sway over all and was pronounced by men who spoke as of right, according to ritual meted out justice and attributed to each its rightful share; it prophesied, not merely announcing what was going to occur, but contributing to its actual event, carrying men along with it and thus weaving itself into the fabric of fate. And yet, a century later, the highest truth no longer resided in what discourse *was*, not in what it *did:* it lay in what was *said.* . . . A division emerged between Hesiod and Plato, separating true discourse from false; it was a new division for, henceforth, true discourse was no longer considered precious and desirable, since it had ceased to be discourse linked to the exercise of power. And so the Sophists were routed. (10)

The fact that the exercise of power was dissociated from discourse does not mean that there was no longer any relationship between power and discourse. Power, according to Foucault, becomes associated with a certain will to truth. The locus of power, then, shifted to the *legomenon* (the content of the *logos*) rather than the being of the *logos (legein)*. How does this shift relate to the division in madness? Only on the basis of the content of the *logos* becoming the primary locus of truth could the words of the mad be excluded from "true discourse." Prior to this development, the relation of the mad to discourse was one of seeing, namely, the madman was said to have a special relation to the discourse of the gods. Although this relationship was one of punishment and destruction,[26] it was still considered to be endowed with strange powers.[27] It is important here to underline Foucault's claim: He does not argue that the mad used to tell the truth in the sense that the content of their discourse corresponded to reality. Their discourse did not refer to anything outside of itself. The mere presence of this discourse folding back onto itself constituted the being of discourse, in other words, its truth. It is a misunderstanding to claim that Foucault sees an original truth in madness, which was subsequently excluded, and that he therefore has a romantic longing for this truth in the past. Foucault's reading of madness cannot be understood in this way, precisely because his reading attempts to question our ordinary understanding of truth. Truth concerns, not the content of an utterance (even if *what is true* may concern such a content), but its very being, its way of presencing.

We can discern an affinity between Foucault and Heidegger concerning the relationship of madness to truth. Both recognize a modification of the question with the beginning of philosophical discourse. Foucault, however, seems to recognize the problematic nature of his own conviction that the Socratic *logos* had no contrary. The Socratic *logos* remains reassuring for Foucault, but thereby constitutes its contrary in this process in the figure of the Sophists. The remainder of this chapter will investigate how Foucault conceives of the relationship between madness and discourse.

How exactly does Foucault think the "folding" of discourse onto itself, the being of discourse, in terms of madness?[28] To respond to this question we have to turn to his early, so called literary writings. Before turning to this question, however, we have to underline two points: First, to demarcate a literary phase in Foucault's thinking gives the impression that Foucault, later in his thinking, did not deal with the questions raised in this earlier phase. This impression is misleading. In fact, the entire project of both archaeology and genealogy, as Foucault will later state, concerns the way in which the subject is constituted in and through a discourse. Hence, Foucault never abandoned thinking the intersection between discourse and the body. Second, Foucault's style referring to this folding of discourse, is not an "exercise of madness," but a staging of the limitation of discourse, including his own. This last point is well worth dwelling upon, because it involves questions of style, as well as of one's relationship to one's own discourse. Perhaps the question of style is nothing but one's own relationship to discourse, and perhaps madness is a question of style (rather than of content).

Toward the end of "Politics and the Study of Discourse,"[29] which is reproduced almost verbatim as the conclusion in *The Archaeology of Knowledge*, Foucault describes his own project in terms of the relationship between discourse and the human being:

> Must we think that the time of discourse is not the time of consciousness extended into the dimension of history, nor the time of history present in the form of consciousness? Must I suppose that, in my discourse, it is not my survival, which is at stake? And that by speaking I do not exorcize my death, but establish it; or rather that I suppress all interiority, and yield my utterance to an outside which is so indifferent to my life, and so *neutral*, that it knows no difference between my life and my death?
>
> I can well understand those who feel this distress. They have doubtless had difficulty enough in recognizing that their history, their economy, their social practices, the language they speak, their ancestral mythology, even the fables told them in childhood, obey rules which are not given to their consciousness; they hardly wish to be dispossessed, in addition, of this discourse in which they think, believe or imagine; they prefer to deny that discourse is a complex and differentiated practice subject to analyzable rules

and transformations, rather than be deprived of this tender, consoling certainty of being able to change, if not the world, if not life, at least their 'meaning', by the sole freshness of a word which comes only from them, and remains forever close to its source. So many things in their language have already escaped them; they do not mean to lose, in addition, *what they say*, the little fragment of discourse—speech or writing, it matters little—whose frail and uncertain existence is necessary to prolong their life in time and space. They cannot bear—and one can understand them a little—to be told: discourse is not life; its time is not yours; in it you will not reconcile yourself with death; it is quite possible that you have killed God under the weight of all that you have said; but do not think that you will make, from all that you are saying, a man that will live longer than he. In each sentence you pronounce—and very precisely in the one that you are busy writing at this moment, you who have been so intent, for so many pages, on answering a question in which you felt yourself personally concerned and who are going to sign this text with your name—in every sentence there reigns the nameless law, the blank indifference: "What matter who is speaking; someone has said: what matter who is speaking." (72)

"In each sentence you pronounce [and a hiatus]—and very precisely in the one that you are busy writing at this moment, you who have been so intent, for so many pages, on answering a question in which you felt yourself personally concerned and who are going to sign this text with your name [and a hiatus]— in every sentence there reigns the nameless law, the blank indifference: 'What matter who is speaking; someone has said: what matter who is speaking.'" In a paragraph in which Foucault is ostensibly addressing those whom he understands, he suddenly begins to talk about the very text he is writing, the text he is going to sign in a minute. This, I think, is the moment of the folding and recoil of the discourse onto itself. It puts the very place of the archaeologist into question. We cannot simply disregard this folding as a self-reflexivity, as a repossession of the discourse. It raises an important question concerning the status of discourse on discursivity. Foucault's discourse can never be regarded as a metadiscourse. Foucault would never deny that his discourse is subject to the rules, transformations, and ruptures he associates with the being of discourse. Thus, it is quite simpleminded to accuse Foucault of being subject to the difficulties associated with discourse. Especially if this accusation is followed by a discourse that attempts to forget these difficulties, attempts to be descriptive.[30] There is a difference between a discourse that is not only aware of the limitations of its own formations but also stages them, and a discourse that simply pretends to describe. Yet how does Foucault stage this folding? How does this question, for Foucault, relate to the question of madness?

These questions include two dimensions: First, they concern what Foucault tries to capture in terms of the experience of madness, in terms of the void, the thought of exteriority and the utterance as play. Second, all these notions concern, to a certain extent, the being of discourse, which, despite different historical configurations (or precisely because of these historical configurations) concerns the question of thinking.

Thus, when Foucault starts his "Madness, the Absence of Work"[31] with the words "perhaps some day we will no longer really know what madness was," he does not express a romantic longing, but the relationship of a discourse to itself. Many interpreters have recognized the fact that Foucault associates a certain conception of literature with madness.[32] Foucault is clear that madness *is* the absence of the work, which implies that works of literature do *not capture* anything like the essence of madness. The relation between the notion of work and madness is not one of representation. Foucault explains this connection in his essay "The Father's No": "The dissolution of a work in madness, this void to which poetic speech is drawn as to its self-destruction, is what authorizes the text of a language common to both."[33] This question brings us back to the connection between madness and Foucault's own work. Foucault does not overlook the problem of writing madness. Indeed, his whole "performance" questions the limits of writing and expression, and investigates madness at the very threshold of the limits of language. Let us return to *Histoire de la folie* and try to articulate the nature of this performance.

Contrary to Derrida, Foucault's entire project (if he has one, that is, if he has only one) can be pinpointed not in his reading of Descartes, but within the tension between two moments in *Histoire de la folie*. The first moment occurs in the last chapter of the book, entitled "The Anthropological Circle."[34] Foucault writes ". . . let us make no mistake here; between madness and the work of art [l'œuvre], there has been no accommodation, no more constant exchange, no communication of languages; their opposition is much more dangerous than formerly; and their competition now allows no quarter; theirs is a game of life and death" (HF, 557). Madness is the absolute break with the work of art . . ." (*l'œuvre*). It is not entirely correct to translate *l'œuvre* as "work of art," as it seems to speak to a more general conception of a work. Yet the translation is not entirely misleading, as the context suggests that Foucault is discussing the works of Nietzsche, van Gogh, and Artaud. Madness is considered to be the absence of the work, as Foucault later repeats. Yet why does Foucault almost always speak of madness in the context of an artist's work? To say that madness is the absence of the work already implies a relationship between the two, however complicated it may be. What exactly is this relationship, and why is this relationship significant in understanding Foucault's thinking?

The second moment occurs in the first chapter of *Histoire de la folie*. As we have already discussed, Foucault appeals to a distinction in the way in which madness was conceived of in plastic and literary forms of art after the second half of the fifteenth century. Even though in both paintings and texts the theme of madness substitutes for the theme of death, pictorial images from this time portray a different conception of madness, namely, a fascination with madness, whereas texts in literary and philosophical forms tame madness in the sense that they reduce the experience of madness to the form of moral satire. As we have already argued, it is on the basis of this taming, which takes the form of an interiorization of madness, that Descartes excludes madness from the domain of reason. This distinction may suggest that Foucault privileges plastic art over literature and philosophy. Yet does not any work of art dissolve in the face of madness? How is it possible to capture, or *present* madness in art if madness *is* the absence of the work? The possible conclusion that Foucault sees a privileged access to madness in plastic art is misleading. Things are much more complicated than privileging one form of art over another. There are at least three points complicating this apparent privileging: First, such a privileging would suggest that Foucault believes that there is a fundamental experience of madness which plastic art can capture or present. This reduces Foucault's interpretation of madness to a romantic longing. But Foucault's fascination with madness cannot be understood as a longing for an originary and founding experience. Moreover, Foucault speaks of a historical configuration of plastic art in the fifteenth century, which does not remain the same in modernity. Second, Foucault's references to Shakespeare and Cervantes at the end of the chapter "*Stultifera Navis*" suggest that he does not believe in a strong distinction between the plastic arts and literature in terms of their respective abilities to make madness present. Finally, "the absence of the work" is a broad category encompassing not simply literary works, but any form of work, including painting. These complications call for a different interpretation of Foucault's relationship to plastic art than that of a straightforward privileging.

Foucault does indeed see a fascination with madness in the plastic art of the fifteenth century, but he does not in any way try to recapture this. Indeed, it is in modern literature that Foucault sees a tendency toward a problematic reflexivity that he tries to articulate as madness. This relationship of a text to its own possibility is how Foucault attempts to read madness. Such a relationship is not only prevalent in the constitution of a text, but ultimately puts any experience, including the experience of madness, into question. Even though Foucault has been accused of appealing to an uncritical conception of madness, this accusation misses a fundamental dimension of Foucault's thinking. His apparent acceptance of this accusation is in fact the very performance of reflexivity that he sees staged by "mad artists." The question still remains, however, as to whether art, or the work, can in any way be said to capture an experience of madness. Foucault's response to this question is too complicated to specify immediately. In what follows, I will try to provide a sketch of this performance.

Foucault's career has been separated into various phases. It appears that today the most significant phase is taken to be the so called later ethical writings leading to the theme of care for the self.[35] This privileging of the ethical writings over Foucault's earlier work may be legitimate in terms of the philosophical questions we face today. Yet we cannot understand the thrust of Foucault's ethics of the care of the self without taking into consideration his earlier preoccupation with madness and the question of alterity. It is especially important to note that Foucault's notion of care for the self is not an attempt to constitute a different concept of the subject in order to preserve the possibility of responsibility and of agency for ethics. Ignoring the significance of Foucault's earlier writings presents special difficulties for the attempt to read Foucault as an ethicist, however qualified this notion may be. I will try to present these difficulties toward the end of this chapter.

One common point to certain paintings that Foucault discusses is a problematic self-reflexivity. The reason that this reflexivity is problematic is because these paintings do not demonstrate the grounds of their possibility, but stage the impossibility of the grounds in terms of which we interpret them. Foucault's most famous discussion of such a painting is that of Velázquez's "Las Meninas" in the first chapter of The Order of Things.[36] Las Meninas, according to Foucault, stages the limits of representation, of the principle in terms of which we try to understand and explain the painting. Foucault's discussion consists of two parts. At the end of the first section, he raises the question of whether it is possible simply to describe this painting in terms of what it represents. After all, we know all the proper names of the persons in the painting. Foucault suspends such a description because "it is in vain that we say what we see; what we see never resides in what we say" (OT, 9). Therefore, Foucault proceeds by "pretending not to know who is to be reflected in the depths of that mirror," (OT, 10) alluding to the mirror in the background of Las Meninas. Yet this question that interrupts his text will come back at the end of his discussion of Las Meninas, and illuminate the subtlety of Foucault's description.

Las Meninas makes it impossible to represent the master who is representing (the painter) and the sovereign who is being represented (the king). Foucault continues:

> Perhaps there exists, in this painting of Velázquez, the representation as it were, of Classical representation, and the definition of the space it opens up to us. And, indeed, representation undertakes to represent itself here in all its elements, with its images, the eyes to which it is offered, the faces it makes visible, the gestures that call it into being. But there, in the midst of this dispersion which it is simultaneously grouping together and spreading out before us, indicated compellingly from every side, is an essential void: the necessary disappearance of that which is its foundation—of the person

it resembles and the person in whose eyes it is only a resemblance. This very subject—which is the same—has been elided. And representation, freed finally from the relation that was impeding it, can offer itself as representation in its pure form. (OT, 16)

Does *Las Meninas represent* the being (the pure form) of representation, and thus illuminate its own ground as a painting, as a representation? It does not, because the being of representation is that which cannot be represented; it necessarily disappears, leaving only a void. In fact, the rest of *The Order of Things* is an interpretation of this disappearance. What disappears, what is erased, is "man," the subject of the modern *episteme*. Foucault's reading of *Las Meninas* aims to demonstrate how this painting operates differently than the modern *episteme*, which grounds its own possibility. What grounds the modern *episteme* and representation necessarily disappears in Velázquez's painting: namely, the subject. The problem of representation relates to the question of the subject: the subject who thinks (i.e., who represents), not only represents the objects, but also represents itself to itself, and thereby grounds the modern *episteme*. For Foucault, the being of thinking (representing), however, cannot be thought (represented). Thinking cannot be reduced to what is thought. There is a void between thinking as an activity and what is thought, a void that cannot be occupied by a subject.[37] It is this intimation that Foucault reads in *Las Meninas* and that extends to literary texts as well. Before discussing Foucault's reading of literary texts as stagings of their own limitations, two questions arise concerning the work of art. It is clear that Foucault refers to exteriority, void, or negativity when he discusses the experience of madness. Madness is the same "experience" as that of the experience of a void that witnesses the dissolution of its own conditions. Does this mean, then, that art works (literary or plastic) that present their own "absence" are products of madness? The answer to this question is a difficult one. Foucault recognizes the difficulty of distinguishing inspiration from hallucination, the pure origins of language from a babble of words. Yet madness *is* the absolute break with the work. Foucault insists on this noncompatibility precisely because the pure origin of language cannot be captured within the language, within the work itself. This conviction not only shows that *Las Meninas* does not represent representation in its pure form, but also folds Foucault's own discourse back onto itself. Thus, we come back to the interruption Foucault introduces in the middle of his discussion of *Las Meninas*. If, as Foucault says, "what we see never resides in what we say," what is the status of Foucault's discourse that discusses *Las Meninas*? Does Foucault capture what *Las Meninas* makes us see, yet is unable to represent? Evidently, Foucault does not privilege the text (his own text) over the image. Thus, we "see" that Foucault stages precisely the same self-reflexivity in his text that he attributes to *Las Meninas*. Foucault undermines the ground of his own discourse that attempts to describe something in words, that is, that which, in a sense, tries to represent or describe the image. He stages this undermining in various ways throughout his career, and this staging is crucial for understanding his later writings concerning the ethics of care for the self.

The question of the status of Foucault's own discourse relates directly to the question of the subject and discourse, and therefore is not extrinsic to the content of his thought. As we have seen, toward the end of "Politics and the Study of Discourse,"[38] Foucault describes his own project in terms of the relationship between discourse and the human being. As we have shown before, Foucault's discourse can therefore never be regarded as a metadiscourse. Foucault would never deny that his discourse is subject to the rules, transformations, and ruptures he associates with the being of discourse. The subject does not own or control the discourse, and this includes Foucault and his own discourse as well. Therefore, Foucault hates commentaries, including the one I am writing right now, because they seem to describe, represent, and explain their origin (or the origin of the original text commented on), the master text, a task which is impossible for Foucault. A text, or a reading that is not aware of that which exceeds the awareness of the author, is naive. Such a text simply reproduces all the discourses that constitute us as the subjects of our own discourses. Hence, attempts to read a new subjectivity in Foucault's later writings in the name of a straightforward ethical concern are precisely what Foucault attempts to avoid throughout his career. In one of his late essays, Foucault describes his entire work as an attempt to analyze how human beings are made into subjects.[39] For Foucault, subjectivity is not simply a question of whether there *is* a subject. The position of the subject is created through a discourse which itself operates in terms of subjectivity. Therefore, it is extremely misleading to ask simply whether Foucault's later writings allow for an ethical subject.[40] Instead, we should perhaps concentrate on the assumption underlying the discourses that ask this very question. They run the risk of simply avoiding what Foucault sees as an inevitable dimension of discourse, namely its folding onto itself, its self-reflexivity, which is not grounded in terms of subjectivity, but undermines its own ground. Perhaps it is only on the basis of this self-dissolving, which is always a permanent task, according to Foucault, that we may start to raise ethical questions. This self-reflexivity is problematic, as I said earlier, precisely because it runs the risk of suggesting self-possession. Foucault describes the same problem in terms of the risk of interiority.

In his essay on Blanchot,[41] Foucault distinguishes two ways in which language folds back onto itself: In the assertion "I lie," the foundation of Greek truth was put into question, whereas the assertion "I speak" puts the whole of modern fiction to the test. Unlike the assertion "I lie," the assertion "I speak" cannot be mastered by simply folding the discourse back onto itself. Thus, any reflexivity involved in "I speak" cannot be understood in terms of an appeal to a metadiscourse. The problem with "I speak" is fundamentally different than with "I lie," because there does not seem to be a problem in "I speak." It is always undeniably true. Despite its apparent clarity, however, the assertion "I speak" opens up a potentially unlimited realm of questions. It requires the existence of another discourse that will provide it with an object. That discourse, however, is missing. In other words, "I speak" tries to represent the one who does the representing. "I" as a sign, however, functions only in the absence of the object of the discourse (i.e., of the "I" as a subject). "I" in "I speak" disappears the instant that I fall silent.[42] "Any possibility of language dries up in the transitivity of its execution" (TO, 11). In the reflexivity of the "I speak," the "I" fragments, disperses, and scatters, disappearing in that naked space that surrounds it: "It is no longer discourse and the communication of meaning, but a spreading forth of language in its raw state, an unfolding of pure exteriority" (TO, 11). It is this doubling back of modern literature that enables it to designate itself. Foucault states that this self-reference is thought to be interiorization to the extreme. However, it is fundamentally a question of a passage to the "outside." It is precisely this *explosion* or passage to the outside that takes place in modern literature. Language escapes the being of discourse, namely discourse qua representation. The "I" cannot represent itself, and thereby opens itself "to the outside." It is this gesture of an incomplete folding, a reflexivity without return, that Foucault attributes to the thinkers of "the thought from outside." In their texts, "language unveils its own being, the sudden clarity reveals not a folding back [a complete recuperation] but a gap, not a turning back of signs upon themselves but a dispersion" (TO, 12). Hence "the being of language appears for itself with the disappearance of the subject" (TO, 15). This relationship of discourse to its own possibility speaks to a thought that stands outside subjectivity. Foucault attributes this thought from outside to Blanchot. The thought from outside speaks to the same experience of madness, an experience that comes forth in its disappearance, and disappears in its coming forth. Yet once again this experience is not by design, is not a movement that goes outside itself only to come back to itself and constitute its own interiority. "Any purely reflexive discourse runs the risk of leading the experience of the outside back to the dimension of interiority" (TO, 21). Thus, Blanchot's language is not a dialectical negation that comes back in order to find itself again, but an erasing of this dialectic as a possible recuperation. This is the insight that Blanchot articulates in terms of the relationship of the text to its "own" being. It is a relationship that constantly displaces possession, yielding it to the outside, and dispossessing the very discourse it appears to be producing. This is perhaps the only possibility of displacing the model that produces the interiority of the subject. And only within (not after, or behind) this dispossession is there a possibility of raising again the ethical question, according to Foucault.

The debate between Foucault and Derrida parallels the confrontation between Heidegger and Hegel. Both Foucault and Heidegger try to think a certain form of negativity—though perhaps it is not appropriate to use this term anymore—that interrupts the continuity of (dialectical) thinking. For Heidegger, nihilation or nothingness designates an unsublatable interruption of dialectical discourse. For Foucault, this interruption takes the form of a thought from outside of a void. Both Foucault and Heidegger emphasize the nonrelatability of this form of negativity, because the very notion of relation overcomes this negativity. Foucault expresses this nonrelational nature of negativity in terms of the unity of being: "The univocity of being, its single-ness of expression, is paradoxically the principal condition which permits difference to escape the domination of identity, which frees itself from the law of the Same as a simple opposition within conceptual elements. Being is always said of difference; it is the Recurrence of difference."[43] For Foucault the univocity of being expresses its fundamental negativity.

To permit difference to escape the domination of identity is not only a conceptual question, but also *the* ethical question. Therefore, the attempt to think negativity becomes explicitly (for Foucault) or indirectly (in the case of Heidegger) an ethical question. The problem of postmetaphysical ethics is to articulate a possibility of alterity without opposition and sameness. Between Hegel and Heidegger implicitly and between Foucault and Derrida explicitly the problem is to interrupt a self-restoring dialectical movement that becomes its other and returns back to the movement itself. If this is the only conception of alterity possible, then there is no possibility of ethics according to Foucault and Heidegger.

CONCLUSION

Madness Is Not a Thing of the Past

~~~~~~

Three dangers threaten thinking.
The good hence healing danger is the neighborhood of the singing poet.
The evil and the keenest danger is thinking itself. It must think against
   itself, which it can only seldom do.
The bad and hence muddled danger is philosophizing.

—Heidegger

It is by *treating differently* every language, by *grafting* languages onto each
other, by *playing* on the multiplicity of languages . . . that one can fight . . .
against the colonizing principle.

—Derrida

AS I STATED in the introduction, this work arrives too late. Madness already
seems to be a thing of the past. Perhaps the more significant question for philosophy today is the question of ethics. The question of ethics emerges as a
result of what becomes designated as the "end of philosophy" in the twentieth
century.[1] Ever since Nietzsche's so called reversal of Platonism, not only has
philosophy shown itself to be incapable of achieving what it had set itself to
accomplish, but also its very contention of being the only way of thinking has
been put into question.[2] This crisis of philosophy manifests itself as a fundamental inability to think the other. The problem of the other emerges not
only as a philosophical problem of thinking the other of the rational and the
logical, but also as a cultural problem of relating to the other of the Western
philosophical tradition. The power of philosophy to assimilate its other
becomes the very issue to be problematized.[3] The question of the other, which
Plato began thinking in terms of ideas at a specific inception of philosophical

thinking, becomes, in the twentieth century, an ethical question of how philosophy must think against its very nature.

Throughout this work I have tried to show that the questions of madness and death are intimately connected with philosophy, rather than being modern topics of philosophical interest. Therefore, the question of madness is also intimately connected with the question of ethics. Indeed, in the final chapter of this work concerning the debate between Foucault and Derrida, we observed the way in which the question of madness leads into that of ethics. One of the interpreters of the Foucault-Derrida debate has observed that both Foucault and Derrida are led to the question of ethics in their own ways after this debate.[4] However, the question of ethics is already implicit within this debate at various levels. First, madness raises the ethical question in terms of the interaction between the rational person and the mad one. In this sense madness is an instance that represents a more general structure of the relationship between the same and the other. The relation between the rational and the mad individual complicates every ethical theory that relies on the rationality of the human being. Second, madness represents a tendency within philosophy understood as a specific historical and cultural discourse. The philosophical tendency of a simultaneous assimilation and exclusion, giving a voice to while silencing the other, represents the relationship of Western culture to other cultures. These two levels of analysis conceptual and historical-cultural, can only be separated analytically.[5] They manifest themselves simultaneously within concrete human existence.

Consequently, the question of madness emerging from the debate between Foucault and Derrida has to be interpreted as a question that speaks to the question of the possibility of ethics. However, madness is not *just* an example of the relationship between the same and the other, but relates to the question of the possibility of ethics in a peculiar way. What we can learn from the debate between Foucault and Derrida concerning the possibility of ethics is that ethics does not concern relations among individuals who share a common history, rationality, and a way of thinking. Indeed, ethics as a possibility has to be thought in relation to those who have nothing in common.[6] A possible ethical relation between the mad and the rational individual does not imply that the mad person must be cured according to standards that are already established on the side of rationality, but demands an abandonment of these standards, and requires that one be open to the possibility of risking one's rationality. The possibility of thinking such an ethics seems to be the only way to displace the "colonial" element in Western philosophical thinking, which already assimilates the voice of the other in advance, rather than being open to this voice.

Foucault and Derrida, in their own ways, try to think the scope of Western philosophical and scientific thinking and how this thinking manifests itself in history. For Foucault, the relationship between rationality and madness is one of exclusion. Specifically, as I tried to show in my last chapter, this exclusion is connected to the emergence of subjectivity as the dominant philosophical discourse. For Derrida, such an explanation suggests that there was a historical moment where this exclusion had not been at work. Indeed, at one point Foucault seems to suggest that the Greek *logos* did not exclude its other. For Derrida, such a privileging of the Greek *logos* assumes that there is a pure moment in Western history, one which is not contaminated by the guilt of domination. For Derrida, to attribute the exclusion of the other to a specific period in history is to affirm the fundamental operation of the metaphysics of presence. On the contrary, Derrida insists that the power of Western metaphysical thinking is not simply one of exclusion, but one of "colonialization." In other words, Western rationality does not exclude madness by silencing it, but rather dominates madness by giving a specific voice to it, namely, the voice of rationality. For Derrida, such an operation is necessary for the possibility of history in general. That is to say, a certain mastery of the other (in this case madness) is a structural necessity for rationality to constitute itself historically. I think that Derrida's insights concerning Western rationality as a structural operation are compatible with Foucault's specific discussion of the exclusion of madness. One can argue that structural mastery can manifest itself as a specific exclusion in history. The question of exclusion in Descartes concerns the question of the continuity of philosophical meditation. For Foucault, the continuity of a certain way of thinking is guaranteed in and through the exclusion of madness. Descartes does not exclude the content of the beliefs of the mad person; rather, he excludes the possibility of philosophical meditation being disrupted. If I were mad, I could not have continued thinking philosophically. I believe that between Hegel and Heidegger a similar question is at stake.

I discuss Hegel and Heidegger after detecting the traces of a certain attitude toward madness and death in Plato. Plato is the first thinker who explicitly connects philosophy with madness. Plato demonstrates the philosophical mastery over madness in two ways: First, philosophy excludes madness from the domain of rational discourse, and second, philosophy appropriates any radical insight madness might possess. In my reading of Plato's *Phaedo* and *Phaedrus*, I suggested that death and madness are related to philosophy in a deconstructive way. Both madness and death are, according to Plato, notions that should be excluded from the domain of philosophy. Plato associates philosophy with a certain presence and with life, as well as with rationality. Yet Plato also incorporates madness and death into philosophy to the extent that they have constitutive roles. Therefore, in Plato we observe a differentiation of the concepts of madness and death, their incorporation into philosophy, as well as their exclusion. In fact, following Derrida, I argue that the simultaneity of this double gesture is what grounds philosophy.

There is a similar gesture in Hegel. Hegel also includes madness and death within philosophy, yet at the same time excludes them. Madness and death are included within the domain of dialectical thinking, yet they are overcome. Hegel's interpretation of madness is connected with the question of truth. For Hegel, madness stands for negativity, always understood cognitively. That is to say that, for Hegel, philosophy is in the final analysis a question of knowing, of consciousness, and of conceptual thinking. Hegel understands madness and death from the perspective of philosophical (or systematic) knowing. I show that in Hegel such an understanding is the result of a certain shape of dialectical thinking, namely, a shape where the previous moments become the content(s) of later stages. Hegel understands not only the structure of thinking but also the structure of reality in terms of this movement. Finally, this dialectical structure also explains Hegel's understanding of the structure of time. Although time in which thinking takes place is not a physical or "objective" time, it nevertheless has a certain structure. It "proceeds" through the completion of the previous moment where this moment is not left behind, but preserved by being negated as a content of the next moment. Therefore, Heidegger states, "for Hegel the former time, the past constitutes the essence of time."[7] Derrida connects Heidegger's insight with Hegel's understanding of truth:

> Consciousness, i.e., the phenomenological, therefore is the *truth* of the soul, that is, precisely the truth of that which was the object of the anthropology. 'Truth,' here, must be understood in a rigorously Hegelian sense. In this Hegelian sense, the metaphysical essence of truth, the truth of the truth, is achieved. Truth here is the presence or presentation of essence as *Gewesenheit*, of *Wesen* as having-been.[8]

I interpret *Being and Time* as an attempt to displace the cognitive movement of Hegel's thinking in general and of the *Phenomenology of Spirit* in particular. I argue that *Being and Time*, as a project, is a failure, but not in the sense that it falls back into the metaphysics of presence that Heidegger criticizes in Hegel's philosophy. *Being and Time* is a failure in that it stages how thinking is destined to fail in its attempt to grasp negativity. Consequently, any constructivist or positive reading of *Being and Time* that tries to explain human existence is misguided, even if, at times, Heidegger himself seems to encourage such an interpretation. Therefore, in a sense, even if I seem to let my reading of Heidegger be entirely dominated by his voice, I believe this chapter carries out a displacement of the author's voice in *Being and Time*. That is to say, a "mad" reading of a text not only allows itself to be dominated by this text, but also lets the master text itself be dominated by displacing the author's alleged intentions. My reading of *Being and Time*, therefore, differs from an attempt to explicate the meaning of the text and the author's intention, even though it seems to be doing just that.

In his later essays, Heidegger acknowledges the difficulty of *Being and Time* and formulates the question of negativity in terms of madness. I argue that Heidegger formulates a different conception of negativity from that of Hegel, but also, to a certain extent, different from his own formulation in *Being and Time*. Heidegger's concern later in his career is to think a different conception of negativity, one which does not rise to the level of cognition. In other words, Heidegger tries to situate his thinking in relation to Hegel's, but also does this in a nonoppositional, noncontradictory fashion. Heidegger, in other words, recognizes that opposing and contradicting Hegel will always be circumvented by a Hegelian economy. Heidegger tries to rethink the structure of madness and futuricity that is given to Kalchas as well as mad (modern) philosophers and poets other than as a negation of the present. Therefore, I argue that Heidegger's understanding of epochality does not remain within the confines of oppositional thinking; madness, for Heidegger, is precisely the recognition of nonoppositional difference, which manifests itself in a different configuration to negativity than a cognitive comprehension. I argue that Heidegger's understanding of madness takes place at a level where the futuricity of the future is not simply taken for granted and is not understood in terms of the present. I argue that such an understanding of the future undermines our philosophical trust that the future is yet to come and thereby refuses to reduce it to the present. I believe this speaks to the same question that I raised at the beginning of the third chapter, namely the question of the continuity of dialectical thinking. For Hegel, the disruption of the dialectic is a problem of finite thinking, whereas for Heidegger, finite thinking has a relation to the futuricity of the future that undermines the dialectical overcoming of finitude. I argue that Heidegger has to transform the language of the condition of possibility in thinking the relationship between his conception of negativity and metaphysical thinking. Any attempt to articulate the possibility of metaphysical thinking in terms of what it presupposes reduces that condition to a movement within metaphysical thinking and thereby surrenders it to a Hegelian economy. I insist that Heidegger tries to displace this predicament. Yet to deny the language of conditions of possibility is not to deny the possibility of the future, but precisely to attempt to articulate it without reducing it to the presence of thought as it has been reduced so many times in the history of philosophy. Therefore, for Heidegger, the question of negativity becomes a question of language. I turned to Heidegger's essay on Trakl's poetry, which I believe should be interpreted not as a reformulation of common Heideggerian themes, but as a fundamental questioning of the language that articulates those themes.

The issue between Hegel and Heidegger, namely the question of negativity, is a complicated one. Throughout this work, I have argued that we should refrain from a simple-minded comparison between Hegel and Heidegger. However, do I not ultimately compare them? Do I not claim that Heidegger achieves something at which Hegel failed? My analysis is not a comparison of the two, because a comparison between two thinkers presupposes that they are trying to think the same thing. I believe that, even though I started with this possibility, I made it explicit that Hegel and Heidegger do not think the same thing by negativity. Heidegger's often misunderstood claim that great thinkers think the same does not mean that first there is such a thing as the same and subsequently two thinkers try to articulate this thing as best as they can. Between Hegel and Heidegger there emerges a problem of understanding not only the question of comparison but also a different way of understanding the task and limits of philosophy. I believe that what Heidegger is trying to show is not that Hegel was wrong, but rather that philosophy is something different than the question of truth or that of knowledge. Philosophy, to the extent that it attempts to think existence, has to be able to disentangle itself from the questions of cognition, of science, and of theory. Therefore, I am engaged in a comparison between Hegel and Heidegger because Heidegger displaces the very ground from which such a comparison would be possible. I believe this displacement speaks to the same problem as Heidegger's attempt to think historical human existence other than dialectically, since the dialectic ultimately remains within the confines of the questions of correctness and of argumentation, and thereby reduces existence to a content of thinking.

I formulate the issue between Hegel and Heidegger as the possibility of the futural nature of thinking and existence. Heidegger contends that the question of the future and possibility in existence, and the way in which this question displaces the present and the possibility of taking for granted the continuity of existence, is what remains to be thought. Hence, for Heidegger, the task of thinking, if there is anything left to think after Hegel, is to think the question of difference. At this point Heidegger's insistence on the ontological difference can be interpreted as the difference between thinking and being. This is not to say that human existence is reducible to thinking, or that the difference between a being and being is the same as being and thinking, but rather that the notion of difference has to be understood from out of a radical future which is not a modification of presence. The understanding of the future in terms of the structure of presence is that which guarantees the continuity of thinking. Therefore, according to Heidegger, Hegel thinks the essence of time not out of the future but out of the past, as that which has already been and which dictates the structure of what is to be. For Heidegger the task of philosophy is to open this question in the most radical fashion, even if this leads to a certain displacement of philosophy. In his lecture course on Hegel's *Phenomenology of Spirit*, Heidegger writes:

> Perhaps in both Kierkegaard and Nietzsche . . . something has been realized which is *not* philosophy, something for which we as yet have no concept. Therefore, in order to understand them and their influence, it is crucial that

we search for that concept instead of pitting them against philosophy. We must keep the possibility open that the time to come, as well as our own time, remains with no real philosophy. Such a lack would not be at all bad.[9]

There is a sense in which my work tries to bring forth, or perform, the implications of the presence of negativity in the form of madness in a work. However, one cannot simply *explain* these kinds of performative gestures. In a sense, simply mentioning their existence displaces what they try to achieve. This work recognizes that madness is, in a sense, a loss of one's voice. Whether madness is excluded, as Foucault believes, or "appropriated," as Derrida suggests, there is a sense in which madness means losing one's voice. Rather than giving a voice to madness, this work tries to perform its silence by letting others speak through it. I recognize that there is a certain madness involved in letting one's work be dominated by what others say. This work, however, tries to refrain from being an execution of an already decided idea or thesis. The absence of a single developing idea is perhaps a lack of its power. Yet there is a sense in which this work sustains a single theme throughout. In this respect, in line with Hegel's definition of madness, this work clings to a single idea even if it appears to be "mad" at times. This work tries to show that the process of thinking is itself subject to various disruptions and that it should not function as a plant reaching its fruition. It would be unfair to accept a consistent continuity from a work that attempts to question this continuity and to show disruptions of thinking. One may still insist that one can consistently show the inconsistencies of thinking. I believe that such an attempt would ultimately not take philosophy seriously. Such an attempt would regard philosophy as an intellectual problem, and not allow it to touch our writing, reading, and thinking. Philosophy should not presuppose a homogenous space for the movement of thinking and the communication of ideas. Philosophy should ultimately interrupt our faith that there is always the possibility of continuing with philosophical thinking.

Yet how is it possible that philosophy itself would interrupt a faith in its own continuation? One can understand this possibility in two senses. The first one would be a Hegelian sense: philosophy always accounts for that which remains outside of it, namely as an interruption that is understood from within philosophy. The second sense would be the ethical question, namely how it is that one can think philosophy in terms of an interruption that cannot be transformed into the binary logic of philosophy. How can one, furthermore, understand this irreducibility other than as opposition? This question, I believe, ties the conceptual problem of alterity with the problem of ethics, as well as with the question of the political. The Western philosophical tradition confronts the question of alterity not only as a conceptual but also as a historical-cultural question. The problem with Western philosophy, as well as the cultural and political tradition that philosophy sustains, is not an exclusion or oppression of its other, but the way in which it understands, interprets, and even produces the alterity of the other. This philosophical way of thinking defines its other in advance, mostly in opposition to itself. Yet the problem is not to restore the dignity of the other within the same framework, but to rethink the very desirability of this framework. Since I see this problem not simply as a conceptual one, but also a political and cultural one, I appeal to a possibility within Foucault's and Heidegger's thinking that interrupts the movement of Western philosophical thinking. I tried to show that both madness and death exemplify the way in which (Western) philosophy (a redundant expression for Heidegger himself, since he believes that philosophy is only Western) constitutes itself in constituting its other. Yet these concepts also designate a possible interruption of the very same thinking. Therefore, madness and death provide us with the possibility of interrupting a certain power of Western philosophy that also sustains the cultural hegemony of Western culture. It is true that both Heidegger and Foucault are thinkers within the same Western tradition. However, one should not totalize "Western philosophical thinking." In fact, unlike Hegel and Derrida, Foucault and Heidegger resist this totalizing tendency of Western philosophy, which circumvents not only its other, but also (and therefore) itself. Ironically, it might be that my work itself ultimately affirms the Western philosophical tradition that it attempts to question. I do not oppose this possibility except perhaps to state that the hegemony of the Western philosophical tradition is not simply a conceptual problem that remains within the paradox of a logical framework, but also a cultural, political, and historical problem that confronts us with ethical and political responsibilities.

In the attempt to think the relationship of philosophy to itself, madness and death point toward the only possibility of continuing to think. If we do not concentrate on the unsublatable negativity exemplified by madness and death, we will merely affirm philosophy as it reaches its culmination in Hegel and is reiterated by Derrida. Consequently, thinking would be simply repeating (perhaps with a difference) the same conceptual framework. This, I contend, would not be thinking, because if thinking were to be understood in terms of its mere continuity, then its possibilities would have been defined in advance. Hence, philosophy not only has the possibility, but also the obligation to interrupt our faith that there is always the possibility of continuing with philosophical thinking. Perhaps we might not call this interruption philosophy anymore, but it is the only possibility for thinking.

Notes

INTRODUCTION
MADNESS AND DEATH

"Here Where Others . . ." *Antonin Artaud: Selected Writings*, trans. H. Weaver (New York: Farrar, Strauss and Giroux, 1976), 59. *Antonin Artaud: Anthology*, trans. J. Hirschman (San Francisco: City Lights Books, 1965), 26.

"There are More Things," in *The Book of Sand*, trans. N. T. Di Giovanni (New York: E. P. Dutton), 51.

1. "Admittedly, we are experiencing today an inflation in discourses on madness." Shoshana Felman wrote these lines more than twenty years ago. In fact, for Felman, the important question is not about madness, but rather "why is everyone today meddling with madness?" *Writing and Madness*, trans. M. N. Evans (Ithaca: Cornell University Press, 1985), 13. The original text was published in 1978.

2. This is, of course, an allusion to Michel Foucault's *Histoire de la folie* which starts with the lines: "At the end of the Middle Ages, leprosy disappeared from the Western World," trans. R. Howard (New York: Vintage Books), 3.

3. At this point I use the designation "philosophical madness" merely to restrict the scope of this study to those works that are considered to be philosophical. However, this study does not presuppose, and in fact tries to displace, a straightforward distinction between madness and mental illness.

4. The terms "cognitive" or "cognition" translate the German word *Erkenntnis*. However, I use the term in a broader sense, designating that which can be made the content of thought. The obvious question is whether anything that is not cognitive in this sense can ever be spoken of philosophically. This question will be important throughout this work.

CHAPTER ONE
PLATO: DEATH AND MADNESS IN THE *PHAEDO* AND *PHAEDRUS*

G. S. Kirk, J. E. Raven, M. Schofield, *The Presocratic Philosophers*, 2nd ed. (Cambridge: Cambridge University Press, 1983), 208.

Philo, Loeb Classical Library, vol. 3, trans. F. H. Olson (Cambridge: Harvard University Press, 1930), 288–289.

1. Concerning the question of definition of philosophy specifically in the context of the *Phaedo*, see Pierre Hadot, *Philosophy as a Way of Life*, ed. Arnold I. Davidson, trans. Michael Chase (Oxford: Blackwell, 1995), 68, and Ronna Burger, *The Phaedo: A Platonic Labyrinth* (New Haven: Yale University Press, 1984), 29ff. I owe this insight to Michael Naas's lectures on Plato at DePaul University and his book *Turning: From Persuasion to Philosophy, A Reading of Homer's* Iliad (Atlantic Highlands: Humanities Press, 1995), 4–12.

2. *Was ist das, die Philosophie?* Translated as *What is Philosophy* by W. Kluback and J. T. Wilde, bilingual edition (New York: Vision, 1956).

3. "Was ist Metaphysik?" in *Wegmarken*, GA. 9 (Frankfurt a.M.: V. Klostermann, 1967). Translated as "What is Metaphysics?" in *Pathmarks*, ed. W. McNeill (Cambridge: Cambridge University Press, 1998), 82–96.

4. At this point by "engagement" I mean a certain involvement with philosophy as a way of life rather than as a form of knowledge. This distinction is difficult to think because one can confuse a thirst for knowledge and a constant struggle to attain knowledge with the philosophical life. However, philosophy can also be thought of as a resistance to this continuous struggle.

5. *What is Philosophy?*, 23.

6. *Pathmarks*, 82.

7. *Phaedo* (Loeb Classical Library, 1914), 61c.

8. At this stage I do want to emphasize that a certain understanding of the beginning is tied to the question of what philosophy is. From the perspective of the *Phaedo*, the question is whether there is a moment that transforms the (sophistical) questioning of death into the philosophical willingness to die. On this question see Michael Naas's *Turning: From Persuasion to Philosophy, A Reading of Homer's* Iliad (Atlantic Highlands: Humanities Press, 1995), 4.

9. Plato expresses this in the *Theaetetus*: ". . . for this feeling of wonder shows that you are a philosopher, since wonder is the only beginning of philosophy . . ." (155d). Or as Aristotle puts it in *Metaphysics*: "[i]t is through wonder that human beings now begin and originally began to philosophize" (982b12) *(dia gar to thaumazein oi anthropoi kai nun kai to proton erxanto philosophein . . .)*, *Metaphysics*, Books I–IX (Cambridge: Harvard University Press, 1933).

10. *What is Philosophy?*, 81.

11. Therefore, I do not enter the debate as to whether Plato himself had a theory of forms or whether this was a later attribution to his thought. Those who argue that Plato never articulates a theory of forms emphasize the dramatic aspect of his dialogues. Although the dramatic aspects of Plato's dialogues are extremely important in understanding his writings, I believe that there is still a necessity of responding to the philosophical question of the relationship between absence and the forms.

12. I take this argument from Jacques Derrida, especially from his "Signature Event Context," where he discusses the relationship between presence and absence in

terms of a homogeneous field. *Margins of Philosophy*, trans. A. Bass (Chicago: University of Chicago Press, 1982), 307–330; see especially 311–321 and 329.

13. The word *"aptomenoi"* is translated as "practice," yet it can also be rendered as "being touched."

14. The word *"orthos,"* which is usually not paid attention to in this sentence, means "rightly," "uprightly," "justly," "truly," or "really." As an adverb it qualifies that there is a right way to pursue philosophy, as well as right way of practicing dying and death. David White recognizes the significance of this word in *Myth and Metaphysics in Plato's* Phaedo (Sellinsgrove: Susquehanna University Press, 1989), 41.

15. Ronna Burger notes that this formulation seems to imply that there is a way of "correctly grasp[ing] philosophy" which, according to Burger "sounds strange." *The* Phaedo: *A Platonic Labyrinth* (New Haven: Yale University Press, 1984), 38.

16. For the distinction between suicide and philosophical willingness to die, see Paul Friedländer, *Plato: The Dialogues, Second and Third Periods*, trans. H. Meyerhoff (Princeton: Princeton University Press, 1969), 41.

17. *Pathmarks*, 82.

18. Pierre Hadot recognizes the relationship between death and the whole in the context of the *Republic* (468a); "here, 'training for death' is linked to the contemplation of the Whole . . ." *Philosophy as a Way of Life*, ed. Arnold I. Davidson, trans. Michael Chase (Oxford: Blackwell, 1995), 97. In the context of the *Phaedrus*, Charles Griswold also recognizes the relationship between the soul and the Whole. *Self-Knowledge in Plato's* Phaedrus (University Park: Pennsylvania State University Press, 1996), 3.

19. Ronna Burger also recognizes that "Socrates begins his account . . . with a presumably self-evident question: Do we believe that death is something?" *The* Phaedo: *A Platonic Labyrinth* (New Haven: Yale University Press, 1984), 39.

20. I leave these questions without answers here, but I will come back to them after following Plato's argument further.

21. Most interpreters recognize the significance of this definition for the rest of the *Phaedo*. See Peter Ahrendorf's *The Death of Socrates and the Life of Philosophy: An Interpretation of Plato's* Phaedo (Albany: State University of New York Press, 1995), 38, and David White's *Myth and Metaphysics in Plato's* Phaedo (Sellinsgrove: Susquehanna University Press, 1989), 44.

22. Ronna Burger recognizes this difficulty in *The* Phaedo: *A Platonic Labyrinth*, 13. See also David White's *Myth and Metaphysics in Plato's* Phaedo (44) on the same question of the separability of the soul and the body.

23. I claim, therefore, that the initial characterization of the forms is that they are not physically present to our senses. Plato refers to justice, beauty, and goodness as *ousia*. *Ousia*, which has been traditionally translated as *substance*, is the participle form of the Greek word *eimi* (I am). Thus, "being" is a more literal translation, which does not presuppose the subsequent translation and philosophical interpretation of this word. I will sometimes use the word *form(s)* instead of *being(s)* as the latter appears awkward in some contexts. *Ousia* is the ground and the cause of particular things.

24. For a discussion of "the metaphysics of opposition" see David White, *Myth and Metaphysics in Plato's* Phaedo, 69ff.

25. Therefore, David Ross argues ". . . in the *Meno* the theory of *anamnesis* is not connected with the knowledge of the Ideas; in the *Phaedo* it is." *Plato's Theory of Ideas,* 2nd ed. (Oxford: Clarendon Press, 1953), 22. For a discussion of the role of equality for equal things see Thomas Gould, *Platonic Love* (New York: Free Press, 1963), 77.

26. David White recognizes the relationship between the Forms and perception in *Myth and Metaphysics in Plato's* Phaedo, 84–90.

27. Concerning the being of the soul, Hans-Georg Gadamer writes: "The being of the soul, however, which understands itself and its own being, is not the numerical being of nature or a *being* harmonious." *Dialogue and Dialectic: Eight Hermeneutical Studies on Plato,* trans. Christopher Smith (New Haven: Yale University Press, 1980), 32.

28. For a more detailed analysis of the question of self-knowledge in Plato, see Edward G. Ballard, *Socratic Ignorance: An Essay on Platonic Self-Knowledge* (The Hague: Martinus Nijhoff, 1965).

29. Gadamer agrees with this interpretation when he writes: "But there could hardly have ever been an interpreter of Plato who could not see that this proof of the ontological relationship of idea, life, and soul, as marvelous as it might be, is incapable of demonstrating anything more than the character of the universal *eide* . . ." *Dialogue and Dialectic: Eight Hermeneutical Studies on Plato,* trans. Christopher Smith (New Haven: Yale University Press, 1980), 36. Also see David White, *Myth and Metaphysics in Plato's* Phaedo, 114.

30. The difficulty of answering this question led most interpreters to suspect that Plato did not believe in the immortality of the individual soul. See Ronna Burger's *The* Phaedo: *A Platonic Labyrinth,* 2ff, Hans-Georg Gadamer, *Dialogue and Dialectic: Eight Hermeneutical Studies on Plato,* 36, and David White, *Myth and Metaphysics in Plato's* Phaedo, 211. Charles Griswold expresses a similar suspicion in his interpretation of the *Phaedrus* in *Self-Knowledge in Plato's* Phaedrus (University Park: Pennsylvania State University Press, 1996), 84.

31. For various relationships between the soul and the body, on the one hand, and life and death, on the other, see David White's *Myth and Metaphysics in Plato's* Phaedo, 115–116.

32. See Ronna Burger, *The* Phaedo: *A Platonic Labyrinth,* 40.

33. For the significance of self-knowledge in the *Phaedrus*, see Charles Griswold's *Self-Knowledge in Plato's* Phaedrus (University Park: Pennsylvania State University Press, 1996), especially 2ff.

34. Concerning the difficulties associated with this definition see Paul Friedländer, *Plato: The Dialogues, Second and Third Periods,* trans. H. Meyerhoff (Princeton: Princeton University Press, 1969), 224ff.

35. For this specific relationship between *eros* and *logos* see John Sallis, *Being and Logos,* 3rd ed. (Bloomington: Indiana University Press, 1996), 127ff, and Charles Griswold, *Self-Knowledge in Plato's* Phaedrus, 67.

36. Later in his speech Socrates will associate being a seer *(mantis)* with madness *(mania)*. Hence, he prepares the context for this connection, in addition to indicating that he will be involved in each kind of madness that he will speak of later.

37. For an interpretation of madness of human origin in the *Phaedrus*, see Martha Nussbaum's "This Story Isn't True: Poetry, Goodness, and Understanding in Plato's *Phaedrus*," in *Plato On Beauty, Wisdom and the Arts*, ed. J. Moravcsik and P. Temko (Totowa: Rowman and Littlefield, 1982), 92ff.

38. Therefore, In *The Birth of Philosophy*, Giorgio Colli claims that madness *(Wahnsinn)* is the origin of wisdom. Taking his point of departure from Nietzsche's distinction between Apollo and Dionysus, Colli argues that Nietzsche's claim that Apollo represents the world of appearances is not exactly true. On the basis of Plato's *Phaedrus* where *mania* is associated with Apollo and the fact that Apollo is the god behind the oracle in Delphi, Colli claims that the origin of Socratic wisdom is madness (an "Apollonian madness"). *Die Geburt der Philosophie* (Frankfurt a.M.: Europäische Verlaganstalt, 1975), 13–20.

39. David White discusses the relationship between madness and disease in *Rhetoric and Reality in Plato's* Phaedrus (Albany: State University of New York Press, 1992), 70.

40. For a discussion of this type of madness, see James Urmson, "Plato and the Poets," in *Plato On Beauty, Wisdom and the Arts*, ed. J. Moravcsik and P. Temko (Totowa: Rowman and Littlefield, 1982), 125–136. Also see Ivan M. Linforth, "Telestic Madness in Plato, *Phaedrus* 244de," in *University of California Publications in Classical Philology*, vol. 13, ed. J. T. Allen et al. (Berkeley and Los Angeles: University of California Press, 1971), 163–172.

41. For an interesting discussion of the different types of madness in the *Phaedrus* see Martha Nussbaum's "This Story Isn't True: Poetry, Goodness, and Understanding in Plato's *Phaedrus*," in *Plato On Beauty, Wisdom and the Arts*, ed. J. Moravcsik and P. Temko (Totowa: Rowman and Littlefield, 1982), 70–124.

42. Concerning the question of whether the ensuing story about the soul can be said to be a proof, see John Sallis, *Being and Logos*, 135–136. Sallis indicates that the word for proof *(apodeixis)* is not simply understood as a proof of formal mathematics, but as a "showing forth" or "exhibiting."

43. For an explanation of this metaphor, see Thomas Gould, *Platonic Love* (New York: Free Press, 1963), 113ff. Julius Moravcsik offers an alternative explanation in "Noetic Aspiration and Artistic Inspiration," in *Plato On Beauty, Wisdom and the Arts*, ed. J. Moravcsik and P. Temko (Totowa: Rowman and Littlefield, 1982), 44ff.

44. The Loeb edition renders this phrase as "truly existing essence," whereas the Hackett translation translates it as "a being that really is what it is."

45. Concerning the difficulty of translating and interpreting this expression see John Sallis, *Being and Logos*, 145ff.

46. Sallis uses this phrase to take issue with the theory of forms attributed to Plato. He rightly suggests that translating this phrase in terms of "absolute essences" already presupposes a particular interpretation of forms. As I said, I refrain from tak-

ing sides in this debate, as the important question in the present work is not whether Plato has a theory of forms or not, but how he interprets absence in the structure of things that are physically present. Plato, I suggest, does indeed interpret this absence in terms of *ousia*, presence.

47. The translation is both from the Loeb edition of *Phaedrus* (249b–c) and from *Being and Logos*, 149. I agree with Sallis that this is one of the most crucial passages in the entire dialogue, albeit for different reasons. See *Being and Logos*, 149ff.

48. David White recognizes the relationship between the *Phaedo* and the *Phaedrus* in this respect. See *Rhetoric and Reality in Plato's* Phaedrus, 109–110.

49. Martin Heidegger, *Nietzsche I* (Pfullingen: Günther Neske, 1961), 224. *Nietzsche I*, trans. D. F. Krell (San Francisco: Harper Collins, 1991), 193. The translation is modified.

50. They are present to thought even though they may not be accessible to finite human existence, that is, even if we may never know them explicitly. The attempts to salvage Plato from Platonism by arguing that Plato never says that forms are accessible to us, are equally problematic once they miss this point.

51. This claim may be said to be a modern, specifically a Kantian, imposition on Plato. However, one should note that Plato's understanding of forms is fundamentally different from Kant's in that Plato does not understand the forms in terms of (human) reason and (human) subjectivity. The problem is similar in that it speaks to the necessity of concepts for perceptual knowledge and for synthesis over time. This synthesis, however, is not the activity of a subject for Plato.

52. Concerning the structure of presence in terms of a symmetrical negative, see Jacques Derrida, "Plato's Pharmacy," in *Dissemination*, trans. B. Johnson (Chicago: University of Chicago Press, 1981), 4ff.

53. This "more radical understanding of madness" is the focus of my concern in this work. Plato refers to this absence *(apousia)* only once in his corpus (. . . *ousias apousian . . . Parmenides* 163c). For Plato the absence of forms is predicated upon their presence. This is the way in which he understands absence in terms of presence. However, I claim that a radical understanding of absence would displace this predication. Thereby, the absence of forms does not simply mean that they are not physically present, nor that human beings cannot know them in the world of becoming. All these claims would indeed be consistent with Platonism. Perhaps the only way of rethinking Platonism along these lines is to claim that absence is the finitude of thinking (divine or mortal), that is, it is a closure of thinking rather than merely its shortcoming.

54. *Orthos* is the same word that Plato uses in characterizing those who are touched by philosophy *rightly*. See *Phaedo*, 64a.

55. For various interpretations of the significance of this designation see G. J. de Vries, *A Commentary on the* Phaedrus *of Plato* (Amsterdam: Hakkert, 1969), and G. R. F. Ferrari, *Listening to the Cicadas: A Study of Plato's* Phaedrus (Cambridge: Cambridge University Press, 1987), 142, where Ferrari responds to de Vries.

56. Concerning the relationship between truth and beauty see Martin Heidegger, "Plato's *Phaedrus*," in *Nietzsche I, The Will to Power as Art*, trans. D. F. Krell (San Francisco: Harper Collins, 1991), 188–199.

57. For the discussion of the notion of *pharmakon*, see Derrida, "Plato's Pharmacy," in *Dissemination*, trans. B. Johnson (Chicago: University of Chicago Press, 1981), 61–172.

CHAPTER TWO
HEGEL: THE MADNESS OF THE SOUL
AND THE DEATH OF THE SPIRIT

Die Weltalter, Ausgewählte Werke (Darmstadt: Wissenschaftliche Buchgesellschaft, 1976), 10, 338. The page number refers to the *Sämtliche Werke* (Stuttgart: Cotta, 1861), 8. The translation is mine.

"The Discourse on Language," in *The Archaeology of Knowledge* (New York: Pantheon, 1972), 235.

Aesthetic Ideology (Minneapolis: Minnesota University Press, 1996), 92.

Aesthetic Ideology, 103–104.

1. I will return to the question of exteriority later.

2. "'To Do Justice to Freud': The History of Madness in the Age of Psychoanalysis," trans P-A. Brault and M. Naas, *Critical Inquiry* 20 (1994): 250.

3. Carl G. Vaught, "Hegel and The Problem of Difference," in *Hegel and His Critics: Philosophy in the Aftermath of Hegel*, ed. W. Desmond (Albany: State University of New York Press, 1989), 35.

4. "Negativity is swallowed in positivity only for metaphysical thinking [*Die Negativität wird nur für das metaphysische Denken in der Positivität verschluckt*]." This is Heidegger's complaint about metaphysical thinking in general and Hegel in particular. See *Hegel*, GA, 68 (Frankfurt a.M.: V. Klostermann, 1993), 15.

5. Concerning the relationship between subjectivity and negativity in Hegel's philosophy, see Joseph Navickas, *Consciousness and Reality: Hegel's Philosophy of Subjectivity* (The Hague: Martinus Nijhoff, 1976), 39–43.

6. Jean Hyppolite agrees with the claim that the question of the subject is not the same as the question of the human being. ". . . Hegelian thought transcends the distinction between pure humanism, the one his unfaithful disciples will develop, and absolute speculative life. Without ignoring the other aspect (pure humanism) and the Hegelian texts that could justify it, we believe that Hegel has chosen the speculative conception, being's self rather than the human self." *Logic and Existence*, trans. L. Lawlor and A. Sen (Albany: State University of New York Press, 1997), 107. To express a similar point Hyppolite writes: ". . . [The absolute as subject] is neither the empirical subject nor even the transcendental subject, but being's universal self." *Logic and Existence*, 145.

7. *Enzyklopädie der philosophischen Wissenschaften im Grundrisse* (1830) Dritter Teil, *Die Philosophie des Geistes. Mit den mündlichen Zusätzen. Werke* 10 (Frankfurt a.M.: Suhrkamp, 1970). *Hegel's Philosophy of Mind: Part Three of the Encyclopaedia of the Philosophical Sciences*, trans. W. Wallace, together with the Zusätze in Boumann's

Text (1845), trans. A.V. Miller (Oxford: Clarendon Press, 1971). Hereafter abbreviated as "Enz." followed by the page numbers to the German and the English translations.

8. The theme of "Anthropology" is the soul. *Phenomenology* and *Logic* inaugurate through the sublation of the individual soul, not through its disappearance, but through its disentanglement from certain questions of subjectivity.

9. For Hegel "even if the non-dialectic difference were possible, it would be absolutely unintelligible." Carl Vaught, "Hegel and the Problem of Difference," 35.

10. Murray Greene, *Hegel on the Soul: A Speculative Anthropology* (The Hague: Martinus Nijhoff, 1972), 121. For Murray's discussion of the relationship between Hegel's notion of insanity and speculative methodology, see *A Speculative Anthropology*, 124ff. For the connection of madness with negativity see also Gerhard Gamm, *Der Wahnsinn in der Vernunft: Historische und Erkenntniskritische Studien zur Dimension des Anders-Seins in der Philosophie Hegels* (Bonn: Bovier Verlag, 1981), 91ff.

11. Timo Airaksinen makes a similar argument: "Hegel's treatment of what he calls subjective mind in the third part of his *Encyclopaedia of the Philosophical Sciences* provides a highly interesting example of the dialectic method, which allows us to see clearly not only some particular aspects of the subjective mind but also the peculiarities of the dialectic philosophizing itself." "Problems in Hegel's Dialectic of Feeling," *Philosophy and Phenomenological Research* 41 (1980): 1.

12. This is because Hegel writes in "Anthropology" that spirit is not susceptible to madness, whereas the soul is. Therefore, there is at least this difference between the two. I do not suggest that spirit is the same as the soul, nor do I intimate that there is a sameness underlying the dialectical movement from subjective to objective spirit. Hegel does say that the soul is subjective spirit. However, the difficulty is to make this statement compatible with the one above, namely, that spirit is not susceptible to madness. Obviously, the solution to this tension would not be to claim that spirit can indeed be mad (and thereby oppose Hegel), but rather to understand *why* and *how* Hegel is consistent in saying that spirit is *not* susceptible to madness.

13. Hegel calls the first stage "magnetic somnambulism," in which there is not yet a differentiation between the soul and the objective world.

14. My argument is neither committed to saying that the soul is an *ens* as Hegel understands it, nor to rejecting Hegel's claim that the soul is subjective spirit. I interpret the designation *"Ding"* in the least controversial sense, namely, as that which becomes an object of thought.

15. At this point I take the word "cognitive" in a broad sense to include consciousness and knowledge. Throughout this chapter "cognitive" is not used in opposition to the practical, nor does it mean "empirical knowledge." In the context of madness "cognitive" means the following: Hegel treats madness as a problem of having certain beliefs concerning the external world. The question of madness, however, is not reducible to such cognitive questions. It is entirely possible for someone to be completely correct in his or her beliefs concerning the external world and yet be mad. Therefore, negativity in madness (not as a methodological question but as an existential designation) is not cognitive.

16. One could argue against my claim that as soon as one thinks about this negativity it becomes cognitive. I think this is not a valid objection insofar as the "one" who thinks in this case is a human subject. Hegel certainly cannot justify an exclusively cognitive relationship to negativity on the basis of human thinking, as if it were the capacity of the human being that secured the continuity of the dialectical movement.

17. *Zerrissenheit* is the same word Hegel uses with respect to spirit when it confronts negativity in the *Phenomenology of Spirit*. For a discussion of *Zerrissenheit* in the *Phenomenology of Spirit* see Gerhard Gamm, *Der Wahnsinn in der Vernunft: Historische und Erkenntniskritische Studien zur Dimension des Anders-Seins in der Philosophie Hegels* (Bonn: Bovier Verlag, 1981), 81ff.

18. Daniel Berthold-Bond points out that "insanity and rationality are not in fact conceived as opposites, but in important respects as kindred phenomena, sharing many of the same underlying structures, each illuminating their other in significant ways." *Hegel's Theory of Madness* (Albany: State University of New York Press, 1995), 3.

19. "Contradiction" here refers to Hegel's claim that "the soul is already *in itself* the contradiction of being an *individual*, a *singular*, and yet at the same time immediately identical with the *universal* natural soul, with its substance" (Enz., 164, 125). Murray Greene explains the nature of this contradiction: "Precisely because it is such a contradiction, according to Hegel, insanity in its speculative considerations marks an advance in the soul's development beyond the forms of immediacy in the magical relation and somnambulism. As a sunderance of the self, insanity is to be viewed both as a sickness state and as part of the soul's liberation struggle from its abstract identity with its natural being as monadic feeling soul." *Hegel on the Soul: A Speculative Anthropology*, 127.

20. The parallel between this conception of madness and Schelling's conception of evil is striking. Schelling, too, characterizes evil as a false unity, rather than as the absence of unity. See Schelling, *Über das Wesen der menschlichen Freitheit, Ausgewählte Werke* (Darmstadt: Wissenschaftlice Buchgesellschaft, 1974). Insanity, therefore, does not erase moral responsibility (even if it may evade legal responsibility). In *Der Wahnsinn in der Vernunft: Historische und Erkenntniskritische Studien zur Dimension des Anders-Seins in der Philosophie Hegels*, Gerhard Gamm discusses the madness of *Eigendünkel*, which in many ways parallels Schelling's conception of evil (Bonn: Bovier Verlag, 1981), 54ff. Gamm also discusses the relationship between Hegel and Schelling on the question of madness, 181ff.

21. For the relationship between negativity and dialectical method, see Charles Taylor, *Hegel* (Cambridge: Cambridge University Press, 1975), 110; Michael Forster, "Hegel's Dialectical Method," *The Cambridge Companion to Hegel*, ed. F. C. Beiser (Cambridge: Cambridge University Press, 1993) 132; Heinz Röttges, *Der Begriff der Methode in der Philosophie Hegels* (Meisenheim: Verlag Anton Hain, 1976), 54; and Michael Rosen, *Hegel's Dialectic and Its Criticism* (Cambridge: Cambridge University Press, 1982), 30–35.

22. "*Wenn ich mich zum vernünftigen Denken erhoben habe, bin ich nicht nur für mich, mir gegenständlich, also eine* subjective *Identität des Subjectiven and Objectiven,*

sondern ich habe zweitens dies Identität von mir abgeschieden, als eine wirklich objective *mir gegenübergestellt"* (Enz., 164, 125, Hegel's emphases).

23. One can see in this structure of relating to the other the problems Levinas, Derrida, and Heidegger identified in Hegel's philosophy. The structure of the relationship to the other is the fundamental starting point of the question of ethics in these thinkers.

24. As Greene explains: "Because regression in insanity is to the feeling-life, while the subjectivity remains simultaneously in the state of waking, insanity, according to Hegel, is a contradiction within each of two levels of selfhood, as well as between the two levels." *Hegel on the Soul: A Speculative Anthropology*, 129.

25. The designation *bei sich*, which I translate as "alongside itself," is important for German Idealism in general and Hegel in particular. It is the way the Greek word *para* is translated into German. This word is significant for two reasons: First *para* is a key word in madness in ancient tragedy. Madness is to be beside oneself; *paranoia*, for example, is to be beside one's mind *(nous)*. See Ruth Padel, *Whom Gods Destroy: Elements of Greek and Tragic Madness* (Princeton: Princeton University Press, 1995), 14. The word *"bei"* is also generally used by German Idealism in characterizing the subject's relationship to itself, which is always related to negativity as it is here in Hegel, but also constitutes the possibility of the subject's movement with regard to different phases of its consciousness. Therefore, by being alongside itself the subject constitutes its subjectivity, that is, to be alongside oneself is a character of the dialectical movement that is the movement of the subject according to Hegel.

26. As Greene puts it, "insanity is thus at once a unity and opposition, a uniting of the self with itself and also a sunderance of the self in its fluid totality. This is the dialectical meaning of self-alienation: not abstract loss of self but a being-with-itself in a form directly contradictory to the *Beisichsein* of Spirit in its notion." *Hegel on the Soul: A Speculative Anthropology*, 128.

27. Thus, one hardly is surprised when Hegel later characterizes the relationship between the doctor and the insane patient in terms of a relation of power. The doctor has to "win their confidence . . . try to obtain proper authority over them. . . . The insane feel their mental weakness, their dependence on the rational person" (Enz., 179, 137).

28. Obviously a desire to change the world is not madness, but is very difficult to distinguish from madness before its realization. Hegel is very clear in distinguishing his conception of madness from a romantic longing for madness. Hegel's attempt to connect the power of imagination *(Einbildungskraft qua Phantasie)* to the power of the concept rather than feeling is important in this context. However, it is impossible for Hegel to understand the fact that "the step back from reason into the abyss of the feelings seems also to contain some strange and mysterious voluntary aspect, since the step back into madness implies that certain individuals actually *choose* insanity." Alan M. Olson, *Hegel and the Spirit: Philosophy as Pneumatology* (Princeton: Princeton University Press, 1992), 92.

29. See Patrick Murray, *Hegel's Philosophy of Mind and Will* (Lewiston: Edwin Mellen Press, 1991), 22.

30. I will show that one fundamental presupposition of negativity as a methodological structure is the same in the *Phenomenology of Spirit* (1807), namely, that it is a question concerning the truth.

31. Jean Hyppolite, "Hegel's Phenomenology and Psychoanalysis," in *New Studies in Hegel's Philosophy*, ed. W. E. Steinkraus (New York: Holt, Rinehart and Winston, 1971), 64. Hereafter abbreviated as HPP in the text, followed by the page number.

32. In his study *Hegel's Theory of Madness*, Daniel Berthold-Bond disagrees with Hyppolite. Bond claims that "not every relationship to the self is an indication of madness . . . [and] madness occupies a categorically different space, the space of feeling rather than reason, of nature rather than spirit" (49ff). Bond disregards the possibility of a more radical question of madness in Hegel's philosophy. It is, to a certain extent, misleading to say that madness does not concern spirit and reason, but rather feeling and nature. As Berthold-Bond himself indicates, madness concerns the struggle between these opposites rather than a conflict within one of them. For a discussion of madness within the context of the *Phenomenology of Spirit*, see Gerhard Gamm, *Der Wahnsinn in der Vernunft: Historische und Erkenntniskritische Studien zur Dimension des Anders-Seins in der Philosophie Hegels* (Bonn: Bovier Verlag, 1981), 64ff. Gamm agrees with Hyppolite that the question of madness can be legitimately asked within the context of the *Phenomenology of Spirit*.

33. This conception of difference is close to Derrida's notion of *différance*. One has to admit, however, that such a notion of difference is unintelligible. Unintelligibility, however, does not mean impossibility. Perhaps madness is precisely unintelligible in this respect.

34. Concerning the relationship between Hegel and Plato see John Findlay, "Hegelianism and Platonism," in *Hegel and the History of Philosophy*, ed. J. J. O. Malley, K. Algozin, and F. G. Weiss (The Hague: Martinus Nijhoff, 1974), 62–76. Findlay recognizes the similarity in the role universals play for Plato and Hegel. According to Findlay, both believe in a subjective soul-life, which is very much geared toward universality.

35. Heidegger's much misunderstood critique of subjectivity takes place precisely at this level. I will return to this question in the next chapter.

36. *Phänomenologie des Geistes. Werke* 3 (Frankfurt a.M.: Suhrkamp, 1970) *Phenomenology of Spirit*, trans. A. V. Miller (Oxford: Clarendon Press, 1977). Hereafter abbreviated as Phen., followed by the page numbers to the German and the English translation. A number of critics recognized the significance of the Preface not only for the *Phenomenology*, but for Hegel's system as a whole. My interpretation of the Preface is informed by the following works: Quentin Lauer, *A Reading of Hegel's* Phenomenology of Spirit (New York: Fordham University Press, 1976); H. S. Harris, *Hegel's Ladder: A Commentary on Hegel's* Phenomenology of Spirit (Indianapolis: Hackett Publishing Company, 1997); Jean H. Hyppolite, *Genesis and Structure of Hegel's* Phenomenology of Spirit, trans. S. Cherniak and J. Heckman (Evanston: Northwestern University Press, 1974); Alexandre Kojève, *Introduction to the Reading of Hegel*, assembled by Raymond Queneau, trans. James H. Nichols, Jr. (New York: Basic Books, 1969); Werner Marx, *Hegel's* Phenomenology of Spirit, *Its Point and Purpose: A Commentary on the Preface and Introduction* (New York: Harper and Row, 1975).

37. Hyppolite, *Logic and Existence*, trans. L. Lawler and A. Sen (Albany: State University of New York Press, 1997), 184. Hyppolite attributes negativity to history rather than to man: "History's real negativity is there, and comprehends itself as the negativity of being in the Logos" (188). Therefore "humanity as such is not the supreme end for Hegel . . . man is an intersection; he is not a natural Dasein which would have a primordial positivity" (186). The conclusion of *Logic and Existence* is an excellent account of negativity in Hegel. See especially 183ff.

38. For the relationship between Hegel and Spinoza, see H. A. Myers, *The Spinoza-Hegel Paradox: A Study of the Choice between Traditional Idealism and Systematic Pluralism* (New York: Burt Franklin, 1944).

39. I believe the question of seriousness is a significant issue between Hegel and Heidegger. In his 1938–1939 lecture course on negativity in Hegel's philosophy, Heidegger claims that "philosophy as ab-solute, as un-conditional must somehow include negativity in itself, and that means at bottom does not take it seriously" *Hegel*, GA 68 (Frankfurt a.M.: V. Klostermann, 1993), 24.

40. Concerning the claim that the presentation and the presented coincide see Sallis, *Delimitations* (Bloomington: Indiana University Press, 1986), 40–62.

41. Indeed, Bataille claims that Hegel's philosophy is a philosophy of death in "Hegel, Death and Sacrifice," *Yale French Studies* 78 (1990): 11.

42. However, I do not interpret Hegel's "entire book as a single theory of knowledge running through different phases from cognition *(Erkennen)* to absolute knowing," as does Tom Rockmore in *Cognition: An Introduction to Hegel's Phenomenology of Spirit* (Berkeley and Los Angeles: University of California Press, 1997), 2. Actually, I disagree with Rockmore that Hegel's *Phenomenology of Spirit* can be reduced to "a unified epistemological theory." I concentrate various configurations of one particular moment in Hegel's system, namely, the confrontation with the negative.

CHAPTER THREE
HEIDEGGER: DEATH AS NEGATIVITY

1. Nevertheless, we do find frequent discussions of such themes as the nothing, the "not" nothingness and nihilism, starting with the essay "What is Metaphysics?" (1929). Giorgio Agamben reflects upon the question of negativity in Hegel and Heidegger in *Language and Death: The Place of Negativity*, trans. K. E. Pinkus with M. Hardt, (Minneapolis: University of Minnesota Press, 1991).

2. Heidegger, Hegel GA. 68: 1. *Die Negativität: Eine Auseinandersetzung mit Hegel aus dem Ansatz in der Negativität* (1938–1939, 1941) 2. *Erläuterung der "Einleitung" zu Hegels "Phänomenologie des Geistes"* (1942) (Frankfurt a.M.: V. Klostermann, 1993). This text has not been translated into English. All translations are mine.

3. On the question of negativity between Hegel and Heidegger, see Jean Paul Sartre, *Being and Nothingness*, trans. Hazel E. Barnes, (London: Meuthen and Co., 1957), 233–252. Sartre distinguishes Hegel's dialectical concept of nothingness from Heidegger's phenomenological concept of nothingness.

4. Hence, I agree with Gerhard Schmitt when he writes: "The difference as to the function of negativity lies at the foundation of their [Hegel and Heidegger] ontological methodologies. . . . To put the same point somewhat figuratively, one might say that in Hegel the death of the spirit is a condition for its resurrection, the Golgatha of the soul a condition for its redemption," in *The Concept of Being in Hegel and Heidegger* (Bonn: Bovier Verlag, 1977), 152–153.

5. Joan Stambaugh argues that Heidegger consistently maintained that being is finite. She immediately recognizes that the finitude of being cannot be understood in terms of a conception of finitude that is only applicable to beings, that is, finitude in space and time. *The Finitude of Being* (Albany: State University of New York Press, 1992), 1.

6. Martin Heidegger, *Zollikoner Seminare: Protokolle-Zwiegespräche-Briefe* (Frankfurt a.M.: V. Klostermann, 1987). I will discuss this text in the next chapter.

7. *Die Grundprobleme der Phänomenologie*, GA. 24 (Frankfurt a.M.: V. Klostermann, 1975). This text consists of Heidegger's lecture course delivered in the summer semester of 1927.

8. Heidegger uses the term *"zerbrochen"* (shattered, or broken down) in the sense of a superficial understanding of these thinkers. *Grundfragen der Philosophie: Ausgewählte Probleme der Logik*, GA 45 (Frankfurt a.M.: V. Klostermann, 1984), 216. *Basic Questions of Philosophy: Selected Problems of Logic*, trans. R. Rojcewicz and A. Schuwer (Bloomington: Indiana University Press, 1994), 182.

9. *Sein und Zeit*, 17th ed. (Tübingen: Max Niemeyer, 1993). Originally published in 1927. Presently there are two English translations of *Sein und Zeit*, the 1962 translation by J. Macquarrie and E. Robinson, *Being and Time* (New York: Harper and Row, 1962) and Joan Stambaugh's 1996 translation, *Being and Time: A Translation of* Sein und Zeit (Albany: State University of New York Press, 1996). I consulted both of these translations. However, the translations are mostly either mine or significantly modified versions of the existing translations. In the main body of the text I refer to *Sein und Zeit* as SZ followed by the page number to the German text. Both of the English translations indicate German pagination in the margins. Therefore, for the sake of brevity I do not indicate the page numbers of the translations.

10. This seems to be Derrida's reading of Heidegger in *Of Spirit*, trans. G. Bennington and R. Bowlby (Chicago: University of Chicago Press, 1989), 9–10. However, Derrida qualifies this claim in light of Françoise Dastur's objection that questioning is not always privileged in Heidegger. Dastur indicates the role of *Zuspruch* in Heidegger's essay "Das Wesen der Sprache," in *Unterwegs Zur Sprache* (Pfullingen: Günther Neske, 1965). See Derrida's long footnote (5) in *Of Spirit*, 129–136.

11. The question of being, however, is not necessarily an explicit, thematic inquiry for Dasein.

12. François Raffoul indicates that "in fact there is no relationship between man and being. Heidegger considers this notion to arise 'from representational thinking' [*Identität und Differenz* (Pfullingen: Günther Neske, 1957), 24], and ultimately from the opposition of subject and object in which we continue to try to enframe the 'relation' between man and being." *Heidegger and the Subject*, trans. D. Pettigrew and G.

Recco (Atlantic Highlands: Humanities Press, 1998), 257. Raffoul's work is a study of the question of the subject in Heidegger's thinking.

13. Heidegger speaks to this problem in the addendum to his essay "The Origin of the Work of Art," when he writes: "In the heading 'the setting-into-work of truth,' in which it remains undecided but decidable who does the setting or in what way it occurs, there is concealed *the relation of being and human being*, a relation which is unsuitably conceived even in this version—a distressing difficulty, which has been clear to me since *Being and Time* and has since been expressed in a variety of versions." *Poetry, Language, Thought*, trans. A. Hofstadter (New York: Harper and Row, 1971), 87.

14. In a marginal note to this sentence, Heidegger writes: "Certainly not. So little that even rejecting this by putting them together is already fatal," SZ, 441.

15. In addition to understanding and discourse. *Befindlichkeit* is a difficult term to translate. Macquarrie and Robinson translate it as "state-of-mind," which has been the subject of criticism, as it has a cognitive connotation. Stambaugh translates it as "attunement," which is confusing, as the word "attunement" seems to be more appropriate for *Stimmung*, which is translated as "mood" by Stambaugh. *Befindlichkeit* can be rendered as "finding oneself disposed." Since this construction is a bit awkward, I use the term "disposition." In general, *Befindlichkeit* is an ontological rendition of attunement, a noncognitive relationality to and with the world that is proper to the being of Dasein.

16. *Phänomenologie des Geistes. Werke* 3 (Frankfurt a.M.: Suhrkamp, 1970), 153. *Phenomenology of Spirit*, trans. A. V. Miller (Oxford: Clarendon Press, 1977), 117.

17. In the second section of *Being and Time*, Heidegger writes that "we always already move in an understanding of being," SZ, 5. This understanding, however, is not a conceptual one.

18. For the relationship between death and time see Françoise Dastur, *Heidegger and the Question of Time*, trans. F. Raffoul and D. Pettigrew (Atlantic Highlands: Humanities Press, 1989), 37.

19. Heidegger connects the question of negativity with existential guilt. In a passage which seems to be an allusion to Hegel's dialectic, Heidegger writes: "Still, the *ontological meaning of the notness* of this existential nothingness *[Nichtigkeit]* remains obscure. But this holds also for the *ontological essence of the 'not' in general*. Ontology and logic, to be sure, have exacted a great deal from the 'not' and thus at times made its possibilities visible without revealing it itself ontologically. Ontology came across the 'not' and made use of it. But is it so self-evident that every 'not' signifies a negativum in the sense of a lack? Is its positivity exhausted by the fact that it constitutes "passing over" *[Übergang]?* Why does every dialectic take refuge in negation, without grounding it *itself* dialectically, without even being able to locate it *as a problem*. Has anyone ever posed the problem of the *ontological source* of notness *[Nichtheit]*, or, *prior to that*, even sought the mere *conditions* on the basis of which the problem of the 'not' and its notness and the possibility of notness could be raised? And where else should they be found *than in a thematic clarification of the meaning of being in general?*" SZ, 285–286. See Giorgio Agamben's *Language and Death: The Place of Negativity*, 3ff, for

a discussion of this passage and its relation to Hegel. Heidegger comes back to the same problem in "What is Metaphysics?" when he writes: "What testifies to the constant and widespread though distorted manifestness of the nothing in our existence more compellingly than negation? But negation does not conjure the 'not' out of itself, as a means for making distinctions and oppositions in whatever is given, inserting itself, as it were, in between what is given. How could negation produce the 'not' from itself when it can negate only if something negatable is already granted to it? But how could the negatable and what is negated be viewed as something susceptible to the 'not' unless all thinking as such has already caught sight of the 'not'? But the 'not' can become manifest only when its origin, the nihilation of the nothing in general, and therewith the nothing itself, is disengaged from concealment. The 'not' does not originate through negation; rather, negation is grounded in the 'not' that springs from the nihilation of the nothing. But negation is also only one way of nihilating, that is, only one sort of comportment that has been grounded beforehand in the nihilation of the nothing." *Pathmarks*, 92. Heidegger continues his discussion of anxiety as an originary mood that confronts nihilation. I think that Heidegger articulates a noncognitive confrontation with negativity in "What is Metaphysics?".

20. In section seven of *Being and Time*, Heidegger asks "now what must be taken into account if the formal concept of phenomenon is to be deformalized to the phenomenological one, and how does it differ from the common concept?" SZ, 35.

21. Heidegger distinguishes his conception of being guilty from its ordinary moral or ethical connotations, SZ, 281–284.

22. For the relationship between the voice of conscience and negativity in Heidegger, see Giorgio Agamben's *Language and Death: The Place of Negativity*, 32–37. Agamben sees the possibility of ethics in Heidegger's philosophy within the context of voice and otherness. Also see Derrida, "Heidegger's Ear: Philopolemology (Geschlecht 4)," in *Reading Heidegger: Commemorations*, ed. J. Sallis (Indianapolis: Indiana University Press, 1993), 163–218.

23. Thus, Dasein should not be understood as a sphere or interiority of any sort, but rather as an exteriority.

24. One can read chapter five of the second division of *Being and Time* as a response to Hegel's notion of thinking as historical. Heidegger's response depends upon the nature of the movement of Dasein's existence historically. Historicity is understood on the basis of finite temporality for Heidegger.

25. Françoise Dastur, *Heidegger and the Question of Time*, trans. F. Raffoul and D. Pettigrew (Atlantic Highlands: Humanities Press, 1998), xxiv.

26. The difficulty of finding a nonobjectifying language preoccupied Heidegger in *Being and Time* and after. Heidegger's notion of *Formale Anzeige* (Formal Indication) seems to be his attempt to develop a language that will resist this objectifying tendency of language. See John van Buren, "The Ethics of *Formale Anzeige* in Heidegger," *American Catholic Philosophical Quarterly: Heidegger*, ed. J. Caputo, 69 (1995): 157–170; Theodore Kisiel, "The Genetic Difference in Reading *Being and Time*," *American Catholic Philosophical Quarterly*, 69:2 (1995): 171–187; James Smith, "Alterity, Transcendence, and the Violence of the Concept: Kierkegaard and Heidegger," *International*

Philosophical Quarterly, 38:4 (1998): 369–381; Ryan Streeter, "Heidegger's Formal Indication: A Question of Method in Being and Time," *Man and World*, 30:4 (1997): 413–430; and Cameron McEwen, "On Formal Indication: Discussion of "The Genesis of Heidegger's 'Being and Time,'" *Research in Phenomenology*, 25 (1995): 226–239.

27. Heidegger recognizes the difficulty of displacing subjectivity and its relation to the problem of exposition: "In *Being and Time* on the basis of the question of truth of Being, no longer the question of truth of beings, an attempt is made to determine the essence of man solely in terms of his relationship to being. That essence was described in a firmly delineated sense as *Da-sein*. In spite of a simultaneous development of a more original concept of truth . . . the past thirteen years have not in the least succeeded in awakening even a preliminary understanding of the *question that was posed.* . . . Above all the path taken terminates abruptly at a decisive point. The reason for the disruption is that the attempt and the path it chose confront the danger of unwillingly becoming merely another entrenchment of subjectivity. . . ." *Nietzsche,* vol. 4, trans. Frank Capuzzi (New York: Harper and Row, 1982), 141.

CHAPTER FOUR
HEIDEGGER: MADNESS, NEGATIVITY, TRUTH, AND HISTORY

Die Fröhliche Wissenschaft, Kritische Studienausgabe, vol. 3, ed. G. Colli and M. Montinari (Berlin: Walter de Gruyter, 1980), 480–481. *The Gay Science,* trans. W. Kaufmann (New York: Vintage Books, 1974), 181.

1. *Zollikoner Seminare: Protokolle-Zwiegespräche-Briefe* (Frankfurt a.M.: V. Klostermann, 1987), 7. *Zollikon Seminars: Protocols-Conversations-Letters,* trans. F. Mayr and R. Aksay (Evanston: Northwestern University Press, 2001). These seminars are edited by Medard Boss and consist of seminars delivered by Heidegger between 1959 and 1969. They consist of discussions with medical doctors and psychiatrists initiated by Boss and mostly held in Boss's house in Zollikon. The seminars are mostly informal, yet philosophically very illuminating in understanding Heidegger's interpretation of modern science, and especially psychiatry as an extension of modern scientific method. All translations are mine.

2. See David F. Krell, *Of Memory, Reminiscence, and Writing: On the Verge,* where he writes that "the name Heidegger chooses for the instant of ecstasis, the temporalizing of existence in each ecstasis as such, is *Entrückung,* rapture. Its seizures are not unidirectional. They move not merely forward into some linear future but also backward. *Rücken* is in fact two words, with two apparently distinct origins: *der Rücken,* 'the back,' *zurück,* 'behind' . . . and the verb *rücken* (or *rücken*), 'the sudden movement.' . . . The 'sudden movement' of ecstatic temporality is not simply a forward leap into future possibilities; it is simultaneously a movement back or recoil to that from which Dasein is thrown." *Of Memory, Reminiscence, and Writing: On the Verge* (Bloomington: Indiana University Press, 1992), 244.

3. "*Der Ursprung des Kunstwerkes,*" in *Holzwege* (Frankfurt a.M.: V. Klostermann, 1950), 55. Translated as "The Origin of the Work of Art," *Poetry, Language, Thought,* trans. A. Hofstadter (New York: Harper and Row, 1971), 66.

4. In *An Introduction to Metaphysics*, Heidegger uses cognates of *rücken* to characterize a similar phenomenon to the one he articulates in "The Origin of the Work of Art." In *An Introduction to Metaphysics*, Heidegger writes: "The violence of poetic saying, of thinking projection, of building configuration, of the action that creates states, is not an operation of capacities that the human has, but a restraining [*bändigen*] and ordering of powers by the strength of which being opens up as such when the human moves into it [*einrückt*]," *Einführung in die Metaphysik* (Tübingen: M. Niemeyer), 120. On page 125 of *An Introduction to Metaphysics*, Heidegger writes: "The uncanniest [*Unheimlichste*] [human] is what it is because, from its ground out, it cultivates and protects the familiar [*Einheimische*] only in order to break out of it and to let what overpowers it break in. Being itself hurls man into the path [*Bahn*] of this tearing-away, which drives him beyond himself forth [*über ihn selbst hinweg*] as the disengaged [*als den Ausrückenden*] towards Being, to set this into a work, and so hold open beings as a whole." Heidegger's description of confronting the work of art is similar to his description of the resoluteness that runs ahead. The noncommunicable aspect of our confrontation with an art work is parallel to Heidegger's insight that the aloneness that is invoked in this confrontation undermines the possibility of a discourse that incessantly continues by being transferred to a public domain.

5. *"Vom Wesen der Wahrheit,"* in *Wegmarken*, GA. 9 (Frankfurt a.M.: V. Klostermann, 1976). The first edition of this essay appeared in 1943. This essay contains the text of a public lecture conceived in 1930 and delivered on different occasions. The 1930 and 1943 versions of this text differ in significant ways.

6. *Grundfragen der Philosophie: Ausgewählte "Probleme" der "Logik,"* GA. 45 (Frankfurt a.M.: V. Klostermann, 1984), 214. Translated as *Basic Questions of Philosophy: Selected "Problems" of "Logic"* by R. Rojcewicz and A. Schuwer (Bloomington: Indiana University Press, 1994). Hereafter abbreviated as GdP in the text followed by the page number of the English translation. The translation is modified.

7. In the *Critique of Pure Reason*, Kant states: "We must . . . make trial whether we may not have more success in the tasks of metaphysics, if we suppose that objects must conform to our knowledge" (B xvii). Consequently ". . . the conditions of the possibility of experience in general are likewise conditions of the possibility of the objects of experience . . ." (A 158, B 197). Therefore, in *Kant und das Problem der Metaphysik*, Heidegger concludes that Kant does not shake the old concept of truth, but "grounds it in the first place." *Kant and the Problem of Metaphysics*, trans. R. Taft (Bloomington: Indiana University Press, 1990), 8.

8. In *Being and Time* Heidegger writes, "To have always already let something be freed for involvement [*Bewandtnis*] is an *a priori perfect*, which characterizes the kind of being of Dasein itself," SZ, 85. In a marginal note to this sentence Heidegger refers to Aristotle's notion of *to ti en einai* (what already was; what always already has presenced in advance, what has been, *Gewesen*, the perfect). Therefore, Heidegger understands essence not as an unchanging form but "that which has always already presenced in advance," SZ, 441.

9. *"Vom Wesen der Wahrheit,"* in *Wegmarken*, GA. 9 (Frankfurt a.M.: V. Klostermann, 1976), 89. Translated as "On the Essence of Truth" by J. Sallis, in *Pathmarks*, ed. W. McNeill (Cambridge: Cambridge University Press, 1998), 148.

10. *"Platons Lehre von der Wahrheit,"* in *Wegmarken*, 143. Translated as "Plato's Doctrine of Truth" by Thomas Sheehan, in *Pathmarks*, 182. The translation is modified.

11. *"Vom Wesen der Wahrheit,"* in *Wegmarken*, 93; "On the Essence of Truth," *Pathmarks*, 151.

12. John Sallis, "Deformatives: Essentially Other Than Truth," in *Reading Heidegger: Commemorations*, ed. J. Sallis (Bloomington: Indiana University Press, 1993), 44–45. In his reading of this text, W. Richardson distinguishes untruth as concealment from untruth as the errancy which has the additional character of "distortion." See "Heidegger and Politics," in *Ethics and Danger: Essays on Heidegger and Continental Thought*, ed. A. B. Dallery and C. Scott (Albany: State University of New York Press, 1992), 12. I don't think that this distinction is ultimately sustainable because, according to Heidegger, errancy holds sway in the simultaneity of disclosure and concealment. "Distortion" gives the impression that somehow a "true" access to concealment is possible. Richardson further wonders why Sallis introduces the theme of madness into the question of truth, and writes, "only he [Sallis] can say." Neither Sallis nor Richardson refers to *Basic Questions of Philosophy*, where Heidegger himself introduces the theme of madness, albeit in a different way than Sallis does. Walter Biemel criticizes Sallis for mistranslating *Verrückung* as "madness," and thereby suggests that there is a pathological derangement in Heidegger. See "Marginal Notes on Sallis's Peculiar Interpretation of Heidegger's *Vom Wesen der Wahrheit*," in *The Path of Archaic Thinking: Unfolding the Work of John Sallis*, ed. K. Maly (Albany: State University of New York Press, 1995), 225. Sallis responds to Biemel's criticism by claiming that his reading of Heidegger's *Vom Wesen der Wahrheit* was not meant as a criticism of Heidegger, because Sallis interprets madness not as mental illness or insanity, but (with Heidegger) in the Greek sense of *mania*, which characterizes the seer, the poet, and the philosopher. Sallis refers to the *Phaedrus* in this context. See ". . . A Wonder that one could never aspire to surpass," in *The Path of Archaic Thinking: Unfolding the Work of John Sallis*, ed. K. Maly (Albany: State University of New York Press, 1995), 273. Indeed, Heidegger himself sees a connection between *Verrückung* and *Verrücktheit* (or even *Wahnsinn*), as we will see in the context of the discussion of *Basic Questions of Philosophy*. Therefore, Sallis seems to be justified in using madness to capture Heidegger's meaning. However, I believe Heidegger's discussion of madness is not in continuity with divine *mania* understood in a Platonic sense. Heidegger resists both clinical and metaphysical interpretations of madness.

13. For an alternative interpretation of negativity in Hegel and Heidegger, see Giorgio Agamben, *Language and Death: The Place of Negativity*, trans. K. E. Pinkus with M. Hardt (Minneapolis: University of Minnesota Press, 1991).

14. In *An Introduction to Metaphysics*, Heidegger contends that the "suspension of the principle of contradiction in Hegel's dialectic is not an end to the domination of *logos* but only its extreme intensification" (143).

15. On this point, see Joseph Flay, *Hegel's Quest for Certainty* (Albany: State University of New York Press, 1984).

16. W. B. Macomber discusses the distinction between Hegel and Heidegger's understanding of truth in its relation to history. Macomber underlines the significance

of history for Hegel's understanding of truth and how it differs from that of Heidegger; For Hegel, the conflict underlying the Western tradition is a conflict within consciousness, whereas for Heidegger such a conception of truth remains inadequate to understanding the historicity of human existence. See *The Anatomy of Disillusion: Martin Heidegger's Notion of Truth* (Evanston: Northwestern University Press, 1967), especially 131–140 and 168–189.

17. See, for example, Robert Williams's *Hegel and Heidegger*, where the author claims that Heidegger's remarks on Hegel are mostly "polemical and critical." For Williams, it is a serious gap in Heidegger's reading of Hegel that he does not have a book length study of Hegel's thought as a whole. It is Heidegger's "failure to make good on his sweeping critical charges leveled at Hegel," in *Hegel and His Critics*, ed. W. Desmond (Albany: State University of New York Press, 1989), 154. Gadamer's interpretation of the relation between Hegel and Heidegger is more sophisticated, as he identifies the problems of truth and historicity in the confrontation of Hegel and Heidegger. See "Hegel and Heidegger," in *Hegel's Dialectic: Five Hermeneutic Studies*, trans. C. Smith (New Haven: Yale University Press, 1971), 100–116. One of the most in depth studies of the relationship between Hegel and Heidegger is Dennis Schmidt's *The Ubiquity of the Finite* (Cambridge: MIT Press, 1988). At the conclusion of this book Schmidt writes that "the temptation to ask for a victor in the confrontation between Hegel and Heidegger is a misguided one."

18. *Logik: Die Frage nach der Wahrheit*, GA. 21 (Frankfurt a.M.: V. Klostermann, 1976), see especially section twenty, entitled *"Hegels Deutung der Zeit in der 'Enzyklopädie.'"* In this 1925–1926 Marburg lecture course, Heidegger's reading concentrates, as in *Being and Time*, on Hegel's determination of time as the negation of negation. Heidegger claims that the fundamental aspects of Hegel's conception of time are already articulated in the *Jena Logic*. Heidegger also contends that the influence of Aristotle's treatment of time in the *Physics* on Hegel's conception of time can be observed in the *Jena Logic*, SZ, 432–433. Derrida problematizes Heidegger's interpretation of Hegel in *"Ousia and Gramme,"* in *Margins of Philosophy*, trans. A. Bass (Chicago: University of Chicago Press, 1982), 29–67.

19. Such an explanation establishes the possibility of thinking a linear connection between the authentic and vulgar conceptions of time, which in turn would render Heidegger's discussion of time continuous with the traditional understanding of time. Heidegger would thereby participate in a further grounding of the metaphysical tradition rather than destructuring it.

20. Perhaps the thinking of difference constitutes Heidegger's last word to Hegel. In *Identity and Difference*, Heidegger criticizes what he calls the "onto-theological" thinking of Hegel for being incapable of thinking the ontological difference between being and beings *out of* their difference. *Identität und Differenz* (Pfullingen: Günther Neske, 1957), 55ff.

21. See especially "Hegels Begriff der Erfahrung," in *Holzwege* (Frankfurt a.M.: V. Klostermann, 1950), 105–192. Translated as *Hegel's Concept of Experience* (New York: Harper and Row, 1970). Hereafter cited as HBE followed by the page numbers of the German text and the translation. This text was composed in 1943 but not published until 1950. This is not the only text that concentrates on Hegel's concept of experi-

ence. In most of his texts Heidegger seems to come back to this concept either directly or indirectly through the dialectical movement of spirit and negativity.

22. Martin Heidegger, *Hegels Phänomenologie des Geistes*, GA. 32 (Frankfurt a.M.: V. Klostermann, 1980). *Hegel's Phenomenology of Spirit*, trans. P. Emad and K. Maly (Bloomington: Indiana University Press, 1988). Hereafter cited as HPS followed by the page number to the translation.

23. At this point it may be helpful to indicate how Descartes' understanding of consciousness as self-consciousness differs from that of Hegel. For Descartes, perception is already a self-perception, as is clear in the famous passage from the *Meditations* in which a perception of wax only "proves" that "I" exist. It is true that one does not explicitly perceive "I think," and Descartes is simply inferring the indubitability of the Cogito. Nevertheless, the perception of the wax does require a looking away from the wax itself, away to the presence, which Descartes understands as "I." The "I" is that which accompanies all the perceptions of the changing characteristics of the wax. It is always alongside the perception and thinking. Hence self-consciousness is an inevitable result of the perspective of the subject, because the subject looks away from the wax as well as from itself as a perceiving subject. However, Hegel's version of consciousness as self-consciousness does not rely on a constant presence of something like an "I," because the experience ultimately is not that of a thinking subject, but of thinking itself.

24. In the second part of *Hegel* GA. 68, entitled *Erläuterung der "Einleitung" zu Hegels "Phänomenologie des Geistes,"* Heidegger presents an informal version of the text, which is published as *Hegel's Concept of Experience*.

25. Concerning the role of sense-certainty and its relation to negativity in Hegel see Giorgio Agamben, *Language and Death: The Place of Negativity*, 11ff.

26. This is the first part of *Hegel* GA. 68, published in 1993. Hereafter abbreviated as H followed by the page number.

27. Since we discussed the Preface to the *Phenomenology of Spirit* at length in chapter three, I do not think that I take these lines out of context: "As regards to the dialectic movement itself, its element is the one Notion; it thus has a content which is, in its own self, Subject through and through," Phen., 61–62, 40.

28. *"Was ist Metaphysik?"* in *Wegmarken*. Translated as "What is Metaphysics?" in *Pathmarks*, ed. W. McNeill (Cambridge: Cambridge University Press, 1998), 94–95.

29. Heidegger draws this distinction between the historicity and eschatology of being in "The Anaximander Fragment," in *Holzwege* (Frankfurt a.M.: V. Klostermann, 1950), 300ff; Translated in *Early Greek Thinking*, trans. D. F. Krell and A. Capuzzi, ed. D. F. Krell (New York: Harper and Row, 1984), 17ff. I will discuss this text later in this chapter.

30. In "The Anaximander Fragment," Heidegger writes: ". . . in the phrase 'eschatology of being' we do not understand the term 'eschatology' as the name of a theological or philosophical discipline. We think eschatology of being in a way corresponding to the way the phenomenology of spirit is to be thought, i.e. from within the history of being. The phenomenology of spirit itself constitutes a phase in the escha-

tology of being, when being gathers itself in the ultimacy of its essence, hitherto determined through metaphysics, as the absolute subjecticity of the unconditioned will to
will." "Der Spruch des Anaximander," in *Holzwege* (Frankfurt a.M.: V. Klostermann,
1950), 302. Translated in *Early Greek Thinking*, ed. D. F. Krell (New York: Harper and
Row, 1984), 18. Heidegger does not think that phenomenology in its Hegelian sense
is a proper way of thinking the history of being. For Heidegger, the unfolding of being
does not "happen" temporally as a sequence of events (or of interpretations) but
eschatologically as an unfolding, which cannot be thought as the unfolding of consciousness or of spirit.

31. "The End of Philosophy and the Task of Thinking," in *Basic Writings*, 449.

32. Homer, *Iliad*, bilingual edition, trans. H. Voss (Augsburg: Weltbild Verlag,
1994). Heidegger cites these lines in "Der Spruch des Anaximander," in *Holzwege*
(Frankfurt a.M.: V. Klostermann, 1950), 318. Evidently Heidegger uses an earlier version of Voss's translation. The translation of "The Anaximander Fragment" is in *Early
Greek Thinking*, ed. D. F. Krell (New York: Harper and Row, 1984), 13–58. References
to "Der Spruch des Anaximander" are hereafter given in the text as SpA followed by
the page numbers of the German original and the translation with modifications.

33. The word *"Gabe"* appears in a revised edition of the Voss translation I quoted
earlier. The translation Heidegger uses differs from the revised edition in the last two
lines: ". . . *der auch her vor Troia der Danaer Schiffe geleitet; durch weissagenden Geist,
des ihn würdigte Phoibos Apollon."*

34. "Die Sprache," in *Unterwegs Zur Sprache* (Pfullingen: G. Neske, 1959), 23.

35. See especially *Sein und Zeit*, 191–196, and my discussion earlier. The difference
between these two ways of being-away is important for understanding Heidegger's modification of the project of *Being and Time*. The being away of madness is not based on the
ecstatic unity of temporality. Through madness, Heidegger displaces a language that
articulates the relation between being-away and existence in terms of conditions of possibility. I will emphasize this modification later in the context of Derrida's reading of
Heidegger's essay "Language in the Poem." Derrida argues, unfairly, I contend, that Heidegger's later philosophy still adheres to the idea of ecstatic temporality as the basis of
thinking. Derrida thereby overlooks a significant modification in Heidegger's thinking.

36. This phrase echoes "What is Metaphysics?" where Heidegger writes: "Dasein
means: being held out into the nothing," in *Pathmarks*, ed. W. McNeill (Cambridge:
Cambridge University Press, 1998), 91ff.

37. "Die Zeit des Weltbildes," in *Holzwege* (Frankfurt a.M.: V. Klostermann,
1950), 104. "The Age of the World Picture," in *The Question Concerning Technology
and Other Essays*, trans. William Lovitt (New York: Harper and Row, 1977), 154.

38. This statement is perhaps Heidegger's most explicit recognition of the historicity of *Being and Time* itself. This is to say that Heidegger recognizes that *Being and
Time* fails if it is understood as describing Dasein's existence as the ground of historicity. In "The Anaximander Fragment," Dasein's ecstatic existence is not that which
grounds historicity, but the most readily experienced correspondence to the epochal
character of being. The difference is that Dasein's ecstatic character is a historical or
rather an epochal phenomenon rather than a structure that grounds historicity.

39. This reference to that which has never been present both refers to and displaces Plato's theory of recollection discussed in the first chapter. For Heidegger, remembrance is a necessary condition for the possibility of vision. However, unlike Plato, Heidegger recognizes that that which has to be remembered must necessarily remain absent. Thus, unlike Plato, Heidegger resists circumventing absence by understanding it as a modification of presence.

40. Hegel's philosophy is based on the productive dimension of thinking. That is, thinking inevitably produces its own object of cognition and reduces negativity to a difference within consciousness.

41. "Die Sprache im Gedicht: Eine Erörterung von Georg Trakls Gedicht," in *Unterwegs zur Sprache* (Pfullingen: Günther Neske, 1959), 35–82. Hereafter abbreviated as S in the text, followed by the page number.

42. Francis M. Sharp argues that "there is indeed a madness in Trakl's poetry . . . [which] resists capture or exhaustion by the conceptual framework of psychiatry." See *The Poet's Madness: A Reading of Georg Trakl* (Ithaca: Cornell University Press, 1981), 40. Also see David Krell, *Lunar Voices: Of Tragedy, Poetry, Fiction, and Thought* (Chicago: University of Chicago Press, 1995), 83–113, and Véronique Foti, *Heidegger and the Poets: Poiesis, Sophia, Techne* (Atlantic Highlands: Humanities Press, 1992), 13–29.

43. The four "Geschlecht" papers are: "Geschlecht: Sexual Difference, Ontological Difference," *Research in Phenomenology*, 13 (1983): 65–83; "Geschlecht II: Heidegger's Hand," in *Deconstruction and Philosophy*, ed. J. Sallis (Chicago: University of Chicago Press, 1987), 161–196; Geschlecht III is not published; "Heidegger's Ear: Philopolemology (Geschlecht IV)," in *Reading Heidegger*, ed. J. Sallis (Bloomington: Indiana University Press, 1993), 163–218. Another text in which Derrida discusses Heidegger's essay on Trakl is *Of Spirit: Heidegger and the Question*, trans. G. Bennington and R. Bowlby (Chicago: University of Chicago Press, 1989), chapters nine and ten.

44. Heidegger will not understand decomposition as the decomposition proper to the sensuous, the earth. Heidegger will retain the term "decomposition," yet apply it to the suprasensuous world, that is, to the world, which is believed to be immune to decomposition. This reversal, however, will not remain a simple reversal of Platonism, but becomes a displacement of the hierarchical structure that overcomes absence in terms of presence.

45. One should not conclude from this move that Heidegger's interpretation depends on an etymological argument, which may or may not be precise. Heidegger does indeed approach Trakl's poetry with the agenda of displacing the Platonic interpretation. However, the fate of this displacement does not depend on a precise account of etymology. It is also important to note that Heidegger's reading does not necessarily target Plato's philosophy. Heidegger is careful in referring to a "Platonism" in his analysis rather than to Plato.

46. *Of Spirit*, 92.

47. *Of Spirit*, 111.

48. "Heidegger's hand" is a reference to Derrida's second paper in the Geschlecht series, entitled "Heidegger's Hand." Derrida characterizes Heidegger's ambivalence toward metaphysics in the figure of hands. Heidegger has two hands, two tendencies with regard to presence.

49. Toward the end of *Of Spirit*, which was initially an oral presentation, Derrida says in a quite extrinsic-sounding fashion: "It is too late and I won't keep you here until morning," *Of Spirit*, 107. Does this mean that Derrida, unlike Heidegger, does not promise a morning, a dawn of a new thinking?

50. Referring back to Heidegger's deconstruction of Western metaphysics in *Being and Time*, Derrida writes: "This retrospective upheaval can seem to dictate a new *order*. One would say, for example, that now everything has to be begun again, taking as the point of departure the en-gage [*l' en-gage*: cf. *langage*] of the *Zusage* so as to construct a quite different discourse, open a quite different path of thought, proceed to a new *Kehre* if not to an *Umkehrung*, and remove a highly ambiguous gesture— the remnant of *Aufklärung* which still slumbered in the privilege of the question," *Of Spirit*, 131 fn.

51. *Of Spirit*, 113.

CHAPTER FIVE
FOUCAULT: THE HISTORY OF MADNESS

1. Michel Foucault, *Histoire de la folie à l'âge classique* (Paris: Gallimard, 1972). *Madness and Civilization: A History of Insanity in the Age of Reason*, trans. R. Howard (New York: Vintage Books, 1965) The English translation is based on Foucault's abridged version of *Histoire de la folie* in the Plon 10/18 series. I use the title *Histoire de la folie* in referring to this text. References are abbreviated as HF followed by the page number for the French text. Jacques Derrida's response to Foucault's book is entitled *"Cogito et Histoire de la folie."* See *L'écriture et la différence* (Paris: Editions du Seuil, 1967), translated as "Cogito and the History of Madness," in *Writing and Difference*, trans. A. Bass (Chicago: University of Chicago Press, 1978). Hereafter abbreviated as CHM followed by the page number to the English translation. Foucault responded to Derrida's criticism of his essay with his remarks published as "Mon corps, ce papier, ce feu," in *Paideia* (September, 1971). This essay is added to *Histoire de la folie à l'âge classique* (Paris: Gallimard, 1972) as an appendix, and is translated by G. Bennington as "My Body, This Paper, This Fire," *Oxford Literary Review* 4 (1975), 9–28. The final word in this debate is Derrida's *"Être juste avec Freud. L'histoire de la folie à l'âge de la psychanalyse,"* "'To do Justice to Freud': The History of Madness in the Age of Psychoanalysis," trans. P-A Brault and M. Naas. This essay was first published in *Critical Inquiry* 20 (1994): 227–266. It also appears in Derrida, *Resistances of Psychoanalysis*, trans. P. Kamuf, P-A Brault, and M. Naas (Stanford: Stanford University Press, 1998), 70–118.

2. Concerning madness and its neurobiological bases, see Louis Sass, *Madness and Modernism: Insanity in the Light of Modern Art, Literature, and Thought* (Massachusetts: Harvard University Press, 1994). See especially the Appendix, entitled "Neurobiological Considerations," 374–397.

3. In Foucault we observe a similar connection between madness and death to that which Heidegger describes. As it seems to be apparent from the excerpt, for Foucault this connection is historical, whereas Heidegger at least initially tries to understand this relationship on the basis of Dasein's temporality. However, I believe the difference between Foucault and Heidegger is not as radical as one might think, because, on the one hand, Heidegger recognizes the significance of the epochal history of being for Dasein's ecstatic temporality. On the other hand, for Foucault, history does not simply mean a linear chain of events.

4. In what follows we are going to see how Foucault's thought of exteriority is related to his understanding of madness.

5. Hence, I disagree with Allan Megill when he writes: ". . . there is a sense of longing, a sense that something originally has been lost," in *Prophets of Extremity: Nietzsche, Heidegger, Foucault, Derrida* (Berkeley and Los Angeles: University of California Press, 1985), 222. This attribution of Romanticism misreads not only Foucault's thinking, but also Romanticism itself. The question of temporality is too difficult an issue both in Foucault and Romanticism to simply claim that there is a longing directed toward the past. If anything, Foucault is concerned with the "yet to come" rather than with going back to a past experience where madness and reason were not radically separated.

6. In fact, Foucault will subsequently modify this claim in "The Order of Discourse," as we will see later. For Foucault, it is Plato who transforms the experience of madness from the saying into the said.

7. The Plon edition of *Madness and Civilization* excludes the beginning of Foucault's second chapter. Therefore, it does not appear in the English translation. I use the unpublished translation by Michael Naas.

8. My designation of Descartes' two conflicting positions as voices is inspired by Foucault's conviction that madness is characterized by the lack of speech. Therefore, whether there can be two voices or whether there is only a modification of a single, meditating, and rational voice, will remain a question, which perhaps amounts to the same question as to whether a dialogue with madness is at all possible.

9. *The Philosophical Writings of Descartes*, vol. II, trans. J. Cottingham, R. Stoothoff, and D. Murdoch (Cambridge: Cambridge University Press, 1985), 13. Hereafter referred to as *Meditations* followed by the page number. An alternative translation is as follows: "How could I deny that these hands or this body are mine, were it not perhaps that I compare myself to certain persons, devoid of sense, whose cerebella are so troubled and clouded by the violent vapors of black bile, that they constantly assure us that they think they are kings when they are really quite poor or that they are clothed in purple when they are really without covering, or who imagine that they have an earthenware head or are nothing but pumpkins or are made of glass. But they are mad, and I should not be any the less insane *(demens)* were I to follow examples so extravagant." *The Philosophical Works of Descartes*, trans. Elizabeth S. Haldane and G. R. T. Ross (Cambridge: Cambridge University Press, 1970), 146.

10. *The Philosophical Writings of Descartes*, vol. II, 13. This translation seems to rely on the Latin version of this paragraph: "*Præclare sane, tanquam non sim homo qui*

foleam noctu dormire, & eadem omnia in fomnis pati, veletiam interdum minus verisimila, quam quæ isti vigilantes." Oeuvres de Descartes, vol. VII (Paris: Leopold Cerf, Imprimeur-Editeur, 1904), 19. Another translation which relies on the French version, indicates more clearly that Descartes indeed posits a counter point in this paragraph: "Nevertheless, I must remember that I am a man, [*Toutesfois j'ay icy à considerer que je suis homme.* See Oeuvres de Descartes, vol. IX (Paris: Leopold Cerf, ImprimeurEditeur, 1904), 14.] and that consequently I am accustomed to sleep and in my dreams to imagine the same things that lunatics imagine when awake, or sometimes things which are even less plausible." *Discourse on Method and Meditations,* trans. Laurence J. Lafleur (Indianapolis: Liberal Arts Press, 1960), 76.

11. "My Body, This Paper, This Fire," *Oxford Literary Review*, 26.

12. *The Philosophical Works of Descartes*, 11. My italics.

13. A Hegelian law seems to follow from Hegel's logic, where the other is always the other of the same. Hence, madness is always the madness of reason. Once cannot have a revolution against reason, because the other of reason is already delimited by reason. Derrida is going to use the same insight in his other essays, including "White Mythology." One can perhaps say that madness for Derrida is both a metaphor and *the* metaphor.

14. Colin Gordon, "*Histoire de la folie:* An Unknown Book by Michel Foucault," in *Rewriting the History of Madness: Studies in Foucault's* Histoire de la folie," ed. A. Still and I. Velody (London: Routledge, 1992), 35.

15. Colin Gordon, "*Histoire de la folie:* An Unknown Book by Michel Foucault," 35.

16. "My Body, This Paper, This Fire," *Oxford Literary Review*, 10.

17. Thus we have to take Derrida seriously when he writes that his dialogue with Foucault (the master) is "in danger of being taken—incorrectly—as a challenge," CHM, 31. Evidently, at a time when every philosophical confrontation is taken to be the collision of two (or more) theoretical positions, Derrida's statement is taken to be simply a disclaimer: "In case I am not successful in challenging Foucault, I will be not be hurt as much, because I have said from the start that this is not my aim." In fact almost all interpreters have ignored Derrida's claim. Perhaps they are right. However, if we desire to "read" the debate without reducing it to theoretical standpoints, we have to take Derrida seriously. He does not challenge Foucault, not because they are saying the same thing, not because Derrida is being polite, but because in the debate there is something else at stake that cannot be reduced to the challenging of a position. Derrida's desire to start speaking at the end of this paragraph, his recognition that the real master may always be absent, clearly indicates that he is aware of the potential problems his discourse is exposed to, CHM, 32.

18. Even though at times Derrida gives the impression of presenting a reductive reading of Foucault's project.

19. Obviously, metaphoricity does not erase the difficulties of Foucault's discourse. Metaphysically, metaphor is only the metaphor of a literal meaning, just as madness is the madness of a meaning, reason, and order.

20. For Derrida, singularity is not opposed to iterability, but rather to other kinds of iteration. "Signature Event Context," in *Limited Inc.*, ed. Gerald Graff (Evanston: Northwestern University Press, 1988), 18.

21. "My Body, This Paper, This Fire," *Oxford Literary Review*, 24.

22. "My Body, This Paper, This Fire," *Oxford Literary Review*, 26.

23. David Carroll discusses the relationship between self-reflexivity and madness in the figure of *mise en abyme* in third chapter of his book *Paraesthetics: Foucault, Lyotard, Derrida* (London: Routledge, 1987), 53–79. See also L. A. Saas, *Madness and Modernism* (Cambridge: Harvard University Press, 1992) for a discussion of the relationship between *mise en abyme* and madness (226, 238, 241, 500).

24. "Orders of Discourse," *Social Science Information* 10:2 (1970): 7.

25. "Orders of Discourse," *Social Science Information* 10:2 (1970): 7.

26. See Ruth Padel, *Whom Gods Destroy: Elements of Greek and Tragic Madness*. "Whom God wishes to destroy, He first makes mad" (5). Padel underlines the fact that madness in the form of emotions "is something coming at you from outside" (8). Hence in Greek tragedy "the gods themselves can cause transgression" (7).

27. Kalchas, therefore, not only had a visionary power, but was also cursed with the inability to intervene into what he could foresee.

28. See "Maurice Blanchot: The Thought from Outside," in *Foucault/Blanchot*, trans. B. Massumi (New York: Zone Books, 1990), 9–13 for Foucault's discussion of "folding" and pp. 15–19 for its connection to madness.

29. *The Foucault Effect*, ed. G. Burchell, C. Gordon, and P. Miller (Chicago: University of Chicago Press, 1991), 53–72.

30. Among others, I have Habermas in mind in this attempt. See *The Philosophical Discourse of Modernity*, trans. F. Lawrence (Cambridge: MIT University Press, 1987).

31. *"La folie, l'absence d'œuvre,"* in *Histoire de la folie à l'âge classique* (Paris: Gallimard, 1972), 575–582. Translation by P. Stastny and D. Şengel in *Foucault and his Interlocutors*, ed A. Davidson (Chicago: University of Chicago Press, 1997), 97–104.

32. David Carroll makes this point quite forcefully in *Paraesthetics*, see chapters three and five, 53–79, 107–129.

33. "The Father's 'No,'" in *Language, Counter-memory, Practice*, trans. D. F. Bouchard (Ithaca: Cornell University Press), 85.

34. In the abridged version, Foucault publishes the following passage in the Conclusion.

35. See especially John Rajchman, *Michel Foucault: The Freedom of Philosophy* (New York: Columbia University Press, 1985).

36. *The Order of Things: An Archaeology of the Human Sciences* (New York: Vintage Books, 1970). Hereafter abbreviated as OT in the text followed by the page number. *Las Meninas*, a 1656 painting by the Spanish artist Diego Velázquez, portrays the king and the queen of Spain in the presence of the infanta Margarita and her atten-

dants. In the tableau itself we can see a self-portrait of Velázquez painting, whereas the king appears through a mirror painted at the back of the room.

37. Evidently, this observation does not mean that Velázquez's painting overcomes subjectivity. Foucault's point here is not that Velázquez's painting in a sense prefigures the disappearance of the modern subject, which historically did not emerge as a category yet. Nevertheless, Velázquez's painting does indeed portray that representing cannot be reduced to what is represented. In this sense, Velázquez does indeed make us aware of the problems of modern subjectivity.

38. *The Foucault Effect,* ed. G. Burchell, C. Gordon, P. Miller (Chicago: University of Chicago Press, 1991), 53–72.

39. "Afterword: The Subject and Power," in *Michel Foucault: Beyond Structuralism and Hermeneutics,* Hubert Dreyfus and Paul Rabinow, 2nd ed. (Chicago: University of Chicago Press, 1982), 208.

40. It seems that today because of the questions concerning the possibility of ethics, there is a growing tendency to try to conceptualize a "different" subject that still supports the problems of responsibility and the necessity of action. I believe that this is a wrong way of approaching the problem of ethics. Indeed, the question of madness is potentially the most promising path toward investigating the questions of ethics. How is it possible to sustain the possibility of ethics in relation to those with whom we have nothing in common? On this issue see Alphonso Lingis, *The Community of Those Who Have Nothing in Common* (Bloomington: Indiana University Press, 1994).

41. "Maurice Blanchot: The Thought from Outside," in *Foucault/Blanchot,* trans. B. Massumi; Maurice Blanchot, "Michel Foucault as I Imagine Him," trans. Jeffrey Mehlman (New York: Zone Books, 1990). Hereafter I abbreviate Foucault's text as TO, followed by the page number.

42. Foucault contrasts "I speak" with "I think," and claims that "I speak" lacks the indubitable certainty of the "I" of "I think." Yet "I think" seems to have the same problem of disappearing the moment it falls silent. Descartes is aware of this problem and institutes God's existence to avoid it. Evidently, in modern fiction such a move is impossible. It is precisely in this sense that Foucault states that Descartes excludes madness, excludes the possibility of the disappearance or interruption of the activity of thinking.

43. "Theatrum Philosophicum," in *Language, Counter-memory, Practice,* trans. D. F. Bouchard (Ithaca: Cornell University Press), 192.

CONCLUSION
MADNESS IS NOT A THING OF THE PAST

Martin Heidegger, *Aus der Erfahrung des Denkens,* GA. 13. (Frankfurt a.M.: V. Klostermann, 1983), 15. Translated by Albert Hofstadter in *Language, Poetry, Thought* (New York: Harper and Row, 1971), 9. The translation is modified.

Jacques Derrida, "La crise de l'enseignement philosophique," in *Du droit à la philosophie,* as cited in Geoffrey Bennington, *Jacques Derrida* (Chicago: University of Chicago Press, 1993), 347.

1. See Martin Heidegger, "The End of Philosophy and the Task of Thinking," in *Basic Writings*, ed. David F. Krell (New York: Harper and Row, 1993), 431–449. In this essay, Heidegger explicitly links the question of the end of philosophy to the question of rationality.

2. Specifically, I have Heidegger's Nietzsche lectures in mind. See especially Heidegger's second volume of Nietzsche lectures, *Nietzsche*, vol. 2 (Pfullingen: Günther Neske, 1961).

3. Concerning the relationship between philosophy and the interaction of cultures, see Derrida's essay "The Ends of Man," in *Margins of Philosophy*, trans. A. Bass (Chicago: University of Chicago Press, 1982), 112.

4. Roy Boyne, *Foucault and Derrida: The Other Side of Reason* (London: Unwin Hyman, 1990), 1–4.

5. As Derrida claims, military or economic violence is in solidarity with linguistic violence. "The Ends of Man," in *Margins of Philosophy*, trans. A. Bass (Chicago: University of Chicago Press, 1982), 135.

6. On this issue, see Alphonso Lingis's *The Community of Those Who Have Nothing in Common* (Bloomington: Indiana University Press, 1994).

7. Heidegger, *Hegels* Phänomenologie des Geistes, GA. 32 (Frankfurt a.M.: V. Klostermann, 1980), 210. *Hegel's* Phenomenology of Spirit, trans. P. Emad and K. Maly (Bloomington: Indiana University Press, 1988), 146.

8. Derrida, "The Ends of Man," in *Margins of Philosophy*, 120.

9. Heidegger, *Hegels* Phänomenologie des Geistes, 19. *Hegel's* Phenomenology of Spirit, 13.

Bibliography

Agamben, Giorgio. *Language and Death: The Place of Negativity*. Translated by Karen E. Pinkus with Michael Hardt. Minneapolis: University of Minnesota Press, 1991.

Ahrensdorf, Peter J. *The Death of Socrates and the Life of Philosophy: An Interpretation of Plato's Phaedo*. Albany: State University of New York, 1995.

Airaksinen, Timo. "Problems in Hegel's Dialectic of Feeling." *Philosophy and Phenomenological Research* 41 (1980): 1–25.

Allen, Jeffner. "Madness and The Poet." *Heidegger and Psychology*. A Special Issue from the *Review of Existential Psychology & Psychiatry*. Edited by Keith Hoeller. Seattle, 1988.

Allen, Michael J. B. *The Platonism of Marsilio Ficino: A Study of His Phaedrus Commentary, It's Sources and Genesis*. Berkeley: University of California Press, 1984.

Allen, R. E. "Anamnesis in Plato's Meno and Phaedo." *Review of Metaphysics* 13 (1959): 165–174.

Archer Hind, R. D. *The Phaedo of Plato*. 2nd ed. London: Macmillan, 1894.

Aristotle. *Metaphysics*, Books I–IX. Translated by Hugh Tredennick. Cambridge: Harvard University Press, 1933.

Artaud, Antonin. *Selected Writings*. Edited by Susan Sontag. Translated by Helen Weaver. New York: Farrar, Straus & Giroux, 1976.

Ballard, Edward G. *Socratic Ignorance: An Essay on Platonic Self-Knowledge*. The Hague: Martinus Nijhoff, 1965.

———. *Philosophy at the Crossroads*. Baton Rouge: Louisiana State University Press, 1971.

Barnett Stuart, editor. *Hegel After Derrida*. London: Routledge, 1998.

Barrett William. *Irrational Man: A Study in Existential Philosophy*. Garden City: Doubleday-Anchor, 1962.

Bataille Georges. "Hegel, Death and Sacrifice." *Yale French Studies* 78 (1990): 9–28.

Beiser, F.C., editor. *The Cambridge Companion to Hegel*. Cambridge: Cambridge University Press, 1993.

Benjamin, Andrew E. *The Plural Event: Descartes, Hegel, Heidegger*. London: Routledge, 1993.

Bennington, Geoffrey. "Cogito Incognito: Foucault's 'My Body, This Paper, This Fire'." *Oxford Literary Review* 4 (1979): 5–8.

——— . *Jacques Derrida*. Chicago: The University of Chicago Press, 1993.

Benvenuto, Bice. "Madness is Philosophy," *Topoi* 12. Kluwer Academic Publishers, (1993): 85–88.

Berthold-Bond, Daniel. *Hegel's Grand Synthesis*. New York: State University of New York Press, 1989.

——— . *Hegel's Theory of Madness*. Albany: State University of New York Press, 1995.

——— . "Intentionality and Madness in Hegel's Psychology of Action." *International Philosophical Quarterly* XXXII, No. 4, (December 1992): 427–441.

Bernasconi, Robert. *The Question of Language in Heidegger's History of Being*. Atlantic Highlands, N.J.: Humanities Press, 1985.

Biemel, Walter. "Marginal Notes on Sallis' Peculiar Interpretation of Heidegger's 'Vom Wesen der Wahrheit'." *The Path of Archaic Thinking: Unfolding the Work of John Sallis*. Edited by Kenneth Maly. Albany: State University of New York Press, 1995. 221–239.

Bigger, Charles. *Participation: A Platonic Inquiry*. Baton Rouge: Louisiana State University Press, 1968.

Blanchot, Maurice. "Michel Foucault as I Imagine Him." *Foucault/Blanchot*. Translated by Jeffrey Mehlman. New York: Zone Books, 1990.

——— . *The Infinite Conversation*. Translated by Susan Hanson. Minneapolis: University of Minnesota Press, 1993.

Boeder, Heribert. *Seditions: Heidegger and The Limit of Modernity*. Translated by Marcus Brainard. Albany: State University of New York Press, 1997.

Bolotin, David. "The Life of Philosophy and the Immortality of the Soul: An Introduction to Plato's Phaedo." *Ancient Philosophy* 7 (1987): 39–56.

Bostock, David. *Plato's Phaedo*. Oxford: Oxford University Press, 1986.

Boss, Medard. *Psychoanalysis and Daseinanalysis*. Translated by Ludwig B. Lefebre. New York: Basic Books, 1963.

Boyne, Roy. *Foucault and Derrida: The Other Side of Reason*. London: Unwin Hyman, 1990.

Burbidge, John. "Man, God, and Death in Hegel's *Phenomenology*." *Philosophy and Phenomenological Research* 42 (1981): 183–196.

Burger, Ronna. *Plato's Phaedrus: A Defense of a Philosophical Art of Writing*. University: University of Alabama Press, 1980.

———. *The* Phaedo: *A Platonic Labyrinth*. New Haven: Yale University Press, 1984.

Burnett, J, editor. *Plato's Phaedo*. Oxford: Clarendon Press, 1911.

Cadava, E., Coonor, P. and Nancy, J-L., editors. *Who Comes After The Subject*. London: Routledge, 1991.

Canguilhem, Georges, "On Histoire de la folie as an Event." Translated by A. Hobart. *Critical Inquiry* 21 (Winter 1995): 282–286.

Carpenter, Jerome. *Mind as Absolute Negativity in Hegel*. Ph.D. Dissertation. Southern Illinois University at Carbondale, 1984.

Carroll, David. *Paraesthetics: Foucault. Lyotard. Derrida*. London: Routledge, 1987.

Chesler, Phyllis. *Women and Madness*. New York: Avon Books, 1972.

Clark, Malcolm. *Logic and System: A Study of the Transition form "Vorstellung" to Thought in the Philosophy of Hegel*. The Hague: Martinus Nijhoff, 1971.

Clark, Timothy. *Derrida, Heidegger, Blanchot: Sources of Derrida's Notion and Practice of Literature*. Cambridge: Cambridge University Press, 1992.

Cobb, Stevens. "Mythos and Logos in Plato's Phaedo." *The Philosophical Reflection of Man in Literature*, Edited by Anna-Teresa Tymieniecka. Boston: Reidel, 1982. 391–406.

Colli, Giorgio. *Die Geburt der Philosophie*. Frankfurt a.M: Europäische Verlaganstalt, 1981.

Comay, Rebecca and McCumber, John, editors. *Endings: Questions of Memory in Hegel and Heidegger*. Evanston: Northwestern University Press, 1999.

Coolidge, Francis P. "The Unity of Platonic Epistemology: Divine Madness in Plato's Phaedrus." *Southwest Philosophy Review* 8 No.1 (1992): 99–108.

Crawford, Claudia. *To Nietzsche: Dionysus, I Love You! Ariadne*. Albany: State University of New York Press, 1995.

Critchley, Simon. *Very Little . . . Almost Nothing*. London: Routledge, 1997.

Critchley, Simon and Dews, Peter, editors. *Deconstructive Subjectivities*. Albany: State University of New York Press.

Dallery, A.B., Scott, C.E. *Ethics and Danger: Essays on Heidegger and Continental Thought*. Albany: State University of New York Press, 1992.

Davis, Michael. "Plato and Nietzsche on Death: An Introduction to Plato's Phaedo." *Ancient Philosophy* 1 (1980): 69–80.

———. "Socrates' Pre-Socratism: Some Remarks on the Structure of Plato's Phaedo." *Review of Metaphysics* 33 (1980): 559–577.

D'Amico, Robert. "Text and Context: Derrida and Foucault on Descartes." *The Structural Allegory: Reconstructive Encounters with the New French Thought*. Edited by John Fekete, Minneapolis: University of Minnesota Press, 1984.

Dastur, Françoise. *Death: An Essay on Finitude*. Translated by J. Llewelyn, London: The Athlone Press, 1996.

————. *Heidegger and the Question of Time*. Translated by F. Raffoul and D. Pettigrew, Atlantic Highlands, N.J.: Humanities Press, 1998.

Davidson, Arnold I (ed). *Foucault and his Interlocutors*. Chicago: The University of Chicago Press, 1997.

Deleuze, Gilles. *Foucault*. Translated by Seán Hand, Minneapolis: University of Minnesota Press, 1988.

De Man, Paul. "Hegel on the Sublime." *Aesthetic Ideology*. Translated by Andrzej Warminski. Minneapolis: University of Minnesota Press, 1996.

————. "Sign and Symbol in Hegel's *Aesthetics*." *Aesthetic Ideology*. Translated by Andrzej Warminski. Minneapolis: University of Minnesota Press, 1996.

Derrida, Jacques. *Aporias*. Translated by Thomas Dutoit. Stanford: Stanford University Press, 1993.

————. *Cinders*. Translated by Ned Loquitur. Lincoln: Nebraska University Press, 1987.

————. "Cogito and The History of Madness." *Writing and Difference*. Translated by Alan Bass. Chicago: University of Chicago Press, 1978. 31–63.

————. *Dissemination*. Translated by Barbara Johnson. Chicago: The University of Chicago Press, 1981.

————. *L'écriture et la différence*. Paris: Tel Quel, 1967.

————. "The Ends of Man." *Margins of Philosophy*. Translated by Alan Bass. Chicago: The University of Chicago Press, 1982. 109–136.

————. "From Restricted to General Economy: A Hegelianism Without Reserve." *Writing and Difference*. Translated by Alan Bass. Chicago: University of Chicago Press, 1978. 251–277.

————. *Given Time: I. Counterfeit Money*. Translated by Peggy Kamuf. Chicago: The University of Chicago Press, 1992.

————. *Glas*. Translated by John P. Leavey, Jr. and Richard Rand. Lincoln: University of Nebraska Press, 1986.

————. "Heidegger's Ear: Philopolemology (Geschlecht 4)." *Reading Heidegger: Commemorations*. Edited by John Sallis. Indianapolis: Indiana University Press, 1993. 163–218.

————. *Limited Inc*. Edited by Gerald Graff. Evanston: Northwestern University Press, 1988.

————. *Margins of Philosophy*. Translated by Alan Bass. Chicago: The University of Chicago Press, 1982.

————. *Memoires for Paul de Man*. Translated by C. Lindsay, J. Culler, E. Cadava and P. Kamuf. New York: Columbia University Press, 1989.

————. *Of Grammatology*. Translated by Gayatri C. Spivak. Baltimore: The Johns Hopkins University Press, 1974.

————. *Of Spirit: Heidegger and The Question*. Translated by G. Bennington, and R. Bowlby. Chicago: The University of Chicago Press, 1989.

————. *On the Name*. Translated by D. Wood, J. Leavey, and I. McLeod. Stanford: Stanford University Press, 1995.

————. "Plato's Pharmacy," *Dissemination*. Translated by Barbara Johnson. Chicago: University of Chicago Press, 1981.

————. *Politics of Friendship*. Translated by George Collins. London: Verso Books, 1997.

————. *Resistances of Psychoanalysis*. Translated by P. Kamuf, P-A. Brault &M. Naas. Stanford: Stanford University Press, 1998.

————. *The Gift of Death*. Translated by David Wills. Chicago: The University of Chicago Press, 1995.

————. *The Post Card*. Translated by Alan Bass. Chicago: The University of Chicago Press, 1987.

————. "'To Do Justice to Freud': The History of Madness in the Age of Psychoanalysis." Translated by P-A Brault and M. Naas. *Critical Inquiry* 20 (Winter 1994): 227–266.

————. *Writing and Difference*. Translated by Alan Bass. Chicago: The University of Chicago Press, 1978.

Descartes, Rene. *Oeuvres de Descartes*. Paris: Leopold Cerf, Imprimeur-Editeur, 1904.

————. *Discourse on Method and Meditations*. Translated by Laurence J. Lafleur. Indianapolis: The Liberal Arts Press, 1960.

————. *The Philosophical Works of Descartes*. Translated by E. S. Haldane and G. R. T. Ross. Cambridge: Cambridge University Press, 1970.

Desmond, William. *Beyond Hegel and Dialectic: Speculation, Cult, and Comedy*. Albany: State University of New York Press, 1992.

De Vries, G. J. *A Commentary on the Phaedrus of Plato*. Amsterdam: Hakkert, 1969.

Dodds, E. R. *The Greeks and the Irrational*. Berkeley: University of California Press, 1951.

Dreyfus, Hubert L. "Foucault's Critique of Psychiatric Medicine." *Journal of Medicine and Philosophy* 12 (November 1987): 311–333.

————. "On the Ordering of Things: Being and Power in Heidegger and Foucault." *Southern Journal of Philosophy* 28. supplement 1989.

Dreyfus, Hubert and Rabinow, Paul. *Michel Foucault: Beyond Structuralism and Hermeneutics*, Second edition. Chicago: Chicago University Press, 1983 .

Dumont, Matthew P. "What is Madness?" *Social Science and Medicine* 2 (1968): 502–504.

Feder, Lillian. *Madness in Literature*. Princeton: Princeton University Press, 1980.

Felman, Shoshana. *Writing and Madness*. Translated by M. N. Evans. Ithaca: Cornell University Press, 1985.

Ferrari, G. R. F. *Listening to the Cicadas: A Study of Plato's* Phaedrus. Cambridge: Cambridge University Press, 1987.

Findlay, John N. *The Philosophy of Hegel: An Introduction and Re-examination.* New York: Collier, 1962.

————. "Hegelianism and Platonism," *Hegel and the History of Philosophy.* Edited by J. J. O'Malley, K. Algozin, F. G. Weiss. The Hague: Martinus Nijhoff, 1974, 62–76.

Flay, Joseph C. *Hegel's Quest for Certainty.* Albany: State University of New York Press, 1984.

————. "Hegel, Heidegger, Derrida: Retrieval as Reconstruction, Destruction, Deconstruction." *Ethics and Danger: Essays on Heidegger and Continental Thought.* Edited by A. B. Dallery, C. E. Scott. Albany: State University of New York Press, 1992. 199–213.

Flynn, Bernard. "Derrida and Foucault: Madness and Writing." *Derrida and Deconstruction.* Edited by H. J. Silverman. London: Routledge, 1989. 201–218.

Forrester, John, "Michel Foucault and the History of Psychoanalysis." *History of Science* 18 (1980): 286–301.

Foucault, Michel, and Ludwig Binswanger. *Dream and Existence.* Edited by Keith Hoeller. Atlantic Highlands, N.J.: Humanities Press, 1993.

Foucault, Michel. *Death and the Labyrinth: The World of Raymond Roussel.* Translated by Charles Raus. Garden City: Doubleday, 1986.

————. *Discipline and Punish: The Birth of the Prison.* Translated by Alan Sheridan. New York: Vintage Books, 1979.

————. "Maurice Blanchot: The Thought from Outside." *Foucault/Blanchot.* Translated by B. Massumi. New York: Zone Books, 1990.

————. *Histoire de la folie: a l'age classique.* Paris: Plon, 1961.

————. *Histoire de la folie: à l'âge classique: suivi de Mon corps, ce papier, ce feu et La folie, l'absence d'oeuvre.* Paris: Gallimard, 1972.

————. *Language, Counter-memory, Practice.* Edited by D. F. Bouchard. Ithaca: Cornell University Press, 1977.

————. *Madness and Civilization: A History of Insanity in the Age of Reason.* Translated by Alan Sheridan. New York: Vintage Books, 1988.

————. *Mental Illness and Psychology.* Translated by Alan Sheridan. Berkeley: University of California Press, 1987.

————. *Michel Foucault: Politics Philosophy Culture.* Edited by Lawrence D. Kritzman. Translated by Alan Sheridan. London: Routledge, 1988.

————. *Power/Knowledge.* Edited by Colin Gordon. Translated by Colin Gordon et. al. New York: Pantheon Books, 1980.

————. *The Archaeology of Knowledge* and *The Discourse on Language.* Translated by Alan Sheridan. New York: Pantheon Books, 1972.

————. *The Birth of the Clinic.* Translated by Alan Sheridan. New York: Vintage Books, 1973.

––––––. *The Foucault Effect: Studies in Governmentality*. Edited by G. Burchell, C. Gordon, P. Miller. Chicago: The University of Chicago Press, 1991.

––––––. *The Foucault Reader*. Edited by Paul Rabinow. New York: Pantheon Books, 1984.

––––––. *The History of Sexuality*, Vol I, An Introduction. Translated by Robert Hurley. New York: Vintage Books, 1978.

––––––. *The Order of Things: An Archaeology of the Human Sciences*. Translated by Alan Sheridan. New York: Vintage Books, 1970.

––––––. *The Use of Pleasure, The History of Sexuality*, Vol II. Translated by Robert Hurley. New York: Vintage Books, 1985.

––––––. *The Care of the Self, The History of Sexuality*, Vol III. Translated by Robert Hurley. New York: Vintage Books, 1986.

––––––. "The Order of Discourse," *Social Science Information* 10 No. 2 (1970): 7–30.

Fóti, Véronique M. *Heidegger and The Poets: Poiesis, Sophia, Techne*. Atlantic Highlands, N.J.: Humanities Press, 1992.

––––––. "Eros, Freedom, and Constraint in Plato's Symposium and Phaedrus." *Auslegung* 5 (1978): 66–100.

Frank, Manfred. "Is Subjectivity a Non-Thing *[Unding]*? On Some Difficulties in Naturalistic Reductions of Self-Consciousness," *The Modern Subject, Conceptions of the Self in Classical German Philosophy*. Edited by K. Ameriks and D. Sturma. Albany: State University of New York Press, 1995. 177–197.

Freud, Sigmund. *Das Ich und Das Es: Metapsychologische Schriften*. Frankfurt am Main: Fischer, 1994.

Friedländer, P. *Plato* (3 vols.) Translated by H. Meyerhoff. Princeton: Princeton University Press, 1969.

Frow, John. *Marxism and Literary Theory*. Cambridge: Harvard University Press, 1986.

Fynsk, Christopher. *Heidegger: Thought and Historicity* (expanded edition). Ithaca: Cornell University Press, 1993.

Gadamer, Hans-Georg. *Dialogue and Dialectic: Eight Hermeneutical Studies on Plato*. Translated by Christopher Smith, New Haven: Yale University Press, 1980.

––––––. *Die Idee des Guten zwischen Plato und Aristoteles*. Heidelberg: Carl Winter Universitätsverlag, 1978.

––––––. *Hegel's Dialectic: Five Hermeneutic Studies*. Translated by Christopher Smith, New Haven: Yale University Press, 1976.

––––––. *Reason in the Age of Science*. Translated by Frederick G. Lawrence. Cambridge: The MIT Press, 1981.

Gamm, Gerjard. *Der Wahnsinn in der Vernunft: Historische und Erkenntniskritische Studien zur Dimension des Anders-Seins in der Philosophie Hegels*. Bonn: Bovier Verlag, 1981.

Gillespie, Michael Allen. *Hegel, Heidegger, and the Ground of History*. Chicago: University of Chicago Press, 1984.

Gordon, Colin. "*Histoire de la folie:* An unknown book by Michel Foucault." *Rewriting the history of madness: Studies in Foucault's* Histoire de la folie. Edited by A. Still and I. Velody. London: Routledge, 1992.

Gould, Thomas. *Platonic Love.* New York: Free Press, 1963.

Greene, Murray. *Hegel on the Soul: A Speculative Anthropology.* The Hague: Martinus Nijhoff, 1972.

————. "Hegel's Conception of Psychology." *Hegel and the Sciences.* Edited by Robert S. Cohen and Mark W. Wartofsky. Dordrecht, Boston: D. Reidel Publishing Company, 1984. 161–191.

————. "'Unhappy Consciousness' and Nietzsche's 'Slave Morality'." *Hegel and the Philosophy of Religion.* Edited by Darrel E. Christensen. The Hague: Martinus Nijhoff, 1970. 125–141.

————. "Natural Life and Subjectivity." *Hegel's Philosophy of Spirit.* Edited by Peter G. Stillman. Albany: State University of New York Press, 1987. 94–117.

Griffiss, James E. *Hegel's Dialectic of Negativity.* PhD. Dissertation. Yale University. 1961.

Griswold, Charles L. *Self-Knowledge in Plato's Phaedrus.* University Park: The Pennsylvania State University Press, 1996.

Hadot, Pierre. *Philosophy as a Way of Life.* Edited by Arnold I. Davidson. Translated by Michael Chase Oxford: Blackwell, 1995.

Harris, H. S. *Hegel's Development: Toward the Sunlight* 1770–1801. Oxford: Clarendon Press, 1972.

————. *Hegel's Development: Night Thoughts* (Jena 1801–1806). Oxford: Clarendon Press, 1983.

————. *Hegel's Ladder* I: *The Pilgrimage of Reason.* Indianapolis: Hackett Publishing Company, 1997.

————. *Hegel's Ladder* II: *The Odyssey of Spirit.* Indianapolis: Hackett Publishing Company, 1997.

Hegel, G. W. F. *Hegel's Philosophy of Mind:* Part three of the Encyclopaedia of the Philosophical Sciences (1830) Translated by W. Wallace, Together with the Zusätze in Boumann's Text (1845). Translated by A. V. Miller. Oxford: Clarendon Press, 1971.

————. *Hegel's Science of Logic.* Translated by A.V. Miller. Atlantic Highlands N.J.: Humanities Press, 1989.

————. *Phenomenology of Spirit.* Translated by A.V. Miller. Oxford: Clarendon Press, 1977.

————. *Werke* in 20 Bänden. Frankfurt a.M.: Suhrkamp, 1970.

Heidegger, Martin. *Aus der Erfahrung des Denkens,* GA 13. Frankfurt am Main: Vittoria Klostermann, 1983.

————. *Basic Writings,* Edited by David F. Krell. New York: Harper & Row, 1977. Second edition 1993.

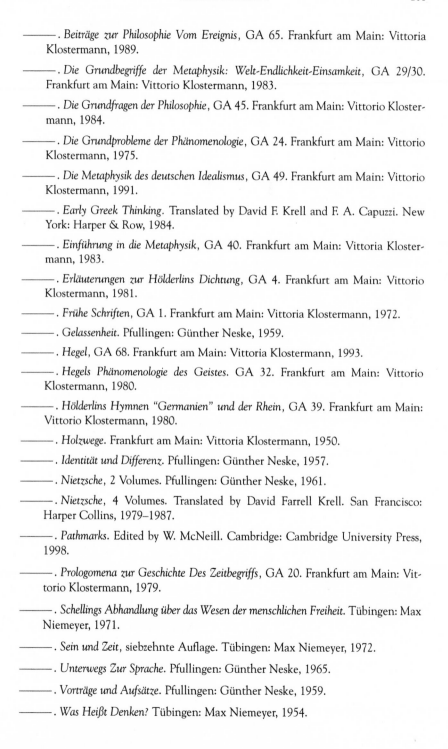

———. *Beiträge zur Philosophie Vom Ereignis*, GA 65. Frankfurt am Main: Vittoria Klostermann, 1989.

———. *Die Grundbegriffe der Metaphysik: Welt-Endlichkeit-Einsamkeit*, GA 29/30. Frankfurt am Main: Vittorio Klostermann, 1983.

———. *Die Grundfragen der Philosophie*, GA 45. Frankfurt am Main: Vittorio Klostermann, 1984.

———. *Die Grundprobleme der Phänomenologie*, GA 24. Frankfurt am Main: Vittorio Klostermann, 1975.

———. *Die Metaphysik des deutschen Idealismus*, GA 49. Frankfurt am Main: Vittorio Klostermann, 1991.

———. *Early Greek Thinking*. Translated by David F. Krell and F. A. Capuzzi. New York: Harper & Row, 1984.

———. *Einführung in die Metaphysik*, GA 40. Frankfurt am Main: Vittoria Klostermann, 1983.

———. *Erläuterungen zur Hölderlins Dichtung*, GA 4. Frankfurt am Main: Vittorio Klostermann, 1981.

———. *Frühe Schriften*, GA 1. Frankfurt am Main: Vittoria Klostermann, 1972.

———. *Gelassenheit*. Pfullingen: Günther Neske, 1959.

———. *Hegel*, GA 68. Frankfurt am Main: Vittoria Klostermann, 1993.

———. *Hegels Phänomenologie des Geistes*. GA 32. Frankfurt am Main: Vittorio Klostermann, 1980.

———. *Hölderlins Hymnen "Germanien" und der Rhein*, GA 39. Frankfurt am Main: Vittorio Klostermann, 1980.

———. *Holzwege*. Frankfurt am Main: Vittoria Klostermann, 1950.

———. *Identität und Differenz*. Pfullingen: Günther Neske, 1957.

———. *Nietzsche*, 2 Volumes. Pfullingen: Günther Neske, 1961.

———. *Nietzsche*, 4 Volumes. Translated by David Farrell Krell. San Francisco: Harper Collins, 1979–1987.

———. *Pathmarks*. Edited by W. McNeill. Cambridge: Cambridge University Press, 1998.

———. *Prologomena zur Geschichte Des Zeitbegriffs*, GA 20. Frankfurt am Main: Vittorio Klostermann, 1979.

———. *Schellings Abhandlung über das Wesen der menschlichen Freiheit*. Tübingen: Max Niemeyer, 1971.

———. *Sein und Zeit*, siebzehnte Auflage. Tübingen: Max Niemeyer, 1972.

———. *Unterwegs Zur Sprache*. Pfullingen: Günther Neske, 1965.

———. *Vorträge und Aufsätze*. Pfullingen: Günther Neske, 1959.

———. *Was Heißt Denken?* Tübingen: Max Niemeyer, 1954.

———. *Wegmarken*. GA. 9. Frankfurt am Main: Vittoria Klostermann, 1967.

———. With Eugen Fink. *Heraklit*. Frankfurt am Main: Vittoria Klostermann, 1950.

———. *Zollikoner Seminare*. Frankfurt am Main: Vittoria Klostermann, 1987.

———. *Zur Sache des Denkens*. Tübingen: Max Niemeyer, 1969.

Hershkowitz, Debra. *The Madness of Epic: Reading Insanity from Homer to Statius*. Oxford: Clarendon Press, 1998.

Hölderlin, Friedrich. *Essays and Letters on Theory*. Edited by Thomas Pfau. Albany: State University of New York Press, 1988.

———. *Hölderlin. Werke und Briefe*, Edited by Friedrich Beissner and Jochen Schmidt Frankfurt a.M.: Insel Verlag, 1969.

———. *Hymns and Fragments*. Translated by Richard Sieburth. New Jersey: Princeton University Press, 1984.

———. *Hyperion*. Translated by Willard R. Trask, Adapted by David Schwarz. New York: The Continuum Publishing Company, 1994.

Hoeller, Keith, editor. *Heidegger and Psychology*. A Special Issue from the *Review of Existential Psychology & Psychiatry*. 1988.

Homer. *The Iliad*, Loeb Classical Library. Massachusetts: Harvard University Press, 1924.

———. *Ilias*, bilingual edition. Translated by H. Voss. Augsburg: Weltbild Verlag, 1994.

Hommes, Jakob. *Zwiespältiges Dasein; die existenziale Ontologie von Hegel bis Heidegger*. Freiburg: Herder, 1953.

Houlgate, Stephen. *Freedom, Truth and History: An introduction to Hegel's Philosophy*. London: Routledge, 1991.

Hoy, David Couzens. "The Owl and the Poet: Heidegger's Critique of Hegel." *Martin Heidegger and the Question of Literature*. Edited by William V. Spanos. Bloomington: Indiana University Press, 1979. 53–70.

Hübscher, Arthur. *Von Hegel zu Heidegger; Gestalten und Probleme*. Stuttgart: Reclam, 1961.

Hyppolite, Jean. *Genesis and Structure of Hegel's Phenomenology of Spirit*. Translated by S. Cherniak and J. Heckman. Evanston: Northwestern University Press, 1974.

———. "Hegel's Phenomenology and Psychoanalysis." *New Studies in Hegel's Philosophy*. Edited by Warren E. Steinkraus. New York: Holt, Rinehart and Winston, INC., 1971, 57–70.

———. *Introduction to Hegel's* Philosophy of History. Translated by B. Harris & J. B. Spurlock. Gainesville: University of Florida Press, 1996.

———. *Logic and Existence*. Translated by L. Lawlor and A. Sen. Albany: State University of New York Press, 1997.

Inwood, M. J. *Hegel*. Arguments of the Philosophers. London: Routledge & Kegan Paul, 1983.

Irigaray, Luce. *An Ethics of Sexual Difference*. Translated by Séan Hand. Ithaca: Cornell University Press, 1995.

———. *The Forgetting of Air in Martin Heidegger*. Translated by Mary B. Mader. London: Athlone, 1999.

———. *Thinking the Difference: For A Peaceful Revolution*. Translated by Karin Montin. London: Routledge, 1994.

Kahn, Charles. *The Verb "Be" in Ancient Greek*. Dordrecht, Boston: D. Reidel, 1973

———. "Some Philosophical Uses of 'to be' in Plato," *Phronesis* 26 (1981): 105–134.

Kant, Immanuel. *Kants Gesammelte Schriften*. Berlin: Königlich Preußische Akademie der Wissenschaften, 1902–. Berlin: Georg Reimer, 1913.

———. *Critique of Judgment*. Translated by Werner S. Pluhar. Indianapolis: Hackett Publishing, 1987.

———. *Critique of Pure Reason*. Translated by Norman Kemp Smith. New York: St. Martin's Press, 1965.

Kiesel, Theodore. *The Genesis of Heidegger's* Being and Time. Berkeley: University of California Press, 1993.

Kiesel, Theodore, and van Buren, John, editors. *Reading Heidegger From the Start*. Albany, State University of New York Press, 1994.

Kirk, G.S. and J.E. Raven and M. Schofield. *The Presocratic Philosophers: A Critical History with a Selection of Texts*, Second Edition. Cambridge: Cambridge University Press, 1983.

Kojève, Alexandre. *Introduction to the Reading of Hegel: Lectures on the* Phenomenology of Spirit. Assembled by Raymond Queneau, edited by Allan Bloom, translated by James H. Nichols, Jr. New York and London: Basic Books, Inc., 1969.

Kolb, David. *The Critique of Pure Modernity: Hegel, Heidegger and After*. Chicago: University of Chicago Press, 1986.

Kraut, Richard, editor. *The Cambridge Companion to Plato*. Cambridge: Cambridge University Press, 1992.

Krell, David F. *Daimon Life: Heidegger and Life Philosophy*. Bloomington: Indiana University Press, 1992.

———. *Intimations of Mortality: Time, Truth and Finitude in Heidegger's Thinking of Being*. Pennsylvania: Pennsylvania State University Press, 1986.

———. *Lunar Voices: Of Tragedy, Poetry, Fiction, and Thought*. Chicago: The University of Chicago Press, 1995.

———. *Of Memory, Reminiscence, and Writing: On the Verge*. Bloomington: Indiana University Press, 1992.

Lacoue-Labarthe, Philippe. *Heidegger, Art and Politics*. Translated by Chris Turner. Oxford: Basic Blackwell, 1990.

———. *The Subject of Philosophy*. Edited by Thomas Trezise. Translated by Thomas Trezise, et. al. (Minneapolis: University of Minnesota Press, 1993.

Laing, R. D. "Sanity and 'Madness'—1: The Invention of Madness." *New Statesman* 16 (June 1967): 843.

Lammi, Walter. "Hegel, Heidegger, and Hermeneutical Experience." *Hegel, History, and Interpretation*, Edited by Shaun Gallagher. Albany: State University of New York Press, 1997. 43–58.

Lauer, Quentin, S.J. *Hegel's Idea of Philosophy*. New York: Fordham University Press, 1971.

———. A Reading of Hegel's "Phenomenology of Spirit." New York: Fordham University Press, 1976.

Linforth, Ivan M. "Telestic Madness in Plato, *Phaedrus* 244de." *University of California Publications in Classical Philology* XIII. Edited by J. T. Allen, et. al. Berkeley: University of California Press, 1971, 163–172.

Lingis, Alphonso. *The Community of Those Who Have Nothing in Common*. Bloomington: Indiana University Press, 1994.

———. *Deathbound Subjectivity*. Bloomington: Indiana University Press: 1989.

Lucas, Hans-Christian. "The 'Sovereign Ingratitude' of Spirit toward Nature: Logical Qualities, Corporeity, Animal Magnetism and Madness in Hegel's 'Anthropology'." *The Owl of Minerva* 23 No. 2 (Spring 1992): 131–150.

Llewelyn, John. "Imadgination," *The Path of Archaic Thinking: Unfolding the Work of John Sallis*. Edited by Kenneth Maly. Albany: State University of New York Press, 1995. 75–88.

Macann, Christopher, editor. *Critical Heidegger*. London: Routledge, 1996.

Malpas, Jeff and Solomon, Robert C., editors. *Death and Philosophy*. London: Routledge, 1998.

Maly, Kenneth, editor. *The Path of Archaic Thinking: Unfolding the Work of John Sallis*. Albany: State University of New York Press, 1995.

Marion, Jean-Luc. *Reduction and Givenness: Investigations of Husserl, Heidegger, and Phenomenology*. Translated by Thomas A. Carlson. Evanston: Northwestern University Press, 1998.

Marx, Werner. *Hegel's "Phenomenology of Spirit," Its Point and Purpose; A Commentary on the Preface and Introduction*. New York: Harper & Row, 1975.

McCumber, John. "Discourse and Psyche in Plato's Phaedrus." *Apeiron* 16 (1982): 27–39.

McNeill, William. "The First Principle of Hermeneutics," *Reading Heidegger From the Start*. Edited by Theodore Kisiel and John van Buren, Albany, State University of New York Press, 1994.

———. *The Glance of the Eye*. Albany: State University of New York Press, 1999.

———. "Spirit's Living Hand," *Of Derrida, Heidegger, and Spirit*. Edited by David Wood, Evanston: Northwestern University Press, 1993.

Megill, Allan. *Prophets of Extremity: Nietzsche, Heidegger, Foucault, Derrida*. Berkeley: University of California Press, 1985.

Melehy, Hassan. *Writing Cogito: Montaigne, Descartes and the Institution of the Modern Subject*. Albany: State University of New York Press, 1997.

Melville, Stephen W. *Philosophy Beside Itself: On Deconstruction and Modernism*. Minneapolis: University of Minnesota Press, 1986.

Meulen, Jan van der. *Heidegger und Hegel; oder, Widerstreit und Widerspruch*. Meisenheim/ Glan: A. Hain, 1953.

Moravcsik, Julius. "Noetic Aspiration and Artistic Inspiration," *Plato On Beauty, Wisdom and the Arts*, Edited by J. Moravcsik and P. Temko. Totowa: Rowman and Littlefield, 1982. 29–46.

Murray, Michael, editor. *Heidegger and Modern Philosophy*. New Haven: Yale University Press, 1978.

Murray, Patrick T. *Hegel's Philosophy of Mind and Will*. Lewiston: The Edwin Mellen Press, 1991.

Myers, Henry A. *The Spinoza-Hegel Paradox: A Study of the Choice between Traditional Idealism and Systematic Pluralism*. New York: Burt Franklin, 1944.

Naas, Michael. "Derrida's Watch, Foucault's Pendulum." *Philosophy Today* 41:1 (Spring 1997): 141–152.

―――. *Turning: From Persuasion to Philosophy, A Reading of Homer's Iliad*. Atlantic Highlands, N.J.: Humanities Press, 1995.

Nancy, Jean-Luc. *The Birth to Presence*. Translated by Brian Holmes et. al. Stanford: Stanford University Press, 1993.

―――. *The Experience of Freedom*. Translated by Bridget McDonald. Stanford: Stanford University Press, 1993.

Navickas, Joseph L. *Consciousness and Reality: Hegel's Philosophy of Subjectivity*. The Hague: Martinus Nijhoff, 1976.

Neumann, Walter. *Die Philosophie des Nichts in der Moderne: Sein und Nichts bei Hegel, Marx, Heidegger und Sartre*. Essen: Blaue Eule, 1989.

Nietzsche, F. *Kritische Studienausgabe*, in zwölf Bänden, Edited by G. Colli and M. Montinari. Berlin: Walter de Gruyter, 1980.

Norman, Richard. *Hegel's Phenomenology: A Philosophical Introduction*. New York: St. Martin's Press, 1976.

Novalis, (Friedrich von Hardenberg). *Werke, Tagebücher und Briefe*. 3 vols. Edited by H-J. Mähl, R. Samuel. München: Carl Hanser Verlag, 1978.

Nussbaum, Martha C. "This Story isn't true": Poetry, Goodness, and Understanding in Plato's *Phaedrus*," *Plato On Beauty, Wisdom and the Arts*, Edited by J. Moravcsik and P. Temko. Totowa: Rowman and Littlefield, 1982. 70–124.

―――. *The Fragility of Goodness: Luck and Ethics in Greek Tragedy and Philosophy*. Cambridge: Cambridge University Press, 1986.

Olson, Alan M. *Hegel and the Spirit: Philosophy as Pneumatology*. Princeton: Princeton University Press, 1992.

Padel, Ruth. *Whom Gods Destroy: Elements of Greek and Tragic Madness.* New Jersey: Princeton University Press, 1995.

Patterson, Robert L. *Plato on Immortality.* University Park: The Pennsylvania State University Press, 1965.

Pheby, Keith C. *Interventions: Displacing the Metaphysical Subject.* Washington D.C.: Maisonneuve Press, 1988.

Philo. *Philo.* Translated by F.H. Colson. Loeb Classical Library. Massachusetts: Harvard University Press, 1930.

Pieper, Joseph. *Enthusiasm and Divine Madness: On the Platonic Dialogue Phaedrus.* New York: Harcourt Brace and World, 1964.

Pinkard, Terry. *Hegel's Dialectic: The Explanation of Possibility.* Philadelphia: Temple University Press, 1988.

Plato. *Euthyphro, Apology, Crito, Phaedo, Phaedrus.* Translated by Harold North Fowler. Loeb Classical Library. Cambridge: Harvard University Press, 1914.

――― . *Laches, Protogoras, Meno, Euthydemus.* Translated by Harold North Fowler. Loeb Classical Library. Cambridge: Harvard University Press, 1924.

――― . *Parmenides.* Translated by Harold North Fowler. Loeb Classical Library. Cambridge: Harvard University Press, 1930.

――― . *Republic.* Translated by Harold North Fowler. Loeb Classical Library. Cambridge: Harvard University Press, 1930.

――― . *Theatetus, Sophist.* Translated by Harold North Fowler. Loeb Classical Library. Cambridge: Harvard University Press, 1921.

Pöggeler, Otto. *Hegels Idee einer Phänomenologie des Geistes.* Freiburg: Karl Alber, 1993.

――― . *Der Denkweg Martin Heideggers.* Pfullingen: Günther Neske, 1963. *Martin Heidegger's Path of Thinking.* Translated by D. Magurshak and S. Barber. Atlantic Highlands, N.J.: Humanities Press, 1987.

――― . *Die Frage nach der Kunst; von Hegel bis Heidegger.* Freiburg: Karl Alber, 1984.

Raffoul, François. *Heidegger and the Subject.* Translated by D. Pettigrew and G. Recco, Atlantic Highlands, N.J.: Humanities Press, 1998.

Rajchman, John. *Michel Foucault: The Freedom of Philosophy.* New York: Columbia University Press, 1985.

Reck, Andrew J. "Substance, Subject and Dialectic." *Studies in Hegel.* Tulane Studies in Philosophy Vol. IX. The Hague: Martinus Nijhoff, 1960.

Richardson, William S.J. *Through Phenomenology to Thought.* The Hague: Martinus Nijhoff, 1963. Second Edition. 1974.

――― . "Dasein and the Ground of Negativity: A Note of the Fourth Movement in the *Beiträge* Symphony." *Heidegger Studies* 9 (1993): 35–52.

――― . "Heidegger among the Doctors." *Reading Heidegger: Commemorations.* Edited by John Sallis. Indianapolis: Indiana University Press, 1993, 49–63.

Roccatagliata, Giuseppe. *A History of Ancient Psychiatry*. New York: Greenwood Press, 1986.

Rockmore, Tom. *Cognition: An Introduction to Hegel's Phenomenology of Spirit*. Berkeley: University of California Press, 1997.

Rosen, George. *Madness in Society*. Chicago: The University of Chicago Press, 1968.

Rosen, Michael. *Hegel's Dialectic and Its Criticism*. Cambridge: Cambridge University Press, 1982.

Ross, David *Plato's Theory of Ideas*. Oxford: Clarendon Press, 1953.

Röttges, Heinz. *Der Begriff der Methode in der Philosophie Hegels*. Meisenheim: Verlag Anton Hain, 1976.

Said, Edward. "The Problem of Textuality: Two Exemplary Positions." *Critical Inquiry* 4 (1978): 673–714.

Sallis, John. *Being and Logos: Reading the Platonic Dialogues*. Third Edition. Indianapolis: Indiana University Press, 1996.

———. *Echoes After Heidegger*. Bloomington: Indiana University Press, 1990.

———. *Delimitations: Phenomenology and the End of Metaphysics*, Second, Expanded Edition. Bloomington: Indiana University Press, 1995.

———, editor. *Deconstruction and Philosophy: The Texts of Jacques Derrida*. Chicago & London: The University of Chicago Press, 1987.

———, editor. *Reading Heidegger: Commemorations*. Indianapolis: Indiana University Press, 1993.

Santas, Gerasimos. *Plato and Freud: Two Theories of Love*. Oxford: Basil Blackwell, 1988.

———. "The Theory of Eros in Socrates' Second Speech." *Understanding the Phaedrus*, Edited by Livio Rossetti. Sankt Augustin, DE: Academia Verlag, 1992. 305–308.

Sartre, Jean Paul. *Being and Nothingness*. Translated by Hazel E. Barnes. London: Meuthen & Co. 1957.

Sass, Louis. *Madness and Modernism: Insanity in the Light of Modern Art, Literature, and Thought*. Massachusetts: Harvard University Press, 1994.

Schacht, Richard. *Hegel and After: Studies in Continental Philosophy Between Kant and Sartre*. Pittsburgh: University of Pittsburgh Press, 1975.

Schelling, F. W. J. *Ausgewählte Werke*. Darmstadt: Wissenschaftlice Buchgesellschaft, 1974.

———. *Die Weltalter*. Edited by Manfred Schröter, München: Biederstein und Leibniz Verlag, 1946.

Schmidt, Dennis. *The Ubiquity of the Finite: Hegel, Heidegger, and the Entitlements of Philosophy*. Cambridge: The MIT Press, 1988.

————. "Economies of Production: Heidegger and Aristotle on *Physis* and *Techne*." *Crisis in Continental Philosophy*, Edited by A. B. Dallery, C. E. Scott & P. H. Roberts. Albany: SUNY Press, 1990. 147–159.

Schmitt, Gerhard. *The Concept of Being in Hegel and Heidegger*. Bonn: Bovier Verlag, 1977.

Schürmann, Reiner. *Heidegger: On Being and Acting: From Principles to Anarchy*. Bloomington: Indiana University Press, 1990.

Scott, Charles. "Heidegger, Madness and Well-Being." *The Southern Journal of Philosophy* 4 (1973): 157–177.

————. "Heidegger and Psychoanalysis: The Seminars in Zollikon." *Heidegger-Studies* (1990): 131–141.

————. *The Question of Ethics*. Bloomington: Indiana University Press, 1990.

Sharp, Francis Michael. *The Poet's Madness: A Reading of Georg Trakl*. Ithaca: Cornell Univertsity Press, 1981.

Siewerth, Gustav. *Gott in der Geschichte. Zur Gottesfrage bei Hegel und Heidegger*. Düsseldorf: Patmos-Verlag, 1971.

Silverman, Hugh J. "Derrida, Heidegger, and the Time of the Line." *Derrida and Deconstruction*. Edited by H. J. Silverman. London: Routledge, 1989, 154–168.

Simon, Bennett. *Mind and Madness in Ancient Greece*. Ithaca & London: Cornell University Press, 1978.

Sinaiko, Herman L. *Love, Knowledge, and Discourse in Plato: Dialogue and Dialectic in Phaedrus, Republic, Parmenides*. Chicago: The University of Chicago Press, 1965.

Sinn, Dieter. *Die Kritik am Identitätsprinzip: von Heidegger zu Hegel*. Bonn: Bouvier, 1988.

Soll, Ivan. *An Introduction to Hegel's Metaphysics*. Chicago: University of Chicago Press, 1969.

Stace, Walter Terence. *The Philosophy of Hegel: A Systematic Exposition*. New York: Dover Publications, 1966.

Stambaugh, Joan. *The Finitude of Being*. Albany: State University of New York Press, 1992.

Steinkraus, Warren E., editor. *New Studies in Hegel's Philosophy*. New York: Holt, Rinehart and Winston, INC., 1971.

Still, Arthur and Velody, Irving, editors. *Rewriting the History of Madness: Studies in Foucault's* Histoire de la folie. London: Routledge, 1992.

Taminiaux, Jacques. *Heidegger and The Project of Fundamental Ontology*, Translated by M. Gendre, Albany: State University of New York Press, 1991.

Taylor, C. *Hegel*. Cambridge: Cambridge University Press, 1975.

Urmson, James O. "Plato and the Poets" in *Plato On Beauty, Wisdom and the Arts*, Edited by J. Moravcsik and P. Temko. Totowa: Rowman and Littlefield, 1982, 125–136.

————. *The Greek Philosophical Vocabulary*. London: Duckworth, 1990.

van Buren, John. "The Ethics of *Formale Anzeige* in Heidegger," in *American Catholic Philosophical Quarterly: Heidegger*. Edited by John Caputo. LXIX, Spring (1995): 157–170.

Vaught, Carl G. "Hegel and the Problem of Difference: A Critique of Dialectical Reflection." *Hegel & His Critics: Philosophy in the Aftermath of Hegel*. Edited by W. Desmond. Albany: State University of New York Press, 1989. 35–48.

Verene, Donald P. *Hegel's Recollection: A Study of images in the* Phenomenology of Spirit. Albany: State University of New York Press, 1985.

Vernant, Jean Pierre. *Mortals and Immortals*. New Jersey: Princeton University Press, 1991.

Veyne, Paul. *Did the Greeks Believe in Their Myths*. Translated by P. Wissing, Chicago: The University of Chicago Press, 1988.

Vosskühler, Friedrich. *Der Idealismus als Metaphysik der Moderne: Studien zur Selbstreflexion und Aufhebung der Metaphysik bei Hölderlin, Hegel, Schelling, Marx und Heidegger*. Würzburg: Königshausen & Neumann, 1996.

Warminski, Andrzej. *Readings in Interpretation: Hölderlin, Hegel, Heidegger*. Minneapolis: University of Minnesota Press, 1987.

Wein, Hermann. *Realdialektik: Von Hegelscher Dialektik zu Dialektischer Anthropologie*. München: R. Oldenbourg Verlag, 1957.

Westphal, Merold. *History and Truth in Hegel's "Phenomenology."* Atlantic Highlands, N.J.: Humanities Press, 1979.

White, David A. *Myth and Metaphysics in Plato's Phaedo*. Sellinsgrove: Susquehanna University Press, 1989.

————. *Rhetoric and Reality in Plato's Phaedrus*. Albany: State University of New York Press, 1992.

Williams, Robert R. "Hegel and Heidegger." *Hegel & His Critics: Philosophy in the Aftermath of Hegel*. Edited by W. Desmond. Albany: State University of New York Press, 1989. 135–157.

Wohlfart, Günter. *Der Augenblick: Zeit und Ästhetische Erfahrung bei Kant, Hegel, Nietzsche und Heidegger mit einem Exkurs zu Proust*. Freiburg: Karl Alber, 1982.

Wood, David. *The Deconstruction of Time*. Atlantic Highlands, N.J.: Humanities Press, 1991.

————, editor. *Of Derrida, Heidegger, and Spirit*. Evanston, Illinois, Northwestern University Press, 1993.

Wyschogrod, Edith. *Spirit in Ashes: Hegel, Heidegger and Man-made Mass Death*. New Haven: Yale University Press, 1985.

Young, William. *Hegel's Dialectical Method*. The Craig Press, 1972.

Ziarek, Krzysztof. *Inflected Language: Toward a Hermeneutics of Nearness, Heidegger, Levinas, Stevens, Celan*. Albany: State University of New York Press, 1994.

Zizek, Slavoj. *Tarrying with the Negative: Kant, Hegel, and the Critique of Ideology.* Durham: Duke University Press, 1993.

Zuckert, Catherine H. *Postmodern Platos: Nietzsche, Heidegger, Gadamer, Strauss, Derrida.* Chicago: The University of Chicago Press, 1996.

Index